To what extent is marriage a contract? What does it offer the parties? What are the difficulties of contractual enforcement and the results of failures in enforcement?

In this book, the authors take an economic approach to marriage and divorce, considering the key role of "incentives" in family law. They highlight the adverse consequences emanating from faulty legal design, while demonstrating that family law needs to provide incentives for consistent and honest behavior. Economists and academic lawyers discuss recent advances in the economic analysis of marriage, cohabitation, and divorce. Chapters are grouped around four topics: the contractual perspectives on marriage commitment; the regulatory framework surrounding divorce; bargaining and commitment issues relating to marriage and near-marriage arrangements; and finally empirical work, which focuses on the impact of more liberal divorce laws.

This important new study will be of considerable interest to lawyers, policymakers, and economists concerned with family law.

ANTONY W. DNES is Associate Dean and Research Professor, University of Hertfordshire, and Visiting Professor, George Mason University Law School. His research has considered the impact of law on the incentives to marry and divorce; he is also the author of an established textbook, *The Economic Analysis of Law* (US version forthcoming in 2002).

ROBERT ROWTHORN is Professor of Economics at Cambridge University and Fellow of King's College, Cambridge. His research has considered inflation, globalization, and employment, as well as female employment and the economics of marriage.

The Law and Economics of Marriage and Divorce

Edited by

Antony W. Dnes
University of Hertfordshire

Robert Rowthorn
University of Cambridge

CAMBRIDGE
UNIVERSITY PRESS

PUBLISHED BY THE PRESS SYNDICATE OF THE UNIVERSITY OF CAMBRIDGE
The Pitt Building, Trumpington Street, Cambridge, United Kingdom

CAMBRIDGE UNIVERSITY PRESS
The Edinburgh Building, Cambridge CB2 2RU, UK
40 West 20th Street, New York NY 10011–4211, USA
477 Williamstown Road, Port Melbourne, VIC 3207, Australia
Ruiz de Alarcón 13, 28014 Madrid, Spain
Dock House, The Waterfront, Cape Town 8001, South Africa

http://www.cambridge.org

First published 2002

Printed in the United Kingdom at the University Press, Cambridge

Typeface Times 10/12 pt.   *System* LATEX 2ε   [TB]

A catalogue record for this book is available from the British Library

Library of Congress Cataloguing in Publication Data
The law and economics of marriage and divorce / edited by Antony Dnes
and Robert Rowthorn.
     p.   cm.
   Includes bibliographical references and index.
   ISBN 0 521 80933 9 (hardback) – ISBN 0 521 00632 5 (paperback)
   1. Domestic relations.   2. Domestic relations – Economic aspects.   I. Dnes,
Antony W.   II. Rowthorn, Robert
K670 .L39 2002
346.01′5 – dc21   2001035640

ISBN 0 521 80933 9 hardback
ISBN 0 521 00632 5 paperback

Contents

Tables and figure

Figure

Tables

Contributors

DOUGLAS W. ALLEN is Professor of Economics at Simon Fraser University, British Columbia, Canada. He is a specialist in transactions cost economics and has written a number of papers on the law and economics of the family, including an important article in the *American Economic Review* on the effect of no-fault divorce on the divorce rate.

MARGARET F. BRINIG is Professor of Law at the University of Iowa, Iowa City, Iowa, USA. She is one of America's leading experts on the law and economics of the family, and is the author of numerous articles and several books, of which the latest is *From Contract to Covenant*.

LLOYD R. COHEN is Professor of Law at George Mason University, Arlington, Virginia, USA. He has written a number of articles on the law and economics of the family. His most influential paper, "Marriage, Divorce and Quasi-Rents, or 'I Gave Him the Best Years of My Life' " was published in the *Journal of Legal Studies* in 1987.

ANTONY W. DNES is Associate Dean and Research Professor at the University of Hertfordshire Business School, UK, and Visiting Professor, George Mason University Law School, Virginia, USA. He has written several articles on the impact of law on the incentives to marry and divorce, and is the author of *The Economic Analysis of Law*.

STEVEN L. NOCK is Professor of Sociology at the University of Virginia, Charlottesville, USA. He writes extensively on the sociology of the family and is the author of a recent book, *Marriage in Men's Lives*.

ALLEN M. PARKMAN is Professor of Management at the University of New Mexico, Albuquerque, New Mexico, USA. He is the author of a major book on American divorce law reform, entitled *Good Intentions Gone Awry: No-Fault Divorce and the American Family*. He has also written a number of academic papers dealing with the impact of divorce law on marital behavior.

ERIC RASMUSEN is Professor of Business Economics and Public Policy and Sub-hedar Faculty Fellow at the Kelley School of Business, Indiana University, Bloomington, Indiana, USA, and during 2000–2001 was Olin Senior Fellow at Harvard Law School. He is the author of the well-known textbook *Games and Information*, and has recently published a paper, "Lifting the Veil of Ignorance: Personalizing the Marriage Contract," with Jeffrey Stake.

ROBERT ROWTHORN is Professor of Economics at the University of Cambridge and Fellow of King's College Cambridge, UK. He is the author of several books on employment and economic growth. He is currently directing a research project on the economics of female labor force participation and is author of a paper "Marriage and Trust: Some Lessons from Economics."

ELIZABETH S. SCOTT is Professor of Law at the University of Virginia, Charlottesville, USA. She has written widely on marriage, including an influential article in the *Virginia Law Review* entitled "Rational Decision-Making about Marriage and Divorce."

IAN SMITH is Lecturer in Economics at the University of St. Andrews, St Andrews, Scotland. He has written a number of papers on divorce, including an econometric analysis of the impact of legal reforms on divorce in the United Kingdom.

KATHERINE SHAW SPAHT is Professor of Law at the University of Louisiana, Baton Rouge, Louisiana, USA. She is the author of many articles on marriage and divorce. She also designed the new covenant marriage law in Louisiana.

MARTIN ZELDER is Director of Health Policy Research at The Fraser Institute, Vancouver, British Columbia, Canada. He has written several papers on the impact of law reform on divorce and marital behavior.

1   Introduction

Antony W. Dnes and Robert Rowthorn

This book is a response to growing public concern about family breakdown, which is associated in the academic world with a burgeoning interest in marriage and divorce. Academic interest has spread beyond the conventional boundaries of socio-legal studies, and a new literature has emerged that draws on economic analysis to illuminate the dynamics of family formation and dissolution. This new approach is distinguished by the importance it assigns to incentives. Whereas other approaches mostly belittle the role of incentives, the economic approach gives them a central place in the analysis of marriage and divorce. Legal and other policy innovations that substantially alter the structure of incentives are presumed to have a significant impact on individual behavior and hence on the formation, operation, and dissolution of families.

Some followers of the economic approach are professional economists, some are specialists in the economic analysis of law, and still others are academic lawyers. They are all represented in this book. The subject matter of the book may be loosely described as "the economic analysis of family law" in so far as it concerns marriage, divorce, and related issues. The literature on this topic tends to be largely American in origin and is scattered around a wide diversity of academic journals. In this book we bring together some of the major authors in the field, who survey and synthesize existing literature and in some cases provide new analyses of their own. The American approach is beginning to catch on in Britain, and the British authors in this book bring a fresh perspective that may be of interest to Americans.

A major impetus behind the growing academic interest in the economics of family law has been the spate of initiatives to reform family law in North America and elsewhere. In the USA, the American Law Institute (ALI) has recently published new guidelines on the law of marital dissolution, which are likely to be highly influential in the design of state-based family law codes. Although the ALI guidelines may seem to fly in the face of economic logic in some areas, such as the arbitrary nature of the rules governing spousal maintenance payments, there is no doubt that debate has been stimulated among observers with economics training. Similarly, in England, the Lord Chancellor's Department has displayed increased interest in exploring the economic basis of the division of marital assets, following its commissioning of a series of reports in the late 1990s.

The growth in marital dissolution witnessed in recent decades has imposed increasing costs on the taxpayer. Some of these costs are associated with the administration of justice. Others arise from the fact that marital breakdown imposes a range of extra demands on the welfare state. These include welfare services for damaged children and depressed adults, financial aid to meet the expense of running an additional household following separation, and the cost of supporting lone parents and their children when the former spouse cannot or will not contribute adequately to their upkeep. The post-war growth in divorce, and the associated fall in marriage rates, also raises wider, non-pecuniary questions about human welfare.

This book draws together recent advances in specialist work on marriage, cohabitation, and divorce. The common thread running through almost all of the contributions is the importance of family law as an influence on the structure of incentives facing individuals. These incentives revolve around the issue of consistent and honest behavior in human relationships. Specialists who apply economics to family law frequently observe that modern family law creates an incentive structure that encourages opportunism and facilitates systematic cheating on interpersonal obligations. Thus, apart from the financial impact of growing divorce rates, there is concern that a badly designed divorce law may undermine the fabric of trust upon which stable marriages depend. If it is badly designed, the law itself may stimulate divorce and contribute to a great deal of human misery. The economic approach takes this kind of issue seriously. It focuses on the incentives associated with alternative legal regimes and on the unintended adverse consequences emanating from faulty legal design.

Interest in the application of economic analysis to family life is not particularly new and dates back at least to the work of Becker and others in the 1960s and 1970s. This earlier work was not primarily concerned with the role of law, but was an application of conventional production and consumption theory to family decision-making in such areas as employment and the domestic division of labor. More recent developments stress the influence of law on family life, and there is now considerable interest in this topic among writers having some background in the economic analysis of law. Family law has become another legal area, along with contract, tort, and property, in which economic analysis has provided new insights. Family law is now set to become a "harder" area of law, akin to contract or tort, as a result of the new approach.

The economic analysis of family law is conducted on two levels. First, the law of marriage and divorce is theoretically analyzed in terms of its incentive structure. For example, following the lead of Lloyd Cohen, a contributor to this book, it is frequently argued that a failure to enforce quasi-contractual obligations between marriage partners encourages opportunistic behavior. Older women, in particular, may be vulnerable to opportunistic abandonment by men, if the legal system renders divorce relatively cheap compared with promised levels of lifetime support. Faced with such a risk, individuals may respond defensively by investing less in their marriage and in their children, thereby damaging the children and destabilizing their marriage. It is easy to see that economics is useful in analyzing such linkages.

In addition to the insights derived from theoretical analysis, it is important to quantify the impact of law on behavior. This requires the application of statistical (econometric) methods to the growing volume of data that is now available. The major application of statistical analysis to family law concerns the impact of divorce law reform during the 1970s. During this period divorce law was liberalized throughout North America and much of Western Europe, and in all cases this change was accompanied by increased divorce rates. The aim of statistical analysis has been to quantify how far legal reform was a causal factor in the growth of divorce. The statistical results provide compelling evidence that in the case of North America the liberalization of divorce law had a permanent impact on divorce rates. In the case of Europe, there is less evidence to go on and the statistical results are less clear-cut. Quantitative analysis is also important for policy formulation. If the statistical evidence consistently rejected the hypothesis that the law had a significant impact, then the design of the law would matter much less. As far as one can tell from the econometric evidence, it matters quite a lot. We therefore offer this book to the reader as a contribution to the debates surrounding the major social changes associated with marriage and divorce in the twenty-first century.

Turning now to the content of this book, we have grouped the papers around four principal themes. The first group covers contractual perspectives on marital commitment (chapters 2 and 3). The next group of papers examines the regulatory framework surrounding divorce (chapters 4, 5, and 6). The third group (chapters 7, 8, and 9) focuses on several bargaining and commitment issues relating to marriage and near-marriage arrangements. The last group (chapters 10, 11, and 12) brings in empirical work, largely on the impact of more liberal divorce laws.

Lloyd Cohen examines the long-term incentive structure in marriage in chapter 2, "Marriage: The Long-Term Contract." His analysis begins from the observation that, although the true nature of marriage is not expressed in the wedding vows, there is a nearly universal expectation that the relationship should endure for the joint lives of the partners. In reality, separation and divorce often invalidate this expectation. He notes that many of the problems inherent in fashioning an efficient and equitable law of divorce, alimony, and property division are similar to the difficulties that surface in the enforcement of commercial contracts. It should be observed that long-term commercial contracts are also replete with complex problems of incentive alignment and broken-down personal relations.

Cohen's contractual analysis of marriage does not yield strong conclusions about the "proper marriage." The nature of the underlying duties assumed by the marriage partners is highly idiosyncratic and not susceptible to bright-line definitions. However, success of the marriage requires the partners to invest heavily in the relationship, asymmetrically over time. They may be able to salvage little of their original investment should the marriage fail, and it is often the wife who has more to lose by divorce. "Insuring" the investments is in the interests of both marriage partners. Cohen finds that neither prenuptial contracts nor the various contemporary legal regimes of divorce and property settlement offer much hope. He argues that much can be claimed for the older reliance on informal social sanctions and the good moral sense of the parties. Our modern need to wrestle with settlement issues may stem from losing this traditional set of checks and loosening the moral value of promise.

In chapter 3, "Marital Commitment and the Legal Regulation of Divorce," Elizabeth Scott criticizes both conservative and liberal views on the legal regulation of marriage and divorce. Conservatives have welcomed the introduction of covenant marriage statutes in a few American states. In these states couples can now choose a more binding marriage option than is allowed under conventional divorce law. Some conservatives are hopeful that this is part of a trend towards a more restrictive divorce regime in which divorce is conditioned on fault. Many liberals see covenant marriage statutes as a threat to personal freedom, because they prevent the easy termination of marriage. Scott argues that one does not have to be a conservative to support legal restrictions on divorce. The legal enforcement of marital commitments is consistent with liberal principles and may enhance the freedom of individuals to pursue their life goals. In marriage, as in commercial contracts, legal commitment can promote cooperation and protect investment in the relationship, to the mutual benefit of the parties concerned. Scott argues that family law reforms since the 1960s increased the freedom of individuals to leave a marriage, but in doing so they have restricted the freedom of individuals to bind themselves so as to achieve the long-term goals they desire.

Scott goes on to consider alternative legal regimes that would facilitate personal commitment in a fashion broadly consistent with liberal principles. Amongst the possibilities that she considers are mandatory premarital and pre-divorce counseling, a mandatory waiting period of two to three years before divorce, and family property trusts to ensure that marital property is used to provide financial security for minor children following divorce. She welcomes covenant marriage because it embodies some of these provisions and because the introduction of this type of marriage offers couples an extra level of precommitment to choose from. However, she rejects fault-based divorce, which is the centerpiece of covenant marriage, on the grounds that judicial determination of fault is both acrimonious and inaccurate. Thus, her initial sympathy for covenant marriage is heavily qualified.

In chapter 4, "Mutual Consent Divorce," Allen Parkman argues that the primary ground for divorce should be mutual consent. A marriage should be dissolved only if both spouses agree it is a failure, which means that two spouses who genuinely wish their marriage to end can dissolve it without difficulty. It also means that a spouse who wishes to terminate a marriage against the initial desire of the other spouse will have to win the consent of the latter. This suggestion mirrors the standard specific-performance remedy for breach of contract, which obliges a party wishing to be released from a contract to pay full compensation. Bargaining over the terms of dissolution might require concessions on such issues as child custody, alimony, or division of the family assets. Such a provision protects spouses against expropriation of their investments in the marriage, since it deters opportunistic desertion and forces a departing spouse to pay full compensation. Like the old fault-based system, mutual consent divorce encourages marital investment and facilitates arrangements that would otherwise be too risky.

Parkman does not consider that mutual consent should be the only route to divorce. The mutual consent provision gives substantial power to spouses who do not want a divorce. To limit abuse of this power, he proposes that unilateral, penalty-free divorce should be available early in the marriage when there are no children. He also believes that fault may have a role to play in exceptional cases. For example, a spouse may be driven out of a marriage by adulterous or cruel behavior, but the guilty spouse may be unwilling to consent to a divorce. Under these conditions, a fault divorce would provide a remedy for the injured spouse. In Parkman's view, such cases are rare and divorce in the case of established marriages would normally be by mutual consent.

In "An Economic Approach to Adultery Law" (chapter 5) Eric Rasmusen provides an economic analysis of sanctions for marital misconduct, of which adultery is one example. He rigorously examines three sanctions: criminal penalties for adultery, a tort action for "alienation of affections," and the self-help remedy of "justification." The penalties are then discussed in a variety of specific applications to past and present law. In modern law, the formal remedy is that the wronged party can file for divorce and force a division of the assets. This really is not a remedy, since under no-fault laws anyone can file for divorce. Other remedies existed in the recent past, of which vestiges continue today. These included criminal penalties, tort actions, and self-help. In general, efficiency requires adultery law that replicates the marriage terms that husband and wife would freely choose at the beginning of a marriage. In the absence of legal penalties, partners may avoid investing in the marriage or may heavily invest in monitoring the other partner. Adultery may be deterred either by the monitoring or by the credible threat of divorce when a partner has not invested in the marriage. There is a very large welfare loss, created by the burden of monitoring and the loss to husband and wife if investments are avoided. There may also be costs attached to concealing adultery in circumstances where it can occur. To deter adultery efficiently, the introduction of a legal penalty must ensure a sufficiently large penalty that, even if the partners spend nothing on monitoring, the expected payoff from adultery will be too low to justify the risks involved. In that case, the partners will be deterred, and they will feel secure in using time investing in the marriage and not in monitoring. Both parties would be happy to accept the possibility of extraordinary penalties for adultery, *ex ante*, knowing that if the penalties are in place deterrence will be complete and no one will have to suffer them.

Katherine Spaht defends the role of fault in chapter 6, "Louisiana's Covenant Marriage Law: Recapturing the Meaning of Marriage for the Sake of the Children." As the person who drafted the covenant marriage law, she is in an ideal position to describe the thinking of those responsible for this reform. In Louisiana couples can now choose between two types of marriage: the conventional type, which permits easy divorce with few penalties; and the new covenant marriage, in which divorce is obtainable only after a substantial delay or on proof of fault. Before entering a covenant marriage couples must undergo counseling, and they must agree to mandatory counseling in the event of difficulties that threaten the marriage. Moreover, a spouse who is guilty of serious misconduct, such as adultery or physical abuse, may be compelled to pay damages in the event of divorce. There may also be damages if a divorce follows a refusal to take "reasonable steps to preserve the marriage, including marriage counseling."

The covenant marriage law unites two distinct strands of thought. It is consistent with the liberal notion that individuals should have the right to make binding commitments if they so choose. This choice is denied to them in states that offer only liberal, no-fault divorce. At the same time, it embodies the communitarian notion that marriage serves important social functions and that marriage law should embody moral principles consistent with these functions. The communitarian influence is especially clear in Spaht's treatment of marital counseling and fault. Under the covenant law, the primary purpose of counseling is to save marriages, and counselors are not expected to be neutral with regard to divorce. Although divorce is legally permissible, it is normally seen as a last option to be chosen only when other avenues have been fully explored. An exception occurs when some behavior by a spouse towards the other is so reprehensible that, despite society's interest in maintaining the marriage, the offended spouse may terminate it without prior counseling. A notable feature of this chapter is Spaht's robust defense of fault. Her grounds are both moral and practical. Marriage law, like ordinary contract law, should embody the moral notion of personal responsibility. She also considers that fault is no more difficult to establish in the case of divorce than in many other legal contexts.

In chapter 7, "Cohabitation and Marriage," Antony Dnes considers why people choose to cohabit rather than marry and the extent to which the law should seek to regulate cohabitation. He argues that many couples deliberately choose to cohabit because they do not want the legal commitments traditionally associated with marriage. The modern legal trend is to impose rights and responsibilities upon such couples irrespective of their wishes. Dnes considers this trend to be largely misguided, since it amounts to compulsory marriage for people who would prefer not to be married. The one exception concerns child support obligations following the dissolution of a cohabiting union. Legal regulation is justified in this case because children are third parties whose interests must be protected. Dnes also points out that people may choose to cohabit because marital law is dysfunctional and offers inadequate protection for spouses who invest in their marriage. He considers various ways in which this might be remedied. One option might be to make divorce contingent on the consent of both spouses (a specific-performance remedy likely to lead to bargaining). Another might be to apply normal contractual principles to marriage, so that damages would be payable for a unilateral breach of the marital contract. Dnes discusses the three standard principles for calculating damages: restitution, reliance, and expectation. He argues that expectation damages are the most efficient in the context of divorce.

In "Marriage as a Signal" (chapter 8) Robert Rowthorn applies the economic theory of signaling to marriage. Apart from a few seminal articles by authors such as William Bishop and Michael Trebilcock, this is a topic that has been largely ignored in the law and economics literature. Following the lead of these authors, Rowthorn argues that in Western culture marriage helps individuals to signal to each other and to the outside world their desire for a sexually exclusive, permanent union. However, modern legal and social trends have greatly reduced the credibility of this signal. It is now much easier to terminate a marriage and the penalties for serious misconduct have been eliminated or greatly reduced. As a result, marriage is no longer such an effective signal of commitment as it once was. This change represents a major loss of information that makes it more difficult to sort out the committed from the uncommitted. Even so, the degree of commitment is still higher, on average, amongst married couples than amongst cohabiting couples, and marriage is still the best predictor of the durability of a relationship. The chapter concludes with an extension of this application of signaling theory to cohabitation and same-sex marriage.

In chapter 9, "For Better or for Worse," Martin Zelder explores the subject of bargaining in marriage and divorce. He is concerned with two issues: the process of bargaining between potential or actual spouses, and the efficiency of the outcome. His chapter covers bargaining before marriage, during marriage, and at the time of divorce. He points out that theoretical analysis in this important area is in its infancy and systematic econometric work is even more limited. The theoretical analysis of bargaining within marriage has developed in opposition to the early assumption that spouses have common preferences. If their preferences differ, then bargaining is likely to play an important role in household decision-making with regard to such items as expenditure, external employment, and the domestic division of labor. Such bargaining may be analyzed as a cooperative game in which the outcome is efficient, in the sense that one spouse could not be made better off without making the other worse off. Alternatively, it may be analyzed as a non-cooperative game in which the outcome may be inefficient, in which case the situation of both spouses could be simultaneously improved under alternative arrangements. Zelder also surveys the literature on bargaining over divorce. Following the lead of Becker, early work on this topic assumed that the legal framework has a negligible influence on the propensity to divorce. A number of authors, including Zelder himself, have recently questioned this assumption and have developed models in which the law has a significant effect on divorce rates.

In "Weak Men and Disorderly Women: Divorce and the Division of Labor" (chapter 10), Steven Nock and Margaret Brinig consider whether the divorce rate has increased because the modern marriage deal is unfair to women. It is a common complaint from women that they must do a double shift. The first comprises their hours of paid work outside the home and their second the long hours of housework when they get home. In considering the role of household labor, Nock and Brinig control for other determinants of dissolution such as age, presence of minor children, education levels, and other socio-economic variables. The effect of the household division of labor turns out to be of great significance. Marriages are strained when either partner does the majority of traditionally female work in the home, and are strengthened by time spent in traditionally male tasks.

In chapter 11, "The Impact of Legal Reforms on Marriage and Divorce," Douglas Allen examines the effects of no-fault divorce laws on three economic decisions: the divorce rate, labor force participation, and the age at which individuals marry. He provides new statistical evidence about age at marriage. A survey of the relevant work shows the effect of divorce laws to be clear but not large in absolute size. Introducing no-fault divorce raises the divorce rate by about 17 percent of the *increased* stock of divorces over the past thirty years. It also increases the age of first time marriage by up to nine months. Finally, it raises married women's labor force participation by around 2 percent. Allen's chapter gives a good illustration of the usefulness of applied (economics) work on family law.

Ian Smith examines the liberalization of divorce laws across Europe in chapter 12, "European Divorce Laws, Divorce Rates, and Their Consequences." Most investigations of the rise in divorce rates have focused on North America. The chapter re-evaluates the association between divorce statutes and divorce rates in the European context. Since many jurisdictions are currently also evaluating rules regarding the division of marital property and child support payments, the chapter also comments on cross-country differences in the financial consequences of divorce. There is significant variation in the evolution of divorce rates and laws across European countries. Although legal innovations reflect and regulate changing behavioral patterns, Smith argues that it is currently difficult to establish a clear causal link between the liberalization of divorce law and rising divorce rates since the late 1960s. He notes that correlation does not automatically imply causation. Both the pattern of divorce rates and the strictness of legislation might be jointly explained by a third factor, for example religion or the economic costs of divorce for women and their children. A rigorous empirical study using a panel of data from European countries is required to permit discrimination between these hypotheses. This is not yet available. The historical trend in legislation is towards facilitating no-fault, separation-based marital dissolution. The trend, he argues, is unlikely to be reversed. There are currently no European initiatives comparable to the introduction of covenant marriage in some American states. Rather than using the law to discourage divorce, European countries (along with most US states) focus on measures that minimize its social and economic costs. Many European countries follow American trends in enforcing child support transfers, setting up after divorce, and the provision of child-care subsidies. Smith notes that insulating women and children from the adverse consequences of divorce may reinforce incentives for marital dissolution.

In commissioning the papers for this collection, we have tried to exhibit something of the range of modern work dealing with the economics of family law. We are confident that the reader will gain valuable insights into the issues surrounding marriage and divorce in the twenty-first century. We hope that this book will stimulate further research in the area.

2   Marriage: the long-term contract

Lloyd R. Cohen

Although far more than a contract from religious, cultural, biological, psycho-logical, and philosophical perspectives, marriage is also a contract, the essence of which is transparent in the marriage vows.[1] The man promises that he will be a husband, the woman that she will be a wife. Each promises that whatever changes are wrought by the winds of time they will continue to perform their respective duties in a spirit of "loving," "honoring," and "cherishing" for the remainder of their lives. In reliance on these assurances, each spouse invests in this marriage, thereby sacrificing current and future love interests and other life choices.

The promise to perform duties in a particular spirit is not merely hortatory; it is a material requirement of the contract. In marriage, more than in any other contract, the spirit counts, and counts a lot. Both the value to the recipient of spousal services and their cost, or value, to the provider are crucially dependent on the attitude with which they are delivered and received.

Some might object to the characterization of marriage as a contract. They observe that marriage seems more like status than contract. That is, it is the state that defines and specifies most of the explicit rights, duties, and privileges of marriage, rather than the parties.[2] They also note the absence of substantial specific obligations voiced at the time of formation. How could this be a contract if there are virtually no specific, explicit duties?

These objections are not fatal to the concept of marriage as contract. They do no more than highlight the peculiarities of this contract. The contractual essence of this institution is that it is a voluntary agreement between two consenting adults, albeit an agreement in which the obligations, rights, and privileges are left largely implicit and defined, if at all, principally by the state rather than

---

[1] This chapter reflects the most current statement of my thought on the subject of marriage and divorce. My earliest and somewhat more complete statement on the subject appears in Cohen (1987). See also Cohen (1998, p. 618) and Cohen (1995).

[2] There has been much discussion in the legal literature of whether marriage is best understood as a contract relation or, alternatively, as a status relation. Some commentators have argued that, "because the law, not the parties, defines the obligations of each spouse," the relationship is truly one of status rather than contract (Babcock, 1978, p. 564). See generally, Clark (1968), esp. section 6.1 at pp. 181–2.

the parties. That the specific acts required of each spouse are not specified at the time of marriage is hardly unique to marriage. Employment contracts are another large class of agreements that generally do not enumerate duties with any specificity. A marriage contract that strove for specificity and detail would make for a clever plot for a Monty Python farce, not a marriage. The complexity, subtlety, and exigent quality of the almost infinite set of duties that each party must perform make it inefficient, if not impossible, to specify them with any precision. The meaning of "husband" and "wife" and the specific rights and duties that attach to each role are normally inferred from the subculture and social class in which the parties were raised, and most importantly from their prenuptial relationship.

Another, more fundamental, objection to the contractual view of marriage is that the state of loving (or perhaps being in love) with another is not a volitional act. Thus the promise to love could be neither intended by the promissor nor believed by the promissee to constitute an enforceable commitment.

There are two responses to this objection. First, we might reinterpret the marriage vow as a promise to assume risk and pay damages. That is, each party is promising the other that they will assume the risk that their love for their spouse dissolves. If that should happen, they accept legal responsibility for the loss to their spouse. Such risk-assuming contracts are not at all unusual. Life insurance, for example, is such a contract. Much in the spirit of a marriage contract, a life insurance contract could be alternatively worded and interpreted as a promise to keep the insured alive for the year, or pay damages for the failure to do so.

A plainer and more basic response to the objection of the non-volitional nature of love is to aver that this is a misinterpretation of the meaning of love in the context of the marriage vow. The vow is a promise not to be in love with one's spouse but rather to act toward them in a manner that displays love, honor, and respect. Thus it is behavior that is being promised not emotion.

Marriage can clearly be regarded as a contract, but what sort of contract is it? What does it offer the parties? What are the difficulties of enforcement? What results from the failure of effective enforcement?

1 The economics of marriage and divorce

Although most of the heart of marriage is not expressed in the wedding vows, at least one expectation is nearly universal and expressly voiced. All marriages are entered into with the promise that the relationship should endure for the joint lives of the parties. Often, however, that promise is broken, and one or both parties seek to dissolve the agreement. Because marriage is a species of contract, many of the problems inherent in fashioning an efficient and equitable law of divorce, alimony, and property division are variations and special cases of the difficulties that surface in the enforcement of commercial contracts.

Marriage, despite being the culmination of romantic love, can be fruitfully analyzed employing the tools of rational choice. It is a voluntary commitment usually undertaken following considerable, albeit imperfect, reflection. The decision to marry a particular woman, even based on so emotional a motive as physical beauty, is at bottom economic – it entails trade-offs and sacrifices.

In the analysis that follows no consideration is given to externalities generated by dissolving a marriage. The principal such externality results from, and is experienced by and through, children. Most observers believe that children themselves experience a massive negative externality from their parents' divorce. The rest of society suffers negative externalities directly from each particular divorce and indirectly from the existence of the option of divorce – with the imperfect remedies to the breach that divorce constitutes or recognizes – on the institution of marriage. These externalities are of immense significance. That said, in this chapter I will analyze marriage assuming an absence of externalities. The theory of marriage as contract is challenging enough to explicate without addressing such externalities, and I can offer no systematic theoretical integration of the externalities of marriage and divorce into a theory of marriage as contract. I will note that marriage is but one path to procreation; it has substitutes. Or, to put it another way, marriage, divorce, child siring, child bearing, and child rearing are all pieces of a jointly endogenous mosaic. The more attractive and secure is marriage, the less the demand for out-of-wedlock birth, and vice versa. Thus the assessment of the external effects of any marriage and divorce regime must include the effect not merely on children of once married couples but also on the children of never married parents as well.

2   Why marry? Specific assets!

We begin with the question of why people choose to marry at all. Given the profound restriction on personal freedom demanded by marriage, and the obvious difficulty of predicting the continuation of one's ardor, the popularity of the long-term contractual commitment of marriage requires an explanation. In most commercial contracts the gains of contracting are purely instrumental, the only joy generated at the formation of the contract arises from the anticipation of its performance. In marriage, by contrast, two significant gains are garnered from the mere formation of the contract. First, the entrance into a consecrated state entailing a spiritual joining of two souls strikes a religious/psychological chord deep in the human soul. Second, the willingness of another to offer one a lifetime commitment indicates a deep and abiding love and is valued as evidence that one is worthy of such love.

That said, it is still the instrumental gains from marriage that are central. By far the most important gain from marriage is that it allows for investment in assets of peculiar value to this relationship. Allow me to elaborate.

The analogy to a long-term contract between a factory owner and a prospective tenant captures some of the flavor of the dilemma faced by a couple seeking to form a union, and especially to procreate. Neither the landlord nor the tenant would desire a long-term contract if no investment by either were to be undertaken that would be of peculiar value to the use of this factory by this tenant. Each would prefer to be free to take advantage of as-yet-unknown opportunities to employ their resources more profitably. Even if the parties anticipate that they will be making "specific asset" investments in this project, as long as (1) those investments are relatively modest and (2) each party knows that the other will make an approximately equal specific investment in this project, although each might desire the protection of a long-term contract they may well be willing to proceed with the project without such protection, relying on the other's self-interest to assure continuing performance. If, however, both parties expect to make major investments in the factory then both would seek the protection of a long-term contract. And *a fortiori*, if one party expects to make significantly greater specific investments in this factory than the other, then that party would be foolish not to insist on a long-term contract to protect the value of their investment from opportunistic appropriation or destruction as a result of the self-interested behavior of their co-venturer.

Imagine that the prospective tenant wishes to employ the factory space to manufacture instrument pads for woodwind instruments made out of pigs' bladders. Let us assume that the renovations required for this operation are unique to this particular manufacturing activity and that the market for such renovated facilities is virtually non-existent. Thus, whichever party undertakes the renovations – landlord or tenant – will lose the value of that investment if the relationship comes to a premature end. And so that party would seek the protections of a long-term contract.

So how does marriage present a similar dilemma? Why should men and women wish to make a long-term contract with one another? Why should they marry? What investments in "specific assets" does marriage entail?

Men and women have much that they can exchange with one another. Each has sex to offer, although men as a rule value it more. Each has procreation to offer, and women as a rule value that more, at least at the specific junctures at which negotiation takes place – their biological clock has a shorter spring. Then there is physical protection and income, of which men typically provide the lion's share, whereas homemaking and child rearing are usually more the province of the lioness. I could go on, but to do so would merely clutter the field. The central point is that men and women each desire the other as providers of vital services. Although in part their joining together yields each with a bit of insurance in the form of a source of *substitute* (symmetrical) services, the most vital part of the relationship centers on the provision of *complementary* (reciprocal) services.

But noting that men and women will seek to exchange does not explain why they should form a contract and certainly not a long-term contract. As suggested above, the drive to form a long-term contract must rest on some meaningful investment in a "specific" asset, that is an asset whose value is substantially diminished if the mutual project comes to a premature end. In the conjugal relationship between a man and a woman, by far the most significant, though not the only, investment in a specific asset is the consequence of procreation – children.

Investing in every good – children included – presents prospective costs and benefits. It is the distinctive character and pattern of those costs and benefits that make children such a peculiar and "specific" asset, and that in turn create the demand for the institution of marriage. What is special about children? More precisely what is it about children that makes them a specific asset that subjects an investor to severe risk of loss if the conjugal relationship terminates prematurely?

First, and most fundamentally, both the cost of, and return from, children span a lifetime. This long-lived quality of the investment is central to its specificity, for it permits its costs and benefits to be altered by the termination of the relationship. Second, whereas in the past (and even in the present in more economically primitive lands) children were something of an investment good, in the sense that the parents could expect a financial or at least a material return on their investment, in modern industrial countries children are principally a costly consumption good. As an investment good the presence of children would serve to hold the marriage together and mitigate damages if one party abandoned the other. The party who left would usually lose the return from the asset. This segues into the third and fourth peculiarities of children. Third, caring for a child may be an onerous burden (cost) to one person but a highly valued consumption activity to another, and neither may have correctly anticipated which it turns out to be. And fourth, the consumption of children can take a variety of forms that differ systematically across individuals, between sexes, and over lifetimes. These differing forms may or may not require having the child in close proximity for extended periods of time – or at all. For example, a father may gain great pleasure merely from knowing that he has children or that they are successful, but actually find the children's presence a burden, whereas the mother may be relatively indifferent to the success of her children but cherish their presence close to her. These two considerations combine to remove the reliability that the self-interest of one's mate will ensure their performance of the contract. Simply put, they may find having children a burden rather than a benefit or they may find them a benefit without requiring their presence, and so they may suffer no loss from leaving their home. Fifth, and finally, the existence of children and more importantly their presence in close proximity (if valued at all) are valued particularly by their natural parents; the presence of other people's children will often be a cost to strangers, especially prospective new mates.

Therefore, when a conjugal relationship between a mother and father terminates, each parent may still have significant costs to bear. But much of the anticipated gain of the procreation may be lost – or not. The loss can take a variety of forms. Access to the children may be reduced or eliminated. Or the reciprocal parenting function may be lost; for example, a mother may find it more difficult to discipline her children effectively, or a father may find it impossible to supply "motherly" love. Or financial support for the custodial parent by the non-custodial parent will be lost. Or homemaking services will be withdrawn; or companionship; or sexual services. More importantly, the children – not merely the expected future sacrifice of time and resources on them, but their very presence – and the mere passage of time since the commencement of the marriage, bringing in its wake changes in one's standing in the market for romantic partners, may make it difficult, if not impossible, substantially to mitigate damages by finding a replacement mate.

Thus a fundamental reason to marry is to allow for optimal investment in assets peculiar to the relationship, primarily, but not exclusively, children. If no long-term contract were available – or enforceable – the parties would not invest as much in the specific assets of the marriage as otherwise. This concern with children as specific assets, the investment in which exposes one to substantial risks, varies across individuals and differs systematically between the sexes. Women as a group have a greater concern for and desire to raise their children than do men. This is almost certainly a result of evolutionary adaptation. It is common to virtually all mammals and certainly to our near relatives – the simians. Further, it is consistent with the relative potential fecundity of men and women. One man could potentially impregnate tens of thousands of women and so has less stake in the outcome of each effort. A woman's stake in each egg and each pregnancy is infinitely greater.

It is not a myth, or an accident, or a socially constructed norm that it is women who are most anxious to obtain the contractual guaranty of marriage before engaging in sex, especially unprotected sex. They typically do not wish to undertake the investment of bearing the children of a particular man unless, and until, they have the promise of lifetime support, commitment, protection, or whatever else they take to be the services that a husband would provide. The significance of children as a specific asset that results in a massive loss at the premature termination of the conjugal relationship is the driving force of marriage. Were it not for the prospect of procreation it is doubtful that the lifetime pledge of the traditional marriage would be anything other than an anomalous high-risk adventure entered into by a few benighted souls.

Although children are the central reason for marriage they are not the only reason. The vow to fulfill one's duty "for richer or for poorer, in sickness and in health" reflects that marriage is also a species of insurance contract. Risk aversion may induce one to give up the opportunity to find a new companion in the event that one's own prospects have improved, in exchange for the other party making a symmetrical sacrifice.

3   The danger of breach

So there are substantial reasons to marry. Over a lifetime, however, the utility functions, information, and opportunities of both marriage partners change, and frequently one or the other will have an incentive to breach the contract. When the marriage contract is breached and terminates in divorce the wronged party loses a lifetime stream of spousal services.

In marriage, as in commercial contracts, examining the costs and difficulties of mitigating damages reveals the magnitude of the loss. The loss that the wronged spouse suffers from divorce is at least the transaction cost of finding a spouse of equivalent *ex ante* "value" the second time around. Often, however, the loss will be much greater, for that equivalent match may no longer be available. Indeed, the very reason that one marries, that is, that one enters into a long-term contract, is that some of the investments one wishes to undertake in a sexual relationship will lose substantial value if the relationship comes to an end. Were it generally possible to successfully mitigate damages by acquiring a substitute mate there would be little reason to marry in the first place.

4   Sharing the risk: reducing opportunism

No long-term contract will ever be formed unless at least one of the parties desires the guaranty provided by such a contract. And no party would insist on such guarantees unless they intended to undertake substantial investment in a specific asset. In commercial contracts it is almost never the case that the hostage investment need be specific to only one party to the agreement. Although the investment must lose value and therefore the owners of the investment must suffer that loss if the relationship is prematurely abandoned, which participant will be the owner and therefore suffer the loss is subject to the contractual relationship between the parties. Rather than the entire risk of the investment falling on but one of the parties, often the parties contractually share the risk.

Consider once more the instrument pad factory. Alice owns a vacant factory; Benjamin would like to rent the factory to manufacture instrument pads made from pig bladders for woodwind instruments. Because of the specialized nature of the production process the factory will require substantial renovations unique to this tiny industry – renovations that would be worthless if the project were abandoned. Benjamin might lease the factory from Alice at the market rate for a vacant space and pay for the renovations himself. If he did so Alice could hold his investments hostage; after he completed them she could threaten to terminate the relationship unless he paid a substantially higher rent. Alternatively, she could agree to undertake the renovations in exchange for his promise to pay a lease rate that capitalized the value of the improvements. In this case it would be Alice who would be vulnerable to appropriation by Benjamin. After she made the renovations, he could threaten to terminate the relationship unless she reduced the rent. The party making the investment in the specific asset is subject to appropriation of their expected quasi-rents by the other.

A long-term contract, *if reliably enforceable*, would protect the party making the investment. However, we live in an imperfect world and, rather than rely on legal protections alone to provide a negative sanction for breach, each party would prefer that the other party be motivated by positive self-interest as well. They can achieve this goal by sharing in the cost of the investment. Thus, Alice and Benjamin could each pay half the price of the renovations, with Benjamin agreeing to a lease rate that capitalized Alice's share of the renovation. Then, neither party's threat to abandon the contract opportunistically would be fully credible; were they to carry through on it they would suffer a substantial loss.

Marriage is different. It offers only the most minimal prospect for a contractual rearrangement that would leave both parties approximately equally vulnerable. This proposition is true not as a theoretical matter, but only as a practical one. Money is fungible. Its transfer from one party to the other could, in theory, make all parties to a contract equally vulnerable. So, in marriage, the party making the smaller real investment in the conjugal relationship could transfer a substantial sum to his or her spouse. These funds could be held as an asset to be passed on to their joint offspring if the marriage lasts, and if it does not then the asset would become the private property of the transferee. The institution of the "bride price" can be understood as a manifestation of this phenomenon. In the modern world the use of a bride price is impracticable. The bride's investment in potential procreation requires such an enormous investment on the part of most brides, in relation to the financial resources of most grooms, that no meaningful transfer is possible to place the parties on an equal footing with respect to the risk of the undertaking and the threat of appropriation of quasi-rents.

5   The market for husbands and wives

As we noted above, men and women are different, and the package of services they offer on the marriage market – husband and wife – differ even more sharply. For a variety of reasons, but principally because of women's more substantial role in the procreation and child-rearing process, it is women who generally make the more substantial investment in a conjugal relationship, and therefore it is they who more often seek the protection of the long-term contract of marriage. And so it is they who suffer most from the failure to enforce such contracts effectively.

Returning to the question of mitigation of damages, women as a rule face far greater difficulties in mitigating damages than do men. Their prospects of replacing a husband with one of equivalent *ex ante* value after an extended marriage punctuated by child bearing are slim. The harsh truth is that women are generally less highly valued in the remarriage market than they were prior to their first marriage. It is not quite, though almost, a corollary to note that men frequently rise substantially in relative value in the remarriage market.

The market for spouses is monopolistically competitive. All men are potential husbands; all women potential wives. Although some men are close substitutes for one another, most others are very imperfect substitutes. Nonetheless, there is substantial choice and competition in this market. Therefore, it is reasonable to view the archetypal party to a marriage as having forgone alternative spouses of nearly equivalent *ex ante* value to the one they actually married.

The loss from breach and divorce – the cost of acquiring a new spouse of equivalent *ex ante* value – is comprised of several distinct parts. We begin with transactions costs. A highly developed market usually results in low transactions costs. The marriage market is indeed highly developed; it offers a rich variety of competing paths to finding a spouse. But, in the case of marriage, the highly developed market, rather than resulting in low transactions costs, is itself the result of the extraordinary difficulty of satisfactorily completing the transaction, i.e. finding a good match.

Why are the costs so high? It is principally because this is a barter market. Men not only face the daunting task of finding a woman to whom they are willing to make a promise of a lifetime conjugal relationship, but also must find a woman who is willing to make the reciprocal promise to them. A careful search is vital for both parties because neither men nor women are fungible.

The participants may see dating, and other such search activities, like many in life, as either consumption or investment. The anecdotal evidence, as well as economic theory, suggests that for most participants dating begins as consumption and frequently mutates into a psychically costly investment with the passage of time and repetition of the experience. Although there is no systematic evidence on the question of how these costs vary between the sexes, there is also no *a priori* reason to assume that they are identical.

But even before one reaches the dating stage of the search process one must overcome two significant barriers. First, there is the problem of signaling one's availability to a sufficient number and appropriate set of market participants on the other side, and/or of acquiring their signals. Second, one must find a means to move from the status of stranger to that of at least acquaintance. To the proverbial Martian these tasks may seem quite straightforward and of minimal cost. But Earthlings who have lived the search know that there is more here than the outward description can capture. The inner sense of these activities is often one of turmoil, uncertainty, embarrassment, and pain. In primitive societies the signaling process is often singular, well known, and highly ritualized. In modern Western countries by contrast one can signal both to the market as a whole and to particular candidates in essentially any manner one wishes. Paradoxically, rather than lowering the cost, this abundance frequently raises it to an astonishing degree. Subtle signals are often lost in the cacophony or are misinterpreted, and grosser "signals" will often lead the recipients to infer a lack of the appropriate social graces or worse. Acting on inferred signals is hazardous on a variety of scores. The most common is leaving oneself open to severe embarrassment. When I seek to purchase an automobile I feel no shame that my offer is rejected because it is of insufficient value. But if my offer of romance is rejected it is a judgment that I am unworthy.

In general, the best environment in which to overcome these barriers is one in which the initial socialization does not suffer the search for mates as its principal purpose. Thus it is at school or at work, environments in which the activities of education and production are in the forefront, that men and women can get the ball rolling in some safety. But the recent rise of the legal category of sexual harassment is both the cause and reflection that all is not perfect even in this environment. Moreover, many people do not find themselves in the appropriate work or school environment when they need to engage in the search for mates. This is particularly true of women – especially mothers – seeking mates in the remarriage market.

Even if transactions costs were zero, it is likely that one party, or both, will not be able to do as well the second time around. Why? First, one spouse may have suffered the stochastic change in value that the marriage vows expressly insured against, for example the great athlete who has been crippled by disease or accident. Second, predictable changes often result from an investment in assets specific to this marriage. Children, being the most significant investment in a specific marital asset, represent the greatest consequent cost in the search for a potential replacement spouse. Women, because they generally gain custody of their children, suffer this cost most heavily. Third, and perhaps most importantly, women usually lose value in the marriage market relative to men solely as a result of ageing.

6   Women's loss of value on the marriage market

Demonstrating the loss of value of women in the remarriage market analytically or empirically is extremely difficult because of the peculiar barter nature of this market. Men and women bear no price tags that state their value, nor are they exchanged for things that can be priced. The only measure of their value is the "quality" of spouses they can acquire, who similarly bear no price tags. The prospective bride is simultaneously the commodity purchased, the currency used to purchase a husband, and the purchaser of the husband. Likewise, the prospective groom is simultaneously the purchased, the currency, and the purchaser. Thus, we are faced with an intractable identification problem. In addition, the lack of transitivity of tastes across purchasers further obscures the issue; Ms. Jones prefers Mr. Smith to Mr. Brown, while Ms. Burns prefers Brown to Smith. Because of these problems, observations from the marriage market are open to multiple interpretations.

Despite these handicaps and qualifications, the available statistical evidence suggests that, with marriage, child bearing, and the passage of time, women lose value on the marriage market relative to men. Four facts stand out: (1) men have higher mortality rates than women at all ages;[3] (2) divorced men remarry at a faster rate than do divorced women for every age group except 14–24;[4] (3) divorced women with children remarry at a slower rate than do those without; and (4) women tend to marry men who are older than themselves, and as they age the gap increases.[5]

Let us consider the impact of different mortality rates. This empirical observation is of a different character than the other three. Whereas the others all suggest that the remarriage market *is* less friendly to women (especially with children), this first observation is powerful evidence of at least one substantial reason of *why* that is the case. It is the hoary notion of supply and demand. One's value on the market is in large part a function of the ratio of the number of men seeking wives to women seeking husbands. In a monogamous culture the numbers of wives and husbands are identically equal. But the numbers of men and women are not usually equal. Although there are slightly more male than female live births, a higher mortality rate for males of all ages (even prenatal) creates an ever-widening abundance of women over men of the same age as age increases.[6]

The gap between the number of men and women is only part of the story. The percentage of men who are married rises steadily as a function of age to age 65. Therefore, the ratio of unmarried women to unmarried men rises faster

---

[3] *Statistical Abstract of the United States*, table 29 (1981).

[4] U.S. Bur. Census, Current Population Reports 55, table 8 (Ser. P-20, No. 223, 1971); and U.S. Public Health Service, Vital Statistics 10, table J (Ser. 21, No. 20, Increases in Divorces, United States, 1967, 1970).

[5] U.S. Bur. Census, U.S. Census of Population: 1960, table 1 (subject Reports, Marital Status, Final Report PC (2)-4E, 1966) cited in Carter and Glick (1976, p. 88). See also Brossard (1933), Glick & Landau (1950).

[6] The life expectancy of American men was 53.6 and of women 54.6 in 1920. In 1983, the respective figures were 71.0 and 78.3. *Statistical Abstract of the United States*, table 102 (1981).

than the overall sex ratio. The ratio of unmarried women to unmarried men is less than 1:1 for 20 year olds and over 2:1 for 55 year olds.[7]

These numbers also fail fully to capture the difficulties that men's higher mortality rates place on women's effort to find a mate as they age. A subset of the unmarried is the relatively unmarriageable. Because of physical handicaps, mental disabilities, imprisonment, etc., they do not have enough to offer to attract a spouse. As the cohort ages, the unmarriageable become an ever-increasing proportion of the age cohort, and a still larger proportion of the unmarried. Further, because of imprisonment and other forms of institutionalization and various disabilities, the unmarriageable become disproportionately more male as the cohort ages. Therefore the female/male ratio of the marriageable unmarried is considerably greater than 2:1 by age 55. Assuming that people generally marry those near their own age (we shall shortly examine this assumption more closely), women have a great deal more competition for potential spouses the second time around than the first.

A sub-issue related to the notion of the unmarriageable is the more general question of the quality of potential spouses left in the market. Those women who have never married tend to be of higher employment status and education level than those who do marry. And so some sociologists have argued that whereas the never-married men tend to be "bottom of the barrel" the women are the "cream of the crop" (Bernard, 1982, p. 158). But this seems implausible. Why should the cream not be skimmed? An alternative explanation is that employment status and education are not the relevant dimensions for measuring the quality of the women as prospective spouses. Beauty, charm, and femininity are particularly pertinent variables for women's success on the marriage market. But why should marital status be negatively correlated with employment and education? Marriage and career are each investment/consumption activities that require substantial commitments of time. They are therefore substitutes. So, it is likely that sexually attractive feminine qualities are negatively correlated with education and occupational status. Women who invest in career invest less in making themselves attractive to men and in searching for men, and women who are less attractive have an incentive to invest more in a career.

Returning to the question of women's fall in value on the marriage market as they age, the relative mortality figures provide evidence that women should fare worse than men as they age, simply as an almost mathematical reflection of the changing supply of and demand for each sex in each age cohort. The remaining three empirical observations may all be taken as evidence that women indeed do fare worse following divorce than men. They marry more slowly, they marry still more slowly if they have children, and they marry older and older men.

---

[7] *Statistical Abstract of the United States*, table 49 (1981).

There are of course commonsense explanations for each of these phenomena that parallel and reinforce the hypothesis that women lose value in the marriage market as they age and bear children. For example, at the time of divorce, women obtain *de facto* even if no longer *de jure* custody of the children in the large majority of cases.[8] Caring for children imposes two significant costs on women in the marriage market. First, it makes it more difficult for them to search and advertise. Second, men usually prefer to marry childless women.[9] And so it is no surprise that the remarriage rate of divorced women with children is significantly lower for the five-year period following divorce than that of divorced women without children.

Although the natural explanation might seem to be men's lesser demand for mothers as marriage partners, we cannot be sure, owing to the identification problem referred to earlier. From the data per se we cannot definitively determine whether we are seeing men's preference for younger childless women or women's preference as they age and have children for (1) older men, (2) a more thorough search of the market, or (3) remaining unmarried.

In addition to the difficulty of distinguishing whether greater time spent on the marriage market is a reflection of a person's greater discrimination or of lesser value, there is the further problem of determining whether he or she is on the market at all. When a person does not seek the company of the opposite sex, does this reflect a preference or is it analogous to the discouraged unemployed who drop out of the labor market? When a person spends a great deal of time dating and going to "singles" events, does this represent: (1) a long and thorough search, (2) difficulty in finding a buyer/partner, or (3) a preference for dating over marriage?

Differing mortality rates and child custody patterns are not the only, and may not be the most important, reason women lose value in the marriage market as they age. What else can we point to as evidence of and explanation for women's relative loss of value on the marriage market? The different mortality rates mean, if we assume that people search only among their immediate contemporaries, that the odds get progressively better for men and worse for women as they age. However, the average age gap between brides and grooms, and more particularly its increase as people age, illustrate that people are not constrained in their search. Why are husbands generally older than wives, and why does the gap increase with age at marriage? This age gap has one explanation with regard to

---

[8] The percentage of times the mother receives custody has been estimated variously from a low of 80 percent (Jacobson, 1959, p. 131) to a high of 95 percent (Goode, 1965, p. 311). According to US census figures, 89.7 percent of the children of divorced parents live with their mother. U.S. Bur. Census, Current Population Reports 5, table E (Ser. P-20, No. 380, Marital Status and Family Status: March 1982).

[9] Socio-biologist Richard Dawkins argues that no strategy of family planning that is indifferent to whether offspring raised by a parent are genetically their own can be evolutionarily stable (Dawkins, 1976, p. 117).

the first marriages of the young, but the gap and its increase require different explanations for older brides and grooms.

Men and women become marriageable at different ages. Being a husband or wife requires certain skills and capacities that do not come to fruition at the same age for men as for women. Sufficient emotional maturity, domestic skills, and fertility can all be well established and apparent in a woman by her middle to late teens. For a man it is different. Even now, a man is expected to support his wife and children. That ability takes more time to establish than the domestic skills required of a wife.

The disparity in the proportion of men versus women who have acquired sufficient human capital to be marriageable at a given age disappears rather quickly once both parties enter their twenties. Why then does the median excess of husbands' ages over wives' increase as the age of the groom increases? If the goal is a joint lifetime of marriage then, given that women tend to outlive men, one would think that the gap would not only shrink but reverse itself, so men would marry women older than themselves.

This increasing age gap of grooms over brides as well as the greater frequency of remarriage of men are best explained by the differing rates and directions of change of attractiveness of men and women to their opposites as they age. The data suggest that older men need not restrict their search to their own direct contemporaries but may instead fish in the likely more attractive pool of younger women. Thus older women have a yet smaller pool of their own contemporaries who are interested in them. Wives and husbands are reciprocal, not symmetrical, roles performed by spouses. Since what a man wants in a wife is different from what a woman wants in a husband, the ability to satisfy these requirements need not, and does not, vary with age at the same rate for wives as for husbands. Women fall in value quite simply because men prefer younger women, whereas women do not have as strong or even a similar age preference with regard to men.[10]

Although this proposition is consistent with the data, it is not proved by them. It is a proposition about tastes and so is not directly observable. That said, the footprints of this common human trait are visible in every byway of the culture. First, we may note that the cultural icons of feminine attractiveness are all young or young looking. Movie starlets, models, showgirls, and dancers are all most admired or desired when young. Women's magazines constantly offer

[10] Judge Richard Neely has observed that "[h]istorically it has been recognized that men are attracted to women of childbearing years. One finds few examples in literature of a man romantically attached to a woman over forty, with a notable exception of Collette's *Cheri*. Anyone who has practiced family law is aware that younger women are in general attracted to rich, powerful and necessarily older men, whilst men are attracted to young, beautiful and adoring women. Domestically, the young, unassertive and impecunious man and the older, homely or overly independent woman are usually the last hired and the first to be fired" (Neely, 1979; see also Posner, 1992).

suggestions on how to maintain one's youthful appearance. Much popular music reflects men's preferences for younger women; for example, from the country and western genre we have "Younger Women, Faster Horses, Older Whiskey" and folk-rock offers "A Younger Girl Keeps Rolling Past My Mind." On the other side of the equation, youth does not carry the same positive connotation when applied to men. Consider the many older actors who successfully played male leads opposite much younger women – Cary Grant, Paul Newman, Robert Redford – or the notion that gray hair makes a man look distinguished. This is little more than a sampling of the multitude of cultural representations of the different age profiles of attractiveness of men and women to those on the other side.[11]

The phenomenon of different age preferences for mates between the sexes is not an idiosyncratic short-lived American cultural peculiarity. The extraordinary attractiveness of young females to males of all ages compared with the more accepting tastes of women with respect to the age of a man is cross-cultural and historically consistent. For example, in polygamous cultures men almost exclusively add younger wives rather than older ones to their harem and, if powerful enough, trade in older ones for younger.

Why do men and women have such markedly different tastes? A powerful evolutionary explanation is available that is also consistent with the ordinary reasons that people give for marriage. Young women are fertile, whereas old women are not. The same is not true for men. Moreover, with age men are generally in a better financial position to support a wife and her offspring. So it would hardly be surprising if men have literally evolved a strong preference for young fertile women and that women's preferences have not evolved in a symmetrical fashion.

7   Breach and appropriable quasi-rents

At the time of formation, the marriage contract promises gains to both parties. Yet the period of time over which these gains are realized is not symmetrical. As a rule, men obtain gains early in the relationship, and women late. This follows from women's relative loss in value. Young women are valued as mates by both old and young men. When they choose to marry a particular man they give up all their other alternatives. And over those early years, as women are wont to

---

[11] Although ordinary language and its analysis may seem a somewhat odd form of argument for either an economist or a lawyer to use, such argument has a reputable intellectual pedigree. As a branch and school of philosophy, "ordinary language analysis" is used to derive and discover definitions of philosophical terms. See, for example, Austin (1979, p. 75). Austin "believed that in general a clear insight into the many subtle distinctions that are enshrined in ordinary language and have survived in a lengthy struggle for existence with competing distinctions could hardly fail to be also an insight into important distinctions to be observed in the world around us" (Edwards, 1967, p. 211).

complain, they give that man "the best years of their lives." At the back end, when their value on the marriage market falls relative to their husbands, they expect to be repaid for their sacrifice. The creation of this long-term imbalance provides the opportunity for strategic behavior whereby one of the parties, generally the man, will perform his obligations under the marriage contract only so long as he is receiving a net positive marginal benefit and will breach the contract unless otherwise constrained once the marginal benefit falls below his opportunity cost.

This problem is well understood in long-term commercial contracts as one of appropriable quasi-rents. A quasi-rent is a return to one party to a contract above what the party would receive if the contract could be dissolved at will at that moment. Much of the law of contract is an effort to design rules and institutions that prevent this kind of strategic behavior, whose control is in the mutual interest of both parties at the time of contract formation.

In a commercial contract the uncompensated breach by one party will usually not affect the *ex post* allocation of resources, but result only in a wealth transfer to the breacher of a large portion of the other's quasi rents. Reasoning by analogy and *wrongly* assuming negotiation between spouses to be a low transactions cost encounter, one would conclude that, if continuing breach and termination of the contract were more costly to the wife (the wronged spouse) than its value to the husband (the breaching spouse), the parties would reach a Coasean bargain in which the wife offers the husband compensation intermediate between the value of breaching to him and the value of continuing the marriage to her.

On occasion, something that bears a passing resemblance to a Coasean bargain is struck: for example, rather than terminate a marriage a wife may accept a husband who is periodically unfaithful or occasionally violent. Even if we could assume that such post-contractual opportunistic adjustments were the norm, breach would not be without its consequences. First, there is the inequity of uncompensated breach. And inequities, when anticipated, will be partially transformed into inefficiencies. That is, even if making post-contractual opportunistic adjustments or declining to renegotiate the contract to forestall breach and recision were *ex post* efficient, their anticipation would generate severe *ex ante* inefficiencies. Women who expect that much of the benefit of the bargain of marriage will not be forthcoming will adjust their behavior *ex ante*. They will: marry less frequently; choose to marry a different sort of man; and invest less in their marriages.

More often than not, however, not even a pale imitation of a Coasean bargain can be reached, and not because breaching is worth more to the husband than it costs the wife. The problems in continuing the marriage under a new arrangement are of two sorts: transactions costs and wealth effects. Normally in a two-person negotiation transactions costs are minimal, but marriage is different. Returning to the second paragraph of this chapter, I remind you that in marriage the spirit counts for a lot. The performance of marital duties loses much value if it is perceived to be in the wrong spirit. Threatening breach and renegotiating the contract will usually poison the relationship. So even if a woman had substantial independent wealth or income and could offer her husband financial compensation to refrain from terminating the marriage, and the marriage, as it had been, was more valuable than the compensation she would have to offer, she likely would not offer to compensate him for refraining from breach and continuing the marriage. For now that negotiations have opened, the marriage can no longer be as it was. Marital duties performed in exchange for financial compensation would have only shadows of their former values. The transactions costs of renegotiating the contract will often be prohibitive, because the very act of renegotiation destroys the value of the services performed.

Even were this not the case, the wife typically lacks the resources with which to bribe her husband to stay in the marriage even if she wished to do so. The problem is a variation on the wealth-effect version of the Coase Theorem. That is, if he must compensate her for breaching he will be unwilling to do so, and if she must compensate him for refraining from breaching she will be unwilling to do so. Her willingness to suffer more in the marriage, that she might thereby suffer less than she would by its termination, will usually be no compensation at all to him; the currency of loss to her does not convert into a currency of benefit to him.

The possibility for substantial breaches of the marriage contract has always existed. Until recent times, though, there were greater costs associated with such breaches. The religious consciousness of the people who participated in and sanctioned the institution placed substantial internal psychological and external social costs on the parties in the event of breach. Rather than the formal legal constraints, which prove to be tenuous and imperfect, it was the informal social and psychological constraints that by and large protected marriages. As those institutions have declined, the probably inherent inadequacies of the legal structures have come to the fore.

Before considering legal responses to the problems of marital breach, let us briefly catalog the private responses to the problem. In many commercial contexts post-contractual opportunism can be anticipated and averted by vertical integration. If the owner of one of the capital assets could purchase the capital asset of the other, the incentive to appropriate the quasi-rents of that capital asset is eliminated. Once more consider the instrument pad factory. The man who wants to produce instrument pads could – and likely would – purchase the factory from its current owner (see Klein, Crawford, and Alchian, 1978).

This solution is not feasible in the context of marriage. The crux of the problem is not the legal prohibition of a person selling him- or herself to another.

It is that the man (or woman) cannot in any meaningful way purchase the person who can be a wife (or husband). He cannot purchase her in such a way that he will have the same stake in her welfare that she has, as a tenant could purchase a building and have the same stake in its condition as the former owner had.

Another contractual device sometimes employed in the commercial sphere is hostage taking (see Williamson, 1983; also Klein and Leffler, 1981, p. 615) This would require the wife to hold something of value of the husband's until she is assured of his performance of the contract. The institution of "bride price" is a form of hostage taking.[12] The shortcomings of instituting a bride price as a form of hostage taking are several. First, the parties may be too young and immature to foresee the possibility of future breach. Second, bridegrooms in our economy are generally far better endowed with human capital than with physical or money capital. Since they cannot transfer their human capital to their wife, they have very little to give as a hostage. Third, couples are likely to spend all their income in the early years of their marriage, therefore, the holding of a substantial amount of property by the wife as a hostage would inefficiently constrain the consumption of the family. Fourth, the need to guarantee performance is partially symmetric. A wife as well as a husband can breach and destroy the quasi-rents of her mate. Finally, bride price is a cultural phenomenon that evolves over many centuries. The institution of bride price grounded in efficiency concerns unconnected to cultural or religious roots would run into the fundamental problem that marriage is not principally a commercial relationship. If one of the parties were to treat it as a commercial contract by insisting on a bride price (or a dowry), this would likely damage the relationship.

But cash is not the only hostage. Children can sometimes serve as hostages. Wives usually receive custody of the children following a divorce. If the husband fears the loss of close contact with his children he may refrain from breach. But, there are severe limitations to the effectiveness of employing children as hostages. They are useless to the childless wife and of only limited value to the wife whose children are adults. Moreover, in order to serve effectively as hostages, the husband must feel their absence as a severe deprivation. If he does not, or if his expected visitation rights following a divorce are liberal enough to mitigate his loss significantly, he may not suffer much cost. And, although it is in the wife's *ex ante* interest to threaten to deprive her husband of access to his children, it is frequently in her *ex post* interest that he should maintain close contact with them. She is more likely to receive child support and maintenance payments if her ex-husband has an

---

[12] For a brief discussion of the economics of bride price in primitive societies, see Posner (1981, pp.186–9).

ongoing relationship with his children. Also she may believe and give weight to the idea that it is better for her children that they maintain contact with their father.

Another strategy women can adopt is to marry an older man than they otherwise would. If a man and a woman are of equal value on the marriage market at age 20 and the woman's value as the capital asset "wife" declines fairly steadily, whereas the man's value as the capital asset "husband" rises initially before declining, then over a large span of the marriage the man's value on the market will exceed the wife's and he will have an incentive to terminate the marriage. By marrying an older man, a woman can protect herself from this relative loss of value. In doing so she in effect is acquiring more current consumption and less investment in a future relationship. This greater consumption may, but need not exclusively, be in the form of higher money income. This strategic choice of a husband by a woman is a species of constrained maximization and thus represents some net social loss. A woman who strategically marries an older man is choosing a man whose market value is higher than his value to her in comparison with other men *in a world in which the marriage contract is secure.* Her choice among men not only reflects her desires but also includes his expected future alternatives.

Finally, there is the default solution. If you cannot protect the quasi-rents that you believe you will receive from investing in assets specific to marriage, then invest less in this marriage or in being married.[13] The tendency of middle-class families to have fewer children and the tendency for women to acquire more marketable skills are of course consistent with and explainable by one another as well as by a variety of other variables of our changing culture. Nonetheless, both phenomena are also consistent with women investing fewer resources in being wives in general and in being one man's wife in particular out of fear of uncompensated breach. Considering the enormous magnitude of the consequence of breach on the value of the specific assets of marriage, it is inconceivable that the greater likelihood of breach has not significantly affected the level of those investments.

Informal devices and state-imposed legal remedies are substitute methods to protect women from the appropriation of quasi-rents. If the informal social mechanisms are insufficient to protect marriage partners, then legal methods of protection increase in importance. The question is: which forms of legal arrangements best prevent the destruction and appropriation of the quasi-rents in marriage? Here it is possible to consider both voluntary prenuptial agreements

---

[13] Elisabeth Landes (1978) found that in states that prohibit alimony there is a statistically significantly lower rate of marriage and a reduced marital fertility rate compared with states that do not restrict alimony awards. She also found a lower rate of marriage in states that exclude considerations of fault in determining alimony awards. See also Becker, Landes, and Michael (1977).

and the standard-form marriage contract that is provided by the state in large measure through its divorce laws.

8   Prenuptial marriage contracts

The use of prenuptial marriage contracts has increased in recent years. These contracts take a variety of forms and are motivated by a variety of forces. The polar forms of these contracts may be characterized as the traditional, the remarriage, the counterculture, and the feminist.

The traditional prenuptial marriage contract was motivated by a desire to protect assets accumulated prior to a marriage from appropriation by the spouse following a divorce. Most often, though not always, it is the groom who seeks such a contract when he has accumulated a great deal of wealth or expects a high income. On occasion the family of one of the marriage partners seeks such a contract.

A variant of this traditional prenuptial agreement frequently arises when one of the parties has offspring from a prior marriage. The blush of romance has faded, and both parties recognize the necessity to protect the future welfare of pre-existing family members. To forestall anxiety and uncertainty, the marriage partners will often negotiate how their property will be divided in the event of both divorce and death.[14]

Counterculture marriage contracts seem to arise out of distaste for traditional marital roles. The panoply of traditional duties that the community implied but did not expressly state in sanctioning marriage is replaced by an express and sometimes detailed statement of duties that the parties agree to. The law, having been unwilling to enforce traditional duties, in the sense of requiring specific performance has also been chary of enforcing the terms of these contracts.

The feminist marriage contract is at least in part motivated by the concerns voiced in this chapter, namely, that women often do not receive a fair shake in a divorce; that is, it recognizes that divorce deprives them of quasi-rents that represent a return to sacrificed opportunities. These contracts seek to shift the weight of post-marital rights, duties, and property division in favor of the wife. Ironically, those women who are most likely to be victimized by the divorce laws – those who embrace the role of the traditional wife – are least likely to negotiate a feminist marriage contract.

These formal prenuptial contracts offer some opportunity to the parties to protect themselves, and, especially with second marriages, they can do quite well in specifying the devolution of property to children after death. Nonetheless, these contracts are of limited use in the case of ordinary marriage, largely because of

---

[14] The creation of a trust prior to remarriage is generally a superior and more secure method of addressing this concern.

the difficulties they face in specifying the appropriate level of damage payments, if any, to be paid in the event of breach. Any such marriage contract must specify a variety of damage amounts, each reflecting the stage in the marriage when the breach occurs, the circumstances of the parties at the time of marriage, and the circumstances at the time of breach. Further, they will still have to contend with the question of whether or not fault should be taken into account and how it is to be determined. The imperfect knowledge of the future cannot be overcome.

9   Public law remedies for breach

What can we make of the legislative approaches to the question of divorce? There are four polar legal structures available for handling the problem of divorce: (1) unilateral divorce with no property settlement, (2) mutual consent divorce with mutually agreed property settlement, (3) indissoluble marriage, and (4) judge-determined divorce and property settlements. These four structures represent the polar forms of which all actual divorce laws are combinations.

Where the law provides for unilateral divorce without property settlement, each party is simply free to walk away from the marriage. As such, the unilateral divorce is the marital analogy to the contract at will. In commercial contexts the at-will contract tends not to be used when either party must make massive investments in specific assets or when the parties must make differential investments, for then the risks of opportunistic behavior or a simple miscalculation of the other party's interest are simply too great.[15] This simple regime of divorce is generally unsuitable for long-term marriage contracts, precisely because usually both parties, but certainly the wife who bears children, must make a massive investment in specific assets, and because it allows one spouse (typically the husband) freely to abandon the marriage after the wife has made her disproportionate contributions to the relationship. The unilateral divorce without property adjustment is therefore the problem that marriage contracts must overcome, rather than the solution.[16]

Mutual consent divorce is the family law analogy to the contractual remedy of specific performance because it requires performance of the contract unless a release is granted. At first blush this solution seems powerful because it appears that no inefficient breaches could occur. Much of the initial attractiveness of mutual consent divorce fades under closer examination. The essential problem is that specific performance is not really available as an enforceable remedy. First, many of the acts that a spouse has implicitly contracted to perform cannot

---

[15] For a discussion of this point, see generally Epstein (1984).

[16] Unilateral divorce more or less corresponds to the modern institution of "no-fault," divorce which was first enacted in California in 1970, and has since swept through the United States and much of the western world, albeit in less radical form. See Foster and Freed (1971, chapter 1); Lichtenstein (1985).

be specified or their performance monitored. Second, as emphasized earlier, the marital duties are to be performed in a certain spirit, and no court can succeed in forcing an unwilling spouse to perform marital duties in a spirit of love and devotion. Therefore, although the law may not permit the party who wishes to breach the marriage agreement to obtain a divorce without the permission of their spouse, nor can it make them meaningfully perform the duties of the contract.

This raises two related problems: breach without divorce, and the destruction of quasi-rents. Because the law can do little to enforce the most meaningful and possibly onerous obligations of a marriage, it is possible for a party to breach the contract while remaining nominally married. If this strategy necessarily imposed substantial costs specifically on the breaching party, an incentive would still remain for the breacher to obtain the consent to divorce from the wronged party. However, the reality is often that a party can breach without obtaining a divorce while simultaneously reaping many of the gains of divorce. In our era of relaxed sexual mores and community values a married man can live separate from, or with, his wife for an indefinite period of time without either party being inordinately restricted in their social and sexual activities.

There is no strong reason for believing that the costs of not obtaining a divorce will bear more heavily on one spouse or the other – breacher or victim, wife or husband. Thus, rather than placing a cost on breachers, inducing a reduction in inefficient breaches of the marriage contract, a requirement for mutual consent for divorce is likely to result in fewer breaches terminating in divorce.

Although the possibility of breach without divorce implies that the costs to not obtaining a divorce are neither specific to the breacher nor excessive, the destructibility of quasi-rents implies that the benefits of not consenting to a divorce are minimal for the party who has suffered a breach. Because marital breach destroys much of the value of the remainder of the contract to the wronged party, often when a marriage is breached neither party wants it to continue. If the marriage is no longer highly valued by either party, it is likely that a property settlement can be worked out that is *ex post* satisfactory. Such an agreement is likely to be far different from what would have been specified *ex ante*.

The breaching spouse often does not merely appropriate the quasi-rents being earned by their partner but actually destroys those rents. This destruction will occur naturally as a result of the breach and need not be the purposeful intent of the breaching spouse. Moreover, such destruction will also occur under a unilateral divorce regime. The problem is exacerbated in the case of mutual consent, however, in that the breaching party gains by destroying the quasi-rents of their partner. The requirement of mutual consent creates an incentive for the breaching party to act more egregiously and thereby destroy more of the rents of their spouse. As the quasi-rents are destroyed, the marriage falls in value to the innocent party, whose consent to a divorce can then be obtained at a lower price.[17]

In light of the shortcomings of unilateral and mutual consent standards of divorce, indissoluble marriages appear to have many virtues. First, the possibility of inefficient divorces is eliminated. Second, extreme incentives are created for the exercise of greater care in choosing a spouse. Third, since the very act of seeking a divorce destroys the quasi-rent being earned by the satisfied spouse in the marriage, making the marriage indissoluble appears to eliminate much of this loss. Fourth, neither party has an incentive to destroy rents solely for the purpose of obtaining the consent of the other to a divorce.

On the other side of the ledger, there are two very substantial costs of indissoluble marriage. First, there indeed are efficient terminations of contract. If the law were to require the parties to carry out the marriage contract in spite of their desire to dissolve it, efficient dissolution of marriages would be sacrificed. In addition to the direct losses to the parties forced to carry out such contracts, some couples at the margin will avoid marrying because these indissoluble contracts are not as valuable to them as dissoluble ones. Because it is possible to breach without obtaining a divorce, some of the costs discussed in the paragraph above and much of the virtue of indissoluble marriage may prove illusory. Although the law can prevent divorce, it is unable to require and enforce performance of the marriage contract in all but a perfunctory sense.[18] Therefore, as in the case of mutual consent divorces, indissoluble marriage allows someone to breach without providing an effective remedy for the wronged party.

The final legislative alternative is to allow the court to grant divorce at its discretion and to determine the property settlement independently of the agreement of the parties. The court would be called on to determine who had breached and the future stream of quasi-rents that the non-breaching party had a right to expect prior to the breach and award them the present value of that future stream. Only *ex ante* efficient divorces would take place, and the demands of both justice and efficiency would be satisfied.

Interestingly, the relationship between this remedy and mutual consent divorce represents a reversal of the usual dichotomy between the liability rule and the property rule. In the typical commercial case a liability rule is a less

---

[17] As a leading jurist in this area, Judge Neely has put it, "[a]lthough an energetic man tied to a woman he married when he was young may find himself bored, fenced in, and unhappy, his wife may be perfectly content with the lifestyle she was encouraged as a child to consider her destiny. Under the liberal grounds for divorce which are becoming acceptable in most states, a man in these circumstances is capable of starting out again with a minimum of either alimony or child support liability. While the woman who had relied to her detriment on society's promise of stable family life can easily find herself in desperate emotional and financial circumstances" (Neely, 1979).

[18] In the entire Marriage section of Am. Jur. 2d (section 52) there is not a single reference to the substantive duties of the parties to a marriage. The only place where spousal duties surface is in the discussion of Divorce and Separation (section 24).

generous vehicle than a property rule for vindicating the rights of the wronged party. The property rule normally permits the wronged party to take a portion of the gain that the breaching party would reap from breach. In the case of marriage, however, because of the personal nature of the duties and the destructibility of quasi-rents, a property rule (i.e. mutual consent divorce) will often leave the wronged party worse off than a liability rule (Dnes, 1998).

There is only one shortcoming to judge-determined divorce: it is much easier to say than to do. In order to implement this regime effectively, courts must determine who breached and the value of the loss to the non-breaching party. The determination of breach is a substantial hurdle but is dwarfed by the difficulties of specifying the loss in quasi-rents occasioned by marital breach. Furthermore, the damages will often be so great that the breacher is in effect judgment proof.

10   Conclusion

The application of the general theory of long-term contracts to the contract of marriage does not yield any obvious or optimistic conclusions as to the proper way to structure the marriage arrangement. The nature of the underlying duties assumed by the marriage partners is not capable of precise definition, much less effective legal enforcement. Yet the success of the marriage often requires the two partners to invest heavily in the relationship even though they may be able to salvage little of their original investment should the marriage turn bad. To make matters more difficult, the roles of men and women are not symmetrical. It is typically the wife who has more to lose by divorce. What, if anything, can be done to insure the integrity of the long-term marriage arrangement, which redounds *ex ante* to the benefit of both marriage partners? Neither antenuptial marriage contracts nor the various legal regimes of divorce and property settlement offer much hope for the general population. It is difficult, therefore, to suggest with any conviction a definitive solution to the marriage problem. There is much to be said for the older view that relies on informal and social sanctions and the good moral sense of the parties for the greatest protection of the marriage relationship.

REFERENCES

Austin, J. (1979), *Philosophical Papers*, 3rd edn, Oxford: Oxford University Press.
Babcock, B.A. (1978), *Sex Discrimination and the Law: Causes and Remedies*, Boston, MA: Little, Brown.
Becker, G., E. Landes and R. Michael (1977), "An Economic Analysis of Marital Instability," *Journal of Political Economy*, 85, 1141–87.
Bernard, J. (1982), *The Future of Marriage*, New Haven, CT: Yale University Press.
Brossard, J.S. (1933), "The Age Factor in Marriage: A Philadelphia Study," *American Journal of Sociology*, 138, 219–24.

Carter, H. and C. Glick (1976), *Marriage and Divorce: A Social and Economic Study*, Cambridge, MA: Harvard University Press.

Clark, H. (1968), *Law and Domestic Relations*, St. Paul, MN: West Publishing Co.

Cohen, L.R. (1987), "Marriage, Divorce and Quasi Rents; or, 'I Gave Him the Best Years of My Life,' " *Journal of Legal Studies*, 16, 267–303.

(1995), "The Unnatural Family, and Women's Work," *Virginia Law Review*, 81, 2275–303.

(1998), "Marriage as Contract," in P. Newman (ed.), *The New Palgrave Dictionary of Economics and the Law*, London: Macmillan.

Dawkins, R. (1976), *The Selfish Gene*, Oxford: Oxford University Press.

Dnes, A. (1998), "The Division of Marital Assets," *Journal of Law and Society*, 25, 336–64.

Edwards, P. (ed.) (1967), *Encyclopedia of Philosophy*, New York: Macmillan.

Epstein, R.A. (1984), "In Defense of the Contract at Will," *University of Chicago Law Review*, 51, 947–87.

Foster, H.H. and D. Freed (1971), *Family Law: Cases and Materials*, 3rd edn, Boston: Little, Brown.

Glick, P. and E. Landau (1950), "Age as a Factor in Marriage," *American Sociological Review*, 517–29.

Goode, W. (1965), *Women in Divorce*, Westport, CT: Greenwood Press.

Jacobson, P. (1959), *American Marriage and Divorce*, New York: Rinehart.

Klein, B., R. Crawford and A. Alchian (1978), "Vertical Integration, Appropriable Rents, and the Competitive Contracting Process," *Journal of Law and Economics*, 21, 297–326.

Klein, B. and K. Leffler (1981), "The Role of Market Forces in Assuring Contractual Performance," *Journal of Political Economy*, 89, 615–41.

Landes, E. (1978), "Economics of Alimony," *Journal of Legal Studies*, 7, 35–9.

Lichtenstein, N.B. (1985), "Marital Misconduct and the Allocation of Financial Resources at Divorce: A Farewell to Fault," *UMKC Law Review*, 54(1), 1–18.

Neely, R. (1979), "Marriage Contracts, for Better or for Worse Marital and Non-marital Contracts," in J.M. Krauskopf (ed.), *Preventative Law for the Family*, Chicago: Section on Family Law of the American Bar Association, 3–11.

Posner, R.A. (1981), *The Economics of Justice*, Cambridge, MA: Harvard University Press.

(1992), *Sex and Reason*, Cambridge, MA: Harvard University Press.

Williamson, O. (1983), "Credible Commitments: Using Hostages to Support Exchange," *American Economic Review*, 73, 519–40.

3 Marital commitment and the legal regulation of divorce

Elizabeth S. Scott

The question of the appropriate role of law in regulating marriage and divorce is the subject of much controversy in the United States – a raging battle of the "Culture Wars" (Hunter, 1991). On one side are social conservatives, who view divorce and family instability as an important source of societal decline. These advocates of "family values" adopt a somewhat punitive tone, arguing that the family can be saved only if the government restricts divorce, by reinstituting fault grounds and discouraging unhappy spouses from selfishly defecting from their responsibilities. Liberals tend to oppose all restrictions on divorce, partly on the ground that they will not be effective in promoting family stability or enhancing the welfare of children. More importantly perhaps, liberals challenge what they view as oppressive constraints on individual freedom.

Recently, conservatives have been encouraged by the introduction of covenant marriage statutes in a few US states.[1] These laws allow couples to choose a marriage option that involves a legal commitment more binding than is allowed under conventional no-fault divorce law. Some proponents of covenant marriage are hopeful that it is part of a trend toward more restrictive divorce reforms – a return to a regime in which divorce is conditioned on fault. Not surprisingly, many liberals view covenant marriage with alarm – for the same reason that conservatives favor these laws. They believe that covenant marriage statutes are coercive legislative initiatives that undermine personal freedom, and that only regulation that prescribes easy termination of marriage is consistent with core liberal values.

In my view, both liberals and conservatives are in error – about covenant marriage and about the law's appropriate role in regulating marriage and restricting divorce generally. The state can play a role in promoting marital stability, but that role should be to assist couples to achieve their goal of a lasting relationship, not to impose the values and preferences of one group in society on the rest, as conservative advocates suggest. On the other hand, contrary to the

---

[1] Louisiana Revised Statutes Annotated, Sect. 9:234; 9:345 (A)(1); 9:224 (C); 9:225 (A)(3) (St. Paul, MN: West Publishing Co., 1999); Arizona Revised Statutes Annotated, Sect. 25-901-906 (St. Paul, MN: West, 1999). Covenant marriage bills are under consideration in legislatures in many other US states.

standard liberal arguments about divorce policy, legal enforcement of marital commitments is compatible with liberal principles, and (paradoxically) easy termination policies can undermine the freedom of individuals to pursue their life goals. As contracts scholars have long recognized, legal enforcement of reciprocal promises expands the freedom of contracting parties by offering them the option of binding commitment (Scott and Leslie, 1997). In marriage, as in commercial contracts, legal commitment can promote cooperation and protect investment in the relationship, enhancing the benefits that the parties derive from the union.

Couples entering marriage face a daunting challenge in their effort to achieve a lasting intimate relationship. Divorce statistics suggest that, for many, the dedication and optimism with which they enter marriage fade with time. Life presents stresses and temptations, and spouses make choices along the way that weaken marital bonds; at some point, the marriage succumbs. Under contemporary no-fault divorce law, the original commitment is "non-binding" and can readily be set aside (Schneider, 1984). Few legal restraints discourage unhappy spouses from leaving marriage, or even encourage them to remain long enough to be certain that dissatisfaction is not transitory (Scott, 1990). Moreover, under current law in most jurisdictions, couples are not permitted voluntarily to undertake a more binding commitment through contracts restricting divorce.

In this chapter, I will examine the ways in which the legal regime regulating divorce in the past generation has destabilized marriage and undermined the ability of couples to achieve their goals for their relationship. Some of the family law reforms since the 1960s simply represent evolving social norms and reflect modern attitudes toward marriage and other intimate relationships. However, in at least three ways, these legal developments have inadvertently weakened the social norms that encourage cooperation in marriage, making more difficult couples' efforts to achieve a successful relationship. First, the reforms have undermined the signaling function of marriage (Bishop, 1984; Trebilcock, 1999). The obligations and commitment of marriage can no longer be sharply distinguished from those of cohabitation unions, in large part because unhappy spouses can exit from marriage without great cost. Thus, the decision to marry is no longer a clear signal of the parties' intentions for the relationship. Second, by removing barriers to divorce, the legal reforms have inadvertently destroyed a useful precommitment mechanism. Traditional divorce law, whatever its deficiencies, discouraged divorce on the basis of transitory dissatisfaction, and thus assisted each spouse to adhere to the long-term goal for a lasting relationship. Precommitment mechanisms that make exit more costly reinforce informal social norms that promote cooperation in marriage and can reduce the risk of marital breakdown (Scott, 1990). Third, no-fault divorce undermines marital commitment, because each spouse knows that the other can leave at any time. Contract theory demonstrates the importance of enforceable commitment, both in reinforcing cooperative norms and as an ultimate sanction for defection (Scott and Scott, 1998).

It is possible that contemporary legal reforms could remedy some of the costly effects of no-fault divorce law. I propose several modern commitment measures that could be implemented either through contract or through statutory creation of alternative marital regimes. Although some restrictions on the freedom of parties to commit are desirable because of the unique attributes of marriage, well-crafted commitment mechanisms could restore the benefits of traditional marital commitment without the element of state coercion. Contemporary covenant marriage statutes represent a promising move in this direction, although the inclusion of fault grounds (a feature of all of the recent statutes to date) seems to me to be a mistake. In part, returning to divorce based on fault is problematic because it smacks of a reactionary social agenda, which many will reject. Indeed, a major impediment to successful reform is created by the close historic association between marital commitment and features of traditional marriage that have been discredited, such as hierarchical gender norms (Scott, 2000). If this hurdle can be overcome, voluntary commitment options such as covenant marriage could provide a legal alternative that, for many people, approximates their psychological commitment to marriage more closely than is possible under contemporary law.

1   Why marriages fail

Although modern family law gives individuals greatly expanded freedom to pursue their personal goals for "the good life," many people seem to fail to achieve the goal of successful marriage. Survey evidence consistently demonstrates that young people aspire to lasting marriage and that most people believe that their own marriage will last a lifetime (Baker and Emery, 1993; Eggars, 2000). Yet divorce statistics over the past generation present a discouraging picture of marital breakdown and family dissolution. How does it happen that so many marriages fail?

The causes of marital failure surely are varied and complex. At the risk of oversimplification, I would suggest that three patterns describe most failed marriages. First, the marriage may be a mistake from the outset, because one or both spouses have inadequate or erroneous information about the other, including information about the intentions for the relationship. Once the information is gained, the marriage flounders. Marriages also fail because one or both spouses change fundamentally over time, with the result that the couple are no longer compatible and no longer share the same values and goals. Anecdotal evidence suggests that a more mundane third pattern is just as common. Many marriages fail because the initial commitment is hard to sustain. Over time, spouses make choices on the basis of immediate preferences that are inconsistent with their long-term goal of lasting marriage, choices that gradually (or suddenly) destroy the relationship.

The third pattern of marital failure requires some clarification. Even though a person has a stable belief that a relationship will be rewarding over a lifetime, she will not always act consistently with that goal. Sometimes the rewards of an enduring relationship seem remote, and are not compatible with immediate desires and preferences. Even in successful marriages, spouses will be tempted to engage in selfish behavior that undermines the stability of the relationship. For example, immersion in career at the expense of family, pursuit of other intimate relationships, disputes over family finances and children, withdrawal, and boredom all can destabilize the cooperative equilibrium. Such behavior can lead to retaliation, estrangement, erosion of the marital commitment, and ultimately to the breakdown of the relationship.

Given the challenge that married couples face in seeking to sustain a cooperative relationship for a lifetime, it might seem that the interesting question is not why marriages fail, but why many succeed. Although the strength of the marital commitment and the compatibility of the parties are critically important, also important are the social norms that promote cooperative behavior in marriage. Elsewhere I have argued that marriage is regulated by an array of "commitment norms," such as reciprocity, altruism, trust, life-long loyalty, and fidelity (Scott, 2000). These norms define the expectations for marital behavior and function in important ways to promote cooperation in this intimate long-term relationship. Commitment norms are internalized by the parties and enforced by the spouses themselves, as well as by the community, and ultimately (for major defections such as abuse and on divorce) by the legal system. The stability of marriage, to a considerable extent, is a function of the strength of these norms in shaping and reinforcing cooperative behavior and in punishing defections.

2   Binding commitment and marital stability

Some marriages will fail whatever the legal regime. For example, when a young couple marries and one or both undergo dramatic changes in personal identity and values, their "later selves" may simply be fundamentally incompatible (Parfit, 1973). In these cases, divorce may be the best outcome. However, for many couples, a legal regime that defines marriage as a special relationship bound by commitment can reinforce the parties' intention for a lifetime union and strengthen the marital norms that promote cooperation; in short, legal enforcement of commitment can reduce the risk of marital failure. In this section, I will explain why binding commitment is important to marital success, by functioning as a signal, as a precommitment, and as a contract.

Marriage as a signal

If marriage has a clear social and legal meaning, with well-understood obligations and enforceable restrictions on entry and exit, the decision to marry signals serious intentions and a desire to undertake a solemn commitment. In effect, prospective spouses announce to one another (and to their community) that they are ready to enter a relationship that only a deeply committed person would choose, because of the attendant obligations, behavioral restrictions, and costs.

This signaling function serves several purposes that together tend to promote cooperation and stabilize the relationship (Bishop, 1984; Trebilcock, 1999). First, it facilitates optimal matching, by allowing those with similar intentions to identify each other as good prospects for successful marriage. Those with shallow attachments will not choose marriage, because marital failure threatens to be very costly. Thus, a clear marriage signal allows parties in an intimate relationship to communicate accurate information to one another about their intentions and reduces the risk of marriage based on misunderstanding. Marital status can also signal to the community that the spouses are unavailable for other relationships and thus should not be pursued. Further, clear community understanding of marriage as a relationship of binding obligation encourages enforcement of commitment norms. This reinforces marital stability by deterring defection. Finally, marital status can enhance reputational status, because it indicates the parties' reliability and adherence to conventional values. Married persons signal that they are "good types" who are ready to undertake obligations and a long-term commitment (Posner, 1999). This reputational benefit reinforces commitment norms by encouraging married persons to conform to the behavioral expectations of the role – and discouraging behavior that could undermine the cooperative equilibrium.

Marriage was an effective signal under traditional law. Its sharp legal boundaries and well-defined obligations and privileges, together with the legal barriers to exit, reinforced its clear social meaning. To a large extent, the terms of the marriage contract were dictated by the state, and couples had little ability to customize the legal relationship. Thus, the legal framework of marriage likely functioned effectively to promote cooperation, despite the deficiencies that ultimately undermined it and led to reforms.

Marriage as a precommitment

I have suggested that many marriages fail because people tend to make choices based on immediate preferences that are inconsistent with their long-term goals and plans. Thus described, marital failure is similar to many other situations in which individuals undermine the fulfillment of important objectives by making choices on the basis of transitory preferences. For example, the desire to lose weight, drink in moderation, or save money for a new home often requires sacrificing pleasures that at the moment seem more compelling than the remote goal. Psychologists and economists generally attribute the penchant to make choices inconsistent with long-term preferences to a tendency to discount the future, so that long-term preferences are devalued as compared with immediate desires (Strotz, 1955–6; Ainslie, 1975). In everyday contexts, people solve problems of inconsistent preferences through the use of precommitment mechanisms. These are self-management strategies that penalize the short-term choice that the individual wants to avoid (eating the chocolate cake) or reward achievement of the goal (losing 10 pounds) (Schelling, 1984; Elster, 1979). By creating, *ex ante*, enforceable penalties or rewards, the individual reinforces the initial commitment and reduces the risk of being diverted by temporarily attractive temptations.

Although the analogy may seem a little strained at first, legal barriers to divorce can function similarly to precommitments in other settings, by reinforcing the initial commitment to marriage and discouraging choices that undermine the relationship. Most directly, precommitments of this kind can influence the decision to divorce by the unhappy spouse. For example, consider a couple who have chosen covenant marriage in a jurisdiction that offers this option. If one spouse becomes dissatisfied, she realizes that she can divorce only by proving fault or by waiting for two years (the mandatory separation period for a no-fault divorce). In effect, by choosing covenant marriage, each prospective spouse agrees to submit to a tax on the decision to leave the marriage – a tax that will reduce the likelihood of divorce unless the costs of remaining married are greater than the (increased) cost of divorce. In short, in the calculation of the costs and benefits of the alternative choices, the precommitment tax weighs in favor of remaining in the marriage. If the benefits of divorce (and costs of remaining married) are shaped by transitory desires, the legal barrier will deter the spouse from a decision that is inconsistent with her ultimate (and constant) goal of lasting marriage. Precommitment theory assumes that, over time, the transitory preference to end the marriage will fade and the satisfaction of lasting marriage will re-emerge (Scott, 1990).

Precommitments that impose costs on divorce can also promote stability in marriage by influencing the couple's attitudes about the kind of commitment they have undertaken, which in turn may affect their behavior during marriage in subtle ways. First, as I have suggested, the decision to undertake a binding commitment signals the seriousness of the parties' intentions for the relationship. Moreover, because both parties recognize that divorce will not be easy, they may be better able to resist the temptation to pursue short-term preferences that undermine the cooperative equilibrium (Scott, 1990). Realizing that the marriage bounded by precommitment cannot be readily abandoned, the spouses may be less inclined to forget their original cooperative intentions during difficult times in the relationship. They may be more likely to conform to the behavioral expectations embodied in commitment norms, so as to avoid choices that could lead them to confront the costly decision to divorce. The day-to-day attitude of such couples might be expressed as follows: "We've made a commitment to this marriage and we are not getting out easily. Since we are in for the duration, we might as well make the best of it." This may seem less than romantic but, remember, being "in for the duration" is the couple's shared objective.

Traditional marriage law created legal precommitments that likely reinforced the sincere intentions of individuals who entered marriage expecting the union to last for life. Divorce was available only upon proof of fault by the spouse or (in some states) after an extended period of separation. Under such a regime, spouses were deterred from leaving marriage on the basis of routine stresses and dissatisfactions that might abate with time. The truly unhappy spouse could end the marriage, but the choice was costly enough (because of legal barriers to exit) that, in general, the decision to divorce came only after long and careful consideration. In these circumstances, precommitment theory holds that divorce was probably the right outcome, because the individual's long-term preferences had changed.

Marriage as a contract

Legal commitment to marriage is more than a self-management strategy. It also establishes reciprocal obligations between the spouses. Whether a couple undertake commitment through a formal contract or marry under a legal regime that creates enforceable obligations and restricts divorce, each spouse benefits because the other is also bound.

In this regard, it is helpful to review the benefits of contract in other settings, benefits that accrue in the marriage context as well. Parties enter contracts when they need the cooperation of others to achieve their own goals (Scott and Leslie, 1997). Thus, the parties give up some future freedom because each believes that the joint benefit produced by binding agreement exceeds the combined benefit that each could achieve individually. Each party can rely on the promised future cooperation of the other, and be assured that her own performance will not be wasted should the other change her mind and defect. Although the parties assume that, ordinarily, legal enforcement of the contract will never be necessary, it provides security for their investment. Without this assurance, the parties might believe that cooperation would be beneficial but be reluctant to undertake the risk.

The benefits of mutually enforceable commitments apply to the marriage contract as well. Each spouse enters marriage with the assurance that the other has undertaken a legally binding commitment that restricts his or her future freedom to defect. The parties realize that, if informal enforcement mechanisms fail to deter major violations of marital norms, legal enforcement is available. This assurance itself deters defection, enhancing mutual trust and encouraging investment of time, energy, emotions, and resources in the marriage. Indeed, for many people, the interdependence required for successful marriage rests on a level of trust that is possible only with binding commitment. Otherwise, spouses may be less inclined to invest wholeheartedly in the marriage because each realizes that the other is free to leave and that the relational investment may be lost. Marriage, in these circumstances, becomes a more limited (and less stable) relationship as each spouse protects against future disappointment.

Under traditional family law, each spouse recognized that the other was bound to the marriage, and thus both enjoyed the security of contractual commitment. By entering marriage, both agreed to restrict their future freedom and to be subject to sanctions for violation of marital promises (in the form of fault grounds for divorce). These constraints provided security for the marital investment and encouraged spousal cooperation. Thus, traditional legal marriage carried many of the benefits of binding commitments in other contractual settings.

Traditional law and marital norms

Restrictions on divorce under traditional law strengthened the social norms that encourage cooperative behavior in marriage by reinforcing the informal enforcement mechanisms with legal compulsion. Fault grounds for divorce – the prohibition of adultery, desertion, and physical cruelty – punished violators of marital commitment norms, amplifying the sanction imposed by spouse and community. Divorce, with its often humiliating public reckoning and financial costs, constituted a threshold across which many spouses might hesitate to cross, and thus served as a powerful outer layer of the complex system that enforced marital norms. Moreover, beyond the content of fault grounds, the fact that divorce law created a substantial barrier to exit underscored for each spouse that marriage was a life-long commitment and reinforced the norm of marital loyalty (Scott, 2000). In general, the legal and normative regulation of marriage under traditional family law formed a coherent and mutually reinforcing system that functioned to enforce obligations and to promote cooperation in marriage.

Despite this positive impact, I am not inclined to revive traditional marriage or the legal regime that supported it. It is important to remember that, under traditional law, parties were not free to customize the marriage contract; life-long commitment was the only option. Marriage was a take-it-or-leave-it proposition dictated by the state, a condition that made this contract quite different from commercial agreements and inconsistent with modern liberal values.

Traditional marriage was inconsistent with contemporary values in another way. The spousal relationship was regulated not only by (beneficial) commitment norms but also by hierarchical gender norms that defined the roles of husbands and wives. Many marital obligations applied differentially to husbands and wives, and married women were economically, socially, and legally subordinated to and dependent on their husbands. Even spousal commitment obligations (such as the adultery prohibition) restricted wives more than husbands, by punishing their defections more harshly (Scott, 2000). Over time, gender norms and commitment norms became intricately interwoven (or "bundled") within a rigid framework of legal regulation.

In the past generation, as egalitarian gender norms have emerged, many dimensions of this legal framework have been discredited. However, as I will suggest in the next section, well-intended legal reforms have inadvertently sacrificed beneficial aspects of traditional law that are quite compatible with the goals and values of modern couples.

3   Marital commitment under modern divorce law

The reform of divorce law

In the relatively brief period since the 1960s, the legal framework that shaped traditional marriage has undergone dramatic change. Some of this change reflects social evolution toward gender equality. Thus, legal support for hierarchical and differentiated gender roles in marriage has been systematically abolished. Family law reforms also reflect adjustments in commitment norms. For most modern persons, lifelong marital commitment has become conditioned not only on the spouse's compliance with behavioral norms (the fault grounds under traditional law) but also on an acceptable level of personal satisfaction in the marriage. Moreover, the notion of a coercive state dictating the terms of the marriage contract and the conditions of termination is incompatible with contemporary norms of privacy and autonomy.

In contrast to the ambitious legal and social agenda to promote gender equality over the past generation, the no-fault divorce reforms in the 1960s and 1970s were treated as routine business and had rather modest objectives. The reformers believed that the removal of fault grounds would reduce the adversarial character of divorce proceedings and protect their integrity, which was threatened by collusion of couples who were in agreement about the desirability of ending their marriage (Jacob, 1988). The reformers also sought to recognize that divorce should be allowed on the basis of relational failure. The reform laws initially permitted divorce on the basis of long-term separation or irretrievable breakdown, as determined by a court or mutually recognized by the parties themselves. Over time, however, almost all restrictions were lifted and divorce became freely available.

Despite the modest goals of the reforms, the legal regulation of divorce has undergone dramatic change. The upshot of the reforms was the abolition of legal enforcement of the marital commitment and a transfer of the authority to regulate the relationship from the state to the individual spouses. In a relatively short period of time the legal norm has become quick, easy, unilateral divorce, reinforced by policies regulating property division and spousal support that facilitate "efficient" termination of marital obligations. Marriage has become functionally a contract terminable at will by either party. Moreover, having rejected the legitimacy of state coercion under the old regime, law makers apparently determined that any legal enforcement of the marriage contract was illegitimate. Thus, in a response curiously inconsistent with the liberal premises of modern regulation of marriage, most courts likely would not enforce voluntary contractual agreements undertaken to reinforce marital commitment by restricting divorce (Haas, 1988; Rasmusen and Stake, 1998). Only recently, with the introduction of covenant marriage laws in some states, have couples been offered the option of legally binding commitments.

The impact of reforms on marital commitment

No-fault divorce law did far more than adjust legal regulation under traditional law to conform to modern notions of commitment. By withdrawing the traditional restrictions on divorce without substituting commitment mechanisms that are more compatible with contemporary values, law makers have inadvertently undermined marital commitment and stability. The reforms were not intended to express a dramatically revised vision of marriage as a casual commitment, and most people do not view the relationship in that way. Nonetheless, this is the account of marriage offered by the modern legal regime, which facilitates easy termination of the relationship while at the same time discouraging contractual commitment. Except in states with covenant marriage laws, couples entering marriage exchange promises of fidelity and loyalty, but these vows can be set aside without penalty. This account is inconsistent with the understanding of marriage held by many people – that of a relationship of mutual commitment and obligation.

The earlier discussion of how legal enforcement of commitment contributes to marital stability suggests how modern divorce law can undermine the couple's efforts to achieve successful marriage. The legal deregulation of marriage has substantially diluted the effectiveness of marriage as a signal. It has also withdrawn a precommitment mechanism that assisted spouses to adhere to their cooperative intentions in the relationship. Finally, parties can no longer rely on the existence of mutually binding commitment to provide assurance that their investment in the costly and somewhat uncertain venture of marriage will not be lost because the other spouse defects. The overall impact of the reforms of divorce law in the past generation has been to undermine the commitment norms that promoted marital cooperation.

The decision to marry no longer signals the choice to undertake a serious commitment to a life-long relationship governed by clear behavioral expectations. Because divorce (or defection from marital obligations) no longer carries serious costs, both those whose intentions are serious and those who seek a more casual relationship might reasonably select marriage. Thus, individuals who aspire to life-long marriage are less able to signal accurately their own intentions and also are less able to evaluate those of the prospective spouse. The pooling of individuals with different tastes for commitment is likely to increase the incidence of inefficient matching in the marriage market (Trebilcock, 1999). Further, because of this pooling phenomenon, it may be unclear whether individuals entering marriage today mean to be subject to the obligations and behavioral expectations that traditionally defined the relationship. Thus, outsiders may be confused about whether spouses are available for other relationships, and community members may be uncertain about what spousal behavior warrants disapproval.

Another effect of the removal of restrictions on divorce under modern law is that the precommitment function of legal enforcement is lost to those spouses whose long-term interest lies with lasting marriage. Because divorce is always an option, the stability and survival of the marriage are dependent on sustained satisfaction with the relationship (as compared with alternatives), and there is less mitigation for temporary fluctuations in commitment. Moreover, the stabilizing effect on behavior during marriage of barriers to divorce is lost under modern divorce law, and, thus, maintaining (and returning to) a cooperative pattern of interactions becomes more difficult. The dynamics of spousal interaction can be intense, and conflict can escalate into a retaliatory pattern that may be harder to reverse if exit is always an option. In contrast, as I have suggested, the realization that the traditional marriage relationship could not easily be abandoned may have disciplined parties to avoid destructive behavior.

Much of the benefit of contract is also lost under modern divorce law. Individuals choose marriage over informal unions, in part, because they can rely more confidently on the partner's commitment (Scott and Scott, 1998). For each spouse, modern marriage is a more risky venture than a traditional union (or than a commercial contract), because it is not protected by legal enforcement. Spouses recognize that they will experience substantial losses should the relationship fail and also that they cannot count on continued cooperation from the partner. Predictably, this should result in less than optimal investment in the relationship and in less trust and interdependence between spouses – all contributing to less satisfactory and less stable marriage.

The no-fault divorce reforms serve the legitimate purpose of releasing unhappy spouses from marriages that cannot be saved. However, contemporary law may also destabilize relationships in which legal reinforcement of commitment norms could assist spouses to achieve their goal of marital fulfillment. The withdrawal of legal enforcement leaves the parties with only informal mechanisms to respond to violations, and such penalties may sometimes prove inadequate. Marital failure may result for some couples whose marriages might have weathered hard times if legal enforcement of commitment norms had been available to deter defection. Thus, in an effort to correct an outmoded expression of commitment, the legal reforms inadvertently destroyed a useful mechanism that encouraged mutually beneficial cooperation for many parties.

The destabilizing effects on marriage of legal regulation are particularly costly if families with children are affected. In the years since divorce has become more common, social scientists have carefully examined the impact of divorce on the development and adjustment of children. The research indicates consistently that, for most children, divorce has a harmful impact on their future social integration, educational and occupational attainment, and psychological well-being (Scott, 1990; Amato and Booth, 1997). Thus, the reassuring justification of the no-fault era – that children are better off if their unhappy parents divorce – no longer seems viable. Unless the level of conflict between parents is intense, children generally are better off if their unhappy parents stay married (Amato and Booth, 1997; Emery, 1982). These research findings suggest, at a minimum, that commitment mechanisms that promote marital stability in families with children may have a social utility that extends beyond the benefits to the spouses.

4   Commitment options: the prospects for reform

There is evidence that the social and legal climate surrounding marriage and divorce may be changing in the United States, in part perhaps because of a growing recognition of the harmful impact of divorce on children. In recent years, law makers have increasingly indicated a willingness to impose family obligations on divorcing parties. The enactment of tough child support enforcement laws and the (tentative) move toward the imposition of more substantial spousal support obligations indicate a changing official attitude toward legal enforcement of marital obligations (American Law Institute, 1999; Scott and Scott, 1998). The recent covenant marriage statutes also represent a more hospitable response toward marital commitment and a recognition that modern couples entering marriage may desire legal commitment options. Moreover, the Uniform

Premarital Agreement Act, the model for regulation of premarital contracts in many states, facilitates premarital contracting and does not prohibit commitment contracts.[2] Whatever barriers to judicial enforcement of such contracts exist are largely psychological rather than doctrinal, and resistance is likely to erode as attitudes toward marriage and divorce change.

Many questions are unresolved, however, about the form and substance of the legal commitment options that couples might adopt. I turn to these matters in the following sections.

The legal structuring of commitment options

Couples entering marriage could undertake a legal commitment through one of two means. First, the parties could execute a premarital agreement, either freely negotiated or through the adoption of a standard form contract. Legislatures could also create alternative marital regimes, so that couples could decide on a level of commitment and follow whatever procedures are required to attain the desired status. The recent covenant marriage statutes embody the second approach. Each of these approaches has advantages, but the second (under certain conditions that I will explore at the end of the chapter) is more likely to be widely utilized.

Premarital agreements. As I have indicated, in many US states, no doctrinal innovation is needed for legal enforcement of commitment agreements under ordinary contract principles. These contracts could be routinely enforced, subject to the conventional contract defenses against enforcement such as fraud, duress, and unconscionability. Courts also have the authority to refuse to enforce contracts that are against public policy, which in this setting might include onerous restrictions on divorce – a subject to which I will return shortly. Contractual freedom is most fully protected if the couple can freely negotiate the customized commitment terms that best reflect their goals. However, standard form contracts might be particularly useful in this setting. Form contracts can offer the couple entering marriage the benefit of the accumulated reflection and experience of others about the effectiveness of various restrictions and about costs and contingencies that the couple may not anticipate. In short, a form contract can include the most effective and beneficial commitment terms.

Premarital commitment contracts offer benefits only if couples contract, and most couples do not execute premarital agreements. Thus, the utility of this means of promoting marital stability is likely to be quite limited unless couples

---

[2] Uniform Premarital Agreement Act, Uniform Laws. Section 3 of the Act, which has been adopted in more than twenty US states, authorizes parties to contract with regard to "(8) any other matter, including their personal rights and obligations, not in violation of public policy."

recognize the value of legal commitment. This could come through educational programs, advertising, or premarital counseling. If commitment contracts are deemed to have social utility, the state could offer incentive schemes, perhaps by giving tax benefits to couples who execute an agreement that involves substantial commitment. The state could also provide forms to couples when they obtain a marriage license, with advice about the benefits that the contract may offer. Such a policy, of course, is quite similar to one of inviting the couple entering marriage to select from alternative marital regimes – the approach to which I turn now.

Alternative marital regimes.   Covenant marriage laws represent an experiment in facilitating marital commitment through alternative marital regimes. Under the covenant marriage model, couples entering marriage are invited to choose between covenant marriage and marriage governed by no-fault divorce law, depending on their plans and objectives. (In theory, the choice could be from a larger menu of marital regimes, but no jurisdiction has been this creative). Those who choose covenant marriage are required to undertake counseling before marriage, and (under some laws) also before divorce. Divorce is available only on the basis of designated fault grounds or after an extended (i.e. two-year) separation. Thus, couples whose commitment is somewhat tentative could choose marriage regulated by no-fault divorce law – the "easy exit" plan – whereas those who desire legal enforcement of their commitment could choose covenant marriage.

Although the covenant marriage model could offer different commitment terms from those available under existing statutes, this legislation provides the framework for a policy offering alternative marital regimes. This approach to facilitating commitment has some attractive features that should be highlighted. First, in contrast to the proposals of conservative reformers who advocate a return to traditional fault-based divorce law, covenant marriage is a voluntary choice by the couple, who also are free to marry without submitting to restrictions on divorce. Thus, the covenant marriage approach does not involve coercive state regulation of intimate relationships and is compatible with the contemporary values of autonomy and privacy. (Indeed, a covenant marriage regime is functionally equivalent to a contractual approach in which couples are presented with standard form contracts with varying commitment terms). Beyond this, covenant marriage statutes serve an information-forcing function, which should promote better matching. By offering couples the choice between two marital commitment options, a legal regime that includes covenant marriage stimulates conversations in which parties are encouraged to consider the options carefully and to disclose their intentions for the marriage. Finally, a covenant marriage regime has several advantages over a policy that permits couples freely to execute premarital agreements. Couples can be directed to consider the commitment options and to make a choice, and thus more couples will undertake commitments. Moreover, legislative deliberation over the terms of covenant marriage is more likely to lead to optimal commitments than couples' executing their agreement without guidance. In this regard, covenant marriage is similar to a standard form contract with an authoritative seal of approval.

The substantive terms of commitment

In theory, any mechanism that imposes a penalty on divorce can function to re-inforce marital commitment to the benefit of both parties. A regime that values freedom of contract will give couples considerable latitude to fashion commitments tailored to their particular goals and circumstances. However, some commitment terms seem particularly useful, and some threaten to have harmful effects that parties might not anticipate and that could outweigh the benefits provided. In this section, I will suggest some useful commitment terms, focusing particularly on the benefits of a mandatory waiting period before divorce or remarriage as the optimal restriction on marriage. Then I will indicate some restrictions on divorce that seem likely to have undesirable effects. Surprisingly, perhaps, I argue against reviving fault grounds, although once they may have served a useful purpose in stabilizing marriage. I end this part on a cautionary note, suggesting that paternalistic restrictions on parties' contractual freedom may be justified in this context because of cognitive biases that may affect decision-making in this context.

Beneficial precommitment restrictions

- *Family property trusts and "super-support".* An agreement that all or most marital property be held in trust after divorce during the minority of the couple's children will serve the dual functions of discouraging divorce and providing for the financial security of children if divorce occurs (Glendon, 1984). Similarly, provisions for high levels of child support (which cannot be reduced based on future family responsibilities) make exit from the family less attractive by clarifying that some obligations of marriage cannot be set aside on divorce. Many spouses, anticipating their parental role, assume that they will want to act in the best interest of their children and readily accept that the role carries serious responsibilities which they expect to fulfill. Thus, *ex ante*, many would willingly undertake divorce costs that benefit their children. For most parents, it is only in the midst of divorce that the interests of their children appear to be in conflict with their own.

As I have suggested, many US states have reformed child support obligation laws to give more weight to the needs of children and (somewhat) less to the freedom of adults. Parents (and spouses) contemplating divorce may consider the decision more carefully if the decision carries a substantial (and continuing) financial penalty, based on nondispensable family obligations.

* *Marital/pre-divorce counseling.* The recent covenant marriage legislation in some US states requires counseling before marriage and before divorce. Premarital counseling can encourage deliberation about the marriage decision. A period of prescribed psychological counseling before a divorce petition can be filed may assist the couple to examine the stresses that have undermined the stability of the marriage. Moreover, counseling can help the dissatisfied spouse to probe the nature of his or her dissatisfaction and to clarify whether the desire to leave the marriage reflects transitory or stable and settled preferences.

* *Mandatory waiting periods before divorce or remarriage.* A mandatory waiting period of some substantial duration before divorce (perhaps two or three years) is the optimal commitment term, in my view, because it serves several functions. First, a prescribed period of delay serves well the standard precommitment purposes. It creates a barrier to divorce that makes leaving the marriage more costly, and thus discourages this choice. At the same time, it defines the relationship as one that is not easily set aside, subtly influencing each spouse's attitudes and behavior during marriage. Beyond this, an extended waiting period promotes better decision-making about divorce. During the waiting period, the spouse who is unhappy in the marriage can more accurately assess whether the decision to leave reflects his/her long-term interest or immediate intense preferences. If the desire to leave the marriage is unchanged after the waiting period, contemporary norms support divorce as the appropriate choice. However, it is also possible that dissatisfaction with the marriage may be transitory, and the unhappy spouse may decide over time not to leave. Finally, a waiting period may deter the divorcing spouse from quickly establishing a new family – a step that dilutes interest in children of an earlier marriage.

Fault as a commitment mechanism.   Under traditional law, fault grounds expressed the behavioral expectations for marriage and punished major violations of commitment norms. They also signaled the scope of marital commitment: spouses were not free to leave the marriage unless the other had committed a grievous offense. Thus, requiring proof of spousal fault served signaling, commitment, and precommitment functions that likely promoted cooperation and contributed to marital stability. These benefits of fault grounds were sacrificed inadvertently by the no-fault divorce reforms. Some modern critics of no-fault divorce law argue for a return to fault grounds, and the recent covenant marriage statutes allow divorce on fault grounds. In my view, however, this trend (if it can be described as such) is problematic.

In some regards, fault grounds would seem to serve quite well as commitment terms in the marriage contract and as mechanisms to enforce marital norms. Including fault terms in a premarital agreement or as the basis of divorce in covenant marriage reminds the spouses of the kind of behavior that is unacceptable and that undermines the relationship. Moreover, the threat of a penalty for violation (a humiliating divorce proceeding, at a minimum) may deter defection, and the requirement of proving fault as a condition of divorce may discourage dissatisfied spouses from that course.

In many regards, however, fault grounds do not function well as commitment terms. First, modern understanding of the dynamics of divorce suggests that, although the failure of some marriages can be attributed solely to the behavior of one spouse, in most cases the responsibility cannot be so clearly assigned. Marriage is a complex web of reciprocal interactions that unfold over a long period of time. It is also a private relationship; much marital behavior is known only to the parties. A failing marriage may involve a pattern of defection and retaliation that is impossible for a third party to sort out and evaluate. In short, the judicial determination of fault will be a vexing task, fraught with the risk of error.

Some of the troublesome aspects of fault grounds that led to the no-fault reform movement should also invoke caution before these restrictions are embraced as commitment terms. Acrimonious divorce litigation surely undermines the parties' future relationship, a worrisome cost if the marriage involves children, whose welfare is linked to their parents' future ability to cooperate. Moreover, the requirement of proving fault before divorce could be granted led to collusion and perjury by many couples, practices that undermined the integrity of the judicial process. Finally, if fault grounds are available as an alternative to a waiting period, they may be utilized to hasten the divorce, undermining the effectiveness of a useful commitment mechanism. For these reasons, I would be hesitant to reintroduce fault as a commitment term.

Protecting vulnerable spouses.   Some commitment terms are theoretically acceptable but may be undesirable where they threaten to penalize one spouse more than the other because of a particular vulnerability. For example, monetary penalties or fines charged to the defecting spouse might seem like a straightforward cost imposed on divorce, but they are problematic if they have a differential impact on the spouses. In many marriages, the spouses do not have equivalent financial assets and earning capacity. Homemaker spouses would be disadvantaged by this type of commitment term, because it creates a greater barrier to exit for them than it poses for their income-earning partners. Further, financial penalties (either direct fines or the withholding of child support) could have a harmful impact on children in some families. In general, the promotion of marital stability takes on a policy importance when the welfare of children is involved, and commitment terms that leave the custodial parent without the means to provide adequately are unacceptable. Similarly, commitment terms that withhold child custody or visitation from the parent who leaves the marriage are impermissible because of their harmful impact on children – although they might be quite effective in deterring divorce in some families. Any restriction that threatens to make devoted parents prisoners in miserable or abusive marriages would surely not be allowed on public policy grounds.

It is important that the implementation of commitment mechanisms provides protection for victims of spousal abuse. Continued cohabitation cannot be required during a mandatory waiting period before divorce, and procedures should be readily available to expedite spousal and child support upon separation in cases involving dependent spouses and minor children. That is not to say, of course, that a period of mandatory delay before final divorce or remarriage cannot be prescribed, but it must transpire under conditions in which financial support for dependants is provided.

Cognitive biases and limitations on the freedom to commit

Decision-making in the premarital context carries unique risks that justify paternalistic restriction of the parties' freedom of contract. Cognitive biases may lead individuals to err in assessing the need for commitment terms to strengthen their relationships. Some couples may be inclined to over-commit, an effect that can have devastating costs in some cases. On the other hand, a policy of informing couples of the benefits of limited commitment may be useful, since some couples may not consider the need to reinforce their marriage against future threats to its stability.

Couples about to be married may tend to be influenced by emotional and cognitive biases that could distort decision-making in this setting. Both parties may be overly optimistic in calculating the prospects for successful and lasting marriage. Moreover, thinking about divorce may generate discomfort and be avoided on that account. Along these lines, researchers suggest that individuals seek to reduce cognitive dissonance when they are confronted with two inconsistent facts or events (Festinger, 1957, 1964). Further, decision makers generally tend to overvalue vivid experiential data that can be readily called to mind and to discount remote abstract information (Tversky and Kahnemann, 1982). In the warm glow of the premarital context, the possibility of divorce or even of serious conflict in the marriage may seem like a distant possibility. Research evidence suggests that couples entering marriage underestimate the possibility that their own marriage will fail (Baker and

Emery, 1993). In general, the period before marriage is not optimal for making decisions about divorce because of predictable cognitive error (Scott, 1990).

The effect of these cognitive biases on decision-making about marital commitment is not easy to predict. Optimism could lead some couples to see no need for binding commitment. If this reaction is widespread, legal commitment mechanisms would simply not be used much – a response that might be characterized as "under-commitment." Other couples may view the adoption of commitment terms as an opportunity to affirm their confidence in the success of the marriage and the depth of their devotion to one another. The latter response might lead to "over-commitment" – the adoption of a more onerous restriction on divorce than most observers would conclude was rational under the circumstances. Thus the couple might agree never to divorce or they might create a prohibitive fine to be imposed on the spouse who ends the marriage. This is not a problem, of course, if the commitment term functions as predicted, reinforcing the stability of a mutually beneficial relationship. It is a serious problem, however, if the agreed-upon commitment terms do not avert marital failure. This might happen, as I have suggested, because the marriage was a mistake from the outset, or because the personal identity, values, and preferences of one or both of the spouses have changed so dramatically that remaining in the marriage is untenable. In these situations, prohibitive barriers to divorce seriously infringe upon the individual's pursuit of his/her ends. Thus, legal restriction of contractual freedom is necessary to ensure that couples undertake commitments that impose only moderate obstacles to divorce and are not a means to self-enslavement.

5   The prospect for legal reform: a cautionary note

If the reformers of traditional family law inadvertently undermined the stability of marriage by abolishing legal commitment mechanisms, it seems likely that contemporary law makers could correct the problem. Along these lines, covenant marriage is promising as a means to assist couples to achieve their objective of stable lasting marriage through a voluntary contractual commitment option. By differentiating marriage with legal commitment from other unions, covenant marriage embodies a clear signal of commitment. Moreover, it offers the precommitment and contractual benefits of traditional marriage, in a form that is compatible with contemporary values of individual autonomy and privacy. Given the aspirations of many couples entering marriage, it is plausible that covenant marriage might be widely chosen by couples with serious intentions for their relationship.

The picture is more complex than it first appears, however. Whether this legislative reform heralds the revitalization of marital commitment is uncertain at this point, because the impact of covenant marriage depends on the social meaning that it comes to assume. The controversy that has surrounded this reform initiative in the political arena reveals that, despite its promise as a commitment mechanism, covenant marriage is viewed in some quarters as an effort to revive disfavored marital norms of an earlier era. This response suggests that, for many people, aspirations for lasting marriage coexist with a deep distrust of legal enforcement of marital commitment.

In my view, this puzzling distaste for legally enforceable commitment can be attributed in part to the lingering association between commitment norms and gender norms, which were intricately bundled in traditional marriage. In theory, disaggregation of these two types of norms, which served very different functions, should be possible. However, the powerful bond that was forged between commitment and gender norms under traditional family law continues to influence attitudes about the law's regulatory role. Today, it is widely understood that gender subordination was coercively imposed on women, most powerfully by the traditional legal regime. Support for gender equality dominates contemporary public discourse. In this climate, many people view legal enforcement of commitment with distrust because it seems to threaten to resurrect discredited spousal gender norms. Policies such as covenant marriage are tainted by the link between commitment and gender hierarchy – a response that is intensified because some conservative supporters of covenant marriage in fact endorse traditional marriage and gender roles. For liberals and feminists, this confirms the suspicion that this "reform" is simply part of a reactionary social agenda.

This is unfortunate. In the context of the political debate over the role of law in regulating marriage and family relationships, the value of legal commitment as a means to assist couples to achieve their personal ends has become obscured. In fact, both liberals and conservatives should support the availability of some form of covenant marriage. An important lesson of my analysis is that liberals and conservatives have a far greater basis for agreement about divorce law reform than the current debate would suggest. In contrast to other divisive social policy issues such as abortion, there is no great value clash about the worth of enduring marriage among those who are most affected by its regulation. Most people would not endorse a return to the *ancien régime,* in which patriarchy reigned and marital commitment was dictated by the state. However, traditional gender norms need play no part in a modern marriage bound by legal commitment, and voluntary contractual commitment is very different from state coercion. Contemporary individuals who aspire to a lasting relationship should welcome a marriage option that promises many of the signaling, contractual, and precommitment benefits of traditional marriage, through legal mechanisms that are compatible with liberal values.

REFERENCES

Ainslie, George (1975), "Specious Reward: A Behavioral Theory of Impulsiveness and Impulse Control," *Psychological Bulletin*, 82, 463.

Amato, Paul and Allen Booth (1997), *A Generation at Risk: Growing up in an Era of Family Upheaval*, Cambridge, MA: Harvard University Press.

American Law Institute (1999), "Compensatory Spousal Payments," *Principles of the Law of Family Dissolution*, Philadelphia, PA: ALI.

Baker, Lynn and Robert Emery (1993), "When Every Relationship Is above Average: Perceptions and Expectations of Divorce at the Time of Marriage," *Law and Human Behavior*, 17, 993.

Bishop, William (1984), " 'Is He Married?' Marriage as Information," *University of Toronto Law Journal*, 34, 245–63.

Eggars, Dave (2000), "Intimacies," *New York Times Magazine*, 5 July, 76–7.

Elster, Jon (1979), *Ulysses and the Sirens: Studies in Rationality and Irrationality*, Cambridge: Cambridge University Press.

Emery, Robert (1982), "Interparental Conflict and the Children of Discord and Divorce," *Psychological Bulletin*, 92, 310.

Festinger, Leon (1957), *A Theory of Cognitive Dissonance*, Evanston, IL: Row Peterson. (1964), *Conflict, Decision and Dissonance*, Stanford, CA: Stanford University Press.

Glendon, Mary Anne (1984), "Family Law Reform in the 1980s," *Louisiana Law Review*, 44, 1553.

Haas, Theodore F. (1988) "The Rationality and Enforceability of Contractual Restrictions on Divorce," *North Carolina Law Review*, 66, 879.

Hunter, James (1991), *Culture Wars: The Struggle to Define America*, New York: Basic Books.

Jacob, Herbert (1988), *The Silent Revolution: The Transformation of Divorce Law in the United States*, Chicago: University of Chicago Press.

Parfit, Derek (1973), "Later Selves and Moral Principles," in A. Montfiere (ed.), *Philosophy and Personal Relations*, London: Routledge & Kegan Paul, 137.

Posner, Eric (1999), "Family Law and Social Norms," in Frank Buckley (ed.), *The Fall and Rise of Freedom of Contract*, Durham, NC: Duke University Press, 256.

Rasmusen, Eric and Jeffrey E. Stake (1998), "Lifting the Veil of Ignorance: Personalizing the Marriage Contract," *Indiana Law Journal*, 73, 454–502.

Schelling, Thomas (1984), "Self Command in Practice and in a Theory of Rational Choice," *American Economic Review*, 74, 1.

Schneider, Carl (1984), "Moral Discourse and the Transformation of American Family Law," *Michigan Law Review*, 83, 1803.

Scott, Elizabeth S. (1990), "Rational Decision-making about Marriage and Divorce," *Virginia Law Review*, 76, 9.

(2000), "Social Norms and the Legal Regulation of Marriage," *Virginia Law Review*, 86, 1901.

Scott, Elizabeth S. and Robert E. Scott (1998), "Marriage as Relational Contract," *Virginia Law Review*, 84, 1225.

Scott, Robert and Douglas Leslie (1997), *Contract Law and Theory*, 2nd edn, Charlottesville, VA: Michie Press.

Strotz, R. H. (1955–6), "Myopia and Inconsistency in Dynamic Utility Maximization," *Review of Economic Studies*, 23, 165.

Trebilcock, Michael (1999), "Marriage as a Signal," in Frank Buckley (ed.), *The Fall and Rise of Freedom of Contract*, Durham, NC: Duke University Press, 245.

Tversky, Amos and Daniel Kahnemann (1982), "Judgment under Uncertainty: Heuristics and Biases," in D. Kahnemann, P. Slovic, and A. Tversky (eds.), *Judgment under Uncertainty: Heuristics and Biases*, Cambridge: Cambridge University Press, 3.

4   Mutual consent divorce

Allen M. Parkman

Voluntary agreements have a central role in the efficient allocation of society's scarce resources. Subject to their constraints, people are assumed to pursue the transactions from which they expect the largest net benefits. Economists generally see little need for legal restrictions on the conditions that the transacting parties impose on themselves except when there are substantial external effects or a party has inordinate market power. Even then, efficiency dictates that legal restrictions force people to recognize the external costs or benefits of their actions or limit the exercise of market power rather than prohibit certain aspects of transactions. Yet when people reach probably the most important agreement of their lives – the decision to marry – they have very little control over the arrangement into which they are entering, owing to legal restrictions imposed on their transaction by the state. They have essentially no control over the basis upon which their agreement will be terminated, and, if it is terminated, the legal system gives them only limited control over the repercussions of the termination. Although a divorce can have external effects on the couple's children and society at large, the law does not address these concerns systematically. Market power is not a concern about these agreements.

In this chapter, I argue that increasing individuals' control over their marriage, especially the circumstances in which their marriage will be dissolved and the financial arrangements if that occurs, would be an improvement over the fault and no-fault grounds for divorce and the statutory requirements for the financial and custodial arrangements that have existed in the United States.[1] Although the grounds for divorce appear to be only one component of a marriage agreement, I argue that they have a fundamental impact on the quality of the relationship. Permitting divorce by the mutual consent of the spouses would also reduce the importance of the current faulty statutory financial arrangements at divorce.

[1] Most industrial countries have also adopted no-fault divorce laws, so the analysis presented here is equally appropriate in those countries. For a more detailed discussion of no-fault divorce in the United States, see Parkman (2000).

The state would still have a role in addressing the external effects of divorce on children.

1   A successful marriage

The essence of a successful marriage is a diligent search for a congenial spouse and then a commitment by all parties to make decisions based on the best interests of their family (Becker, 1991). The most obvious benefit from a diligent search is a reduction in the likelihood that the couple will experience the pain and anguish associated with divorce. Most adults want to marry and, among those who marry, essentially all believe that they would benefit from and are making a long-term commitment to their spouse (Glenn, 1996). People marry when they expect to be better off in that state and they divorce when at least one spouse concludes that has not been the result.

A divorce is more likely to occur if there is a faulty investigation of prospective spouses prior to marriage. After marriage, people obtain information about their spouse and other alternatives that cause some to conclude that their earlier optimism about the relationship was incorrect (Becker, Landes, and Michael, 1977). Some of this information could not have been anticipated during courtship, such as a dramatic change in a spouse's health, and, therefore, would not have altered their decision to marry. Other information, however, could have been obtained with a more thorough inquiry into fundamental issues, such as their mate's views on the desirability and number of children. A diligent search that revealed this type of information prior to marriage could alter at least one party's expectation about marriage to a particular person.

Although a successful marriage is clearly fostered by love and sexual attraction, it also benefits from the spouses making a stronger commitment to the welfare of other family members than they make to participants in markets or social activities. Marriage involves an ongoing relationship between people that seldom exists in other settings, so that many decisions by someone within a family have effects on the other family members. To the extent that these effects – which frequently follow from the parties' assuming more specialized roles – increase the welfare of the family members and, therefore, reflect the gains from marriage, they should be encouraged. A major source of their encouragement is the expectation of reciprocal actions then or later. A meal cooked by one spouse benefits all family members, as does the income earned by another spouse. In a market setting, a person seldom has the same incentives to address the concerns of others because the relationship is usually temporary.

The benefits of a strong commitment to marriage are especially important if a couple want children. Most adults want children and children present substantial opportunities for a couple to enhance their welfare. However, this welfare will usually follow from the parents' assuming more specialized roles. A married couple who do not have children can continue to have careers and domestic roles that are similar to those that they had before marriage. Children change this situation by increasing the pressure for a couple to specialize within a relationship. The arrival of children usually results in one parent increasing the emphasis that he or she places on household activities. Because parents usually view having happy and well-adjusted children as being important, they may be tempted to share the responsibilities for child rearing. However, on closer inspection most conclude that a higher income will result from just one parent altering his or her employment rather than both altering their employment. Higher-paying jobs often require unexpected overtime and travel. If both parents reject that type of employment, they may be worse off than if only one parent – usually the one with the higher income-earning potential – makes that choice and the other, if he or she is employed, accepts employment that accommodates child care. The family, therefore, benefits from the couple's assuming more specialized roles.

Although searching diligently for a spouse and considering the welfare of other family members have obvious benefits, these choices can also impose costs on a party. The search for someone with whom you want to spend a significant part of your life can be costly in terms of time, money, and forgone opportunities. The time and money are obvious costs. Also, because it is often difficult to investigate new relationships while having an established one, a potential cost of additional search is the sacrifice of a current situation.

Making decisions during a marriage based on the best interest of one's family also can be costly. One spouse may have the opportunity for a career relocation that will impose adjustment costs on the other spouse. A psychological commitment to a spouse can be particularly devastating if eventually a person discovers that his or her spouse has not made a similar commitment. The cost of a long-term commitment to marriage is particularly apparent when a couple have children. Increased specialization within a relationship can impose long-term costs on a party. A couple can often avoid this type of specialization until they have children. They can maintain their careers, while dividing the responsibilities within their household. The specialization that results from parenthood can have longer-lasting effects than those commonly associated with people living together. Although this specialization is usually in the best interest of the parents and their children while a relationship lasts, it can be revealed as costly if the relationship ends. Skills developed in one household may have little value in another relationship and even less value in the marketplace, leaving a spouse who has emphasized domestic work vulnerable at divorce.

Although this can be a problem in a marriage of short duration, it is particularly a concern in longer marriages. If spouses specialize in income earning, that skill will be intact if the relationship ends. Those persons would lose their share of the household commodities provided by their spouse, but those commodities may have decreased in value after any children have grown up and left the home. During the relationship, the spouses who worked in the home may have developed skills producing household commodities that do not have substantial value outside their relationship, and their income-earning capacity has deteriorated because of their working primarily at home. They may be worse off if the relationship is dissolved, compared with the situation they would be in if they had never entered the relationship in the first place.

When people make these critical decisions about marriage, they would be expected to weigh the benefits and costs of their choices with their being expected to pursue activities only so long as the benefits exceed the costs. They will search only as long as the benefits of additional search exceed the costs. Two particular problems occur in this decision-making process during marriage. First, some of the benefits are external to the decision maker and fall on other family members. Second, the benefits and costs of actions may not be simultaneous, with the costs frequently occurring before the expected benefits. Over the duration of a marriage, the potential contributions of both spouses create the incentives that are the basis for the marriage, but the asymmetry of their contributions can create incentives for income-earning spouses, for example, to dissolve their marriage later (Cohen, 1987). To increase the gains from marriage, it is important to encourage spouses to search diligently for a spouse, to appreciate the benefits of their actions to others, and to anticipate that their sacrifices will be reciprocated by the actions of others.

2   The legal environment

The quality of the decisions that people will make prior to and during marriage is very much a reflection of the incentives that they face, and those incentives in turn are very much a product of the legal environment. In marriage, the most relevant legal constraints are the grounds for divorce and the associated financial and custodial arrangements at divorce. Throughout most of American history, it was difficult to dissolve a marriage except when a spouse had committed acts that were so fundamentally detrimental to the marriage that he or she was held to be at fault for the failure of the marriage. These acts were usually adultery, desertion, or cruelty. During the period from 1969 to 1985, all the states in the United States replaced those grounds with the no-fault grounds of irretrievable breakdown or incompatibility or added the no-fault grounds to the existing fault grounds. Although technically the change was from fault to no-fault, the important change was from divorces being based on mutual consent to their being available to either spouse unilaterally.

The fault divorce system was predicated on the belief that the failure of a marriage could be traced to the actions of one spouse. However, marriages frequently failed because they did not meet the expectations of at least one spouse, especially if the conditions discussed above did not occur: there was not a diligent search or both spouses did not make a strong commitment to the relationship. Seldom did a marriage fail just because one party had committed adultery, deserted their spouse, or been unacceptably cruel to their spouse. Even if these particular acts occurred, the reasons for the failure of the marriage were often more complex. Adultery could be the result of a belligerent attitude toward sexual relations by the other spouse, causing a spouse to look for satisfaction elsewhere. Desertion could be caused by a spouse being driven out of the home for a variety of reasons such as excessive drinking or drugs. Last, physical acts of cruelty could be the result of less obvious verbal acts, such as revealing an extramarital sexual relationship. Although these statutes recognized the type of acts that are detrimental to a successful marriage, the reasons for the failure of most marriages lay elsewhere.

More likely, when a marriage failed it was due to the spouses being exposed to new information about each other and their relationship as well as opportunities outside their marriage. If a divorce required evidence of fault and neither spouse had committed those acts, or at least their commission could not be proven, then a divorcing couple had to agree to fabricate testimony to establish the grounds. As the divorce rate rose under fault divorce, especially in the period after World War II, it became more common for couples to fabricate testimony to establish the fault grounds (Rheinstein, 1972, p. 247). That is not to say that they did this harmoniously. Frequently, only one spouse initially wanted the marriage to end and he or she was forced to make concessions to obtain his or her spouse's cooperation. These concessions, being based on the agreement of the parties, could ignore the arrangement provided by law. A spouse who had limited a career for the benefit of the marriage and faced the prospect of a fall in income if the applicable statutes were applied could demand more compensation to participate in the divorce. A combination of the reality of the marriage and these concessions was important in obtaining both spouses' cooperation.

Fault divorce was attractive because it encouraged spouses to make sacrifices that benefited their family based on the expectation that the marriage was a long-term commitment. The spouses knew that it would be difficult for their partner to dissolve the marriage without their cooperation. On the other hand, it gave substantial power to a spouse who did not want a divorce, potentially imposing a large cost on a spouse who made a mistake by incorrectly estimating the gains from this marriage. If the courts had limited divorces to unambiguous, non-fabricated evidence of fault, the outcome would have been a disaster. Numerous couples who eventually recognized that they had made a mistake would have been forced to continue a marriage that by any reasonable standard was a failure. By permitting fabricated evidence of fault, the courts permitted couples to dissolve marriages by mutual agreement when the net benefits to all parties were probably negative.

The difficulty of obtaining a divorce under fault without committing perjury led to a reform movement that resulted in the enactment of the no-fault divorce laws (Parkman, 2000). Initially, some states anticipated that courts would determine if the no-fault grounds had been established. Courts quickly realized that determination was a futile exercise and divorces became available automatically, based often on the preferences of only one spouse.

The laws regulating the financial arrangements at divorce have been ignored in the deliberations about the change in the grounds for divorce. The statutory arrangements can consist of a division of any marital property, child support from the non-custodial parent to the custodial parent, and short-term rehabilitative spousal support. These arrangements have practical problems because couples frequently have only limited marital property and child and spousal support are often difficult to collect.

In addition to these practical problems, the statutes covering the financial arrangements at divorce tend to underestimate the costs of divorce (Parkman, 1998–9). An obvious omission at divorce is a systematic consideration of the effect that the marriage had on the spouses' income-earning capacities. Frequently, spouses have limited a career during marriage so that they cannot anticipate a future income similar to the one that they would have had if they had not married or had not limited their career during marriage. If they are not compensated for the reduction in their income-earning capacity, all the costs of the divorce are not being recognized. Less frequent, but still a concern, is the situation in which an income-earning spouse's future income has increased as a result of the marriage. If this occurred, one spouse may have incurred a cost in making investments in the primary income-earning spouse. Lack of compensation for these investments can also be a cost of the divorce. Although these omissions might be addressed with new statutes, there are other costs of divorce that the courts are incapable of estimating. Even with the knowledge that the other spouse wants to dissolve the marriage, the divorced spouse may still be strongly attracted to that person and their children. The loss of or reduction in these relationships will be a cost to that spouse. The current marriage was potentially the result of a long and costly search. Now, the divorced spouse is going to be exposed to a new and undesired search for a new living arrangement. Last, the quality of life of any children is potentially going to deteriorate relative to what would still be possible if their parents stayed together.

The likelihood of an inefficient outcome increases if the costs of an alternative are underestimated. This can be illustrated with commercial agreements. Economists have generally found contract law attractive because it attempts to confront a party who wants to terminate an agreement with the alternatives of performing or compensating the non-breaching party for the costs that he or she is about to incur (Posner, 1992). Therefore the parties to the contract have an incentive to breach it only if the benefits of breaching exceed the costs of performance. If the costs of a breach are underestimated, the contract may be breached when the net benefits are negative.

Similarly, if the arrangements at divorce underestimate the cost of divorce, a divorce can occur when the net benefits of all affected parties are negative. Consequently, with no-fault divorce, a divorce can easily occur when the benefits to all family members are less than their costs. Still, as far as divorcing spouses are concerned, their benefits exceed their costs, so the divorce seems reasonable and rational to them.

No-fault divorce is attractive to some people because it permits someone who made an incorrect decision about a relationship to escape from his or her commitment at a fairly low cost. As the costs of poor decisions are reduced, rational people respond by expending less effort to avoid them. Predictably, the result is more poor decisions about prospective spouses. No-fault divorce can also reduce the compensation to people who have made sacrifices based on their marriage being a long-term commitment. Consequently, people have weaker incentives to make these sacrifices. In terms of incentives, no-fault divorce has to be viewed as a very unattractive system. Because a marriage can be dissolved unilaterally, often at a very low cost, people have less incentive to search diligently for a spouse, and after marriage they have less incentive to make sacrifices for the benefit of the family.

In summary, the fault divorce statutes were usually employed by parties to limit divorces to circumstances in which the spouses mutually agreed to dissolve their marriage. This encouraged people to search diligently and to make the sacrifices that lie at the core of the gains from marriage. The major problem with fault divorce was that it made it potentially costly for a spouse who had made an ill-advised decision to marry. Meanwhile, from the perspective of incentives, there is little to say in defense of no-fault divorce because it discourages diligent search and commitment to marriage. It does have the advantage of reducing the costs of making a mistake when choosing a spouse.

3 The preferred grounds for divorce

The preferred grounds for divorce should limit a divorce to situations in which the net benefits for all parties are positive. Mutual consent is most likely to produce this result for established marriages. Since spouses often receive important new information about each other early in marriage when the costs of divorce are small, no-fault divorce can be attractive at that time. A requirement for mutual consent could lock a spouse into an abusive relationship whose dissolution would yield substantial benefits, but the abusing spouse will not cooperate. In that case, fault divorce would meet the criterion established above.

A combination of no-fault, mutual consent, and fault grounds for divorce will provide a major improvement in the incentives that face adults who want to marry. States have traditionally been reluctant to become involved in the normal interactions within a family and that is a position that is supported here.[2] The state's role in protecting children is obvious, so it is appropriate for states to have statutes that establish rules for protecting children during and after a marriage. It is important to recognize that the conditions that accompany the dissolution of marriage have far greater effects on the quality of the marriage itself than has been commonly accepted because they strongly influence the quality of search before marriage and the commitment that the spouses make to their family after marriage.[3]

Mutual consent divorce

Mutual consent should be the primary ground for divorce. A marriage should be dissolved only if both spouses agree that it is a failure. The opponents of fault divorce – and more recently those who support no-fault divorce – do not appear to have given serious consideration to mutual consent divorce (Kay, 1987). Among those willing to consider a change, the normal alternative to no-fault divorce that is considered is fault divorce rather than mutual consent divorce (Ellman, 1996; Bradford, 1997; and Ellman and Lohr, 1997). If we recognize that the problem with the current laws is their permitting unilateral divorce, then the appropriate alternative to consider is mutual consent divorce rather than fault divorce.

The debate over the grounds for divorce represents the triumph of the obvious over the subtle. No-fault divorce is defended because it protects people who have made a miscalculation by marrying someone with whom they no longer want to live – the obvious case of the unfortunate women who would be locked into loveless marriages if the grounds for divorce were either mutual consent or fault (Coontz, 1997, p. 82).[4] Ignored – because it is a great deal subtler – are the gains from encouraging and rewarding those who have made or are attempting

---

[2] Traditionally, the American family has been viewed as the cornerstone of society, with the result that the state legislatures and courts have been reluctant to intervene in family affairs. See, e.g., *Maynard v. Hill*, 125 U.S. 190, 205 (1888). Still, if a legislature wanted to intervene, its powers were viewed as broad until 1965. In *Griswold v. Connecticut*, 381 U.S. 479 (1965) the Supreme Court held that the Connecticut statute forbidding the use of contraceptives was unconstitutional as applied to married couples.

[3] Since the state controls the grounds for divorce, people who do not like the legally prescribed ease of and arrangements at divorce have been forced to turn to premarital agreements. These agreements traditionally were difficult to enforce, but that situation has improved in the states that have passed the Uniform Premarital Agreement Act, 9B U.L.A. 369 (1987); see Bix (1998). Still, premarital agreements are not attractive for most couples because they do not have a clear idea of the range of potential future events and what are the conditions that they want to attach to these events. Also see Alexander (1998).

[4] Others argue that no-fault divorce protects children from the mistakes of their parents without recognizing the benefits to children from parents having incentives to make better decisions. See Gordon (1998).

to make better decisions. They want to search diligently for a congenial spouse and then after marriage they want to make the decisions that increase their and their family's gains from marriage.

Knowing that the ground for divorce for established marriages is mutual consent would encourage spouses to make sacrifices that benefit their marriage. Meanwhile, not all established marriages are successful and, if a couple is questioning the durability of their marriage, mutual consent would increase the incentives for them to recognize and place a value on the collective benefits and costs of marriage and, potentially, divorce.

Under mutual consent divorce, a party who does not want a divorce would have an incentive to require compensation for these costs as a basis for agreeing to the divorce. This point can be illustrated with two examples. A husband who is being asked for a divorce by his wife may feel that he is no longer strongly attracted to her, he could continue to have a satisfactory relationship with his children, he has not made substantial sacrifices for the sake of the family, and he could find someone just as attractive with a limited amount of effort, and he may believe that any children would not be adversely affected by a divorce. He might therefore be willing to reach a divorce agreement at a small cost to his wife. Since the benefit of the divorce exceeds the cost, social welfare would be improved by permitting the divorce. Alternatively, he may still be strongly attracted to his spouse, and he might feel that the quality of his relationship with his children would deteriorate substantially, that he has made substantial sacrifices based on his expectation that the marriage was going to last, and that only a long and costly search would find another comparable spouse or living situation, and he may believe that the children would suffer compared with the quality of life that is still possible if the parents stay together. He might in those circumstances ask for a level of compensation that the other spouse is unwilling to provide. In other words, the party who wants the divorce does not value the divorce as much as the other spouse and the children value the continuation of the marriage. In that case, social welfare is improved by continuing the marriage.

One of the attractive aspects of mutual consent divorce is the increased likelihood that both parents will address the costs incurred by their children as a result of a divorce. These costs go far beyond just maintenance, which is covered by child support. If the divorcing spouses are forced to recognize the full costs of their divorce, some parents might be able to make their marriage work and, thereby, provide benefits to their children.[5] The parents who expect custody of any children after a divorce are most likely to recognize the costs that the children will incur. If the children are less happy after divorce, their attitudes will affect the welfare of the custodial parent. These changes in the

---

[5] Under no-fault divorce, many divorces occur when there has been only a minor discord between the spouses. See Amato and Booth (1997, p. 220).

welfare of the children and the custodial parent are a cost that mutual consent divorce would encourage those parents to address when considering a divorce.

Another attraction of mutual consent divorce is the incentives it creates for couples to consider the rules that are appropriate for their marriage. If people knew that mutual consent was the primary ground for dissolving an established marriage, that knowledge might increase the incentive for them to negotiate premarital and postmarital agreements. Neither fault divorce nor no-fault divorce provides marrying individuals with the opportunity to construct their own grounds for the dissolution of their marriage. With mutual consent divorce, the dissolution of marriage would be based on the parties' criteria rather than those of the state. In those circumstances, the parties might be more inclined to specify their own grounds for divorce, such as a career conflict, at the time of marriage. Any agreement of the spouses should be subject to regulations that attempt to protect the interests of any children.

Mutual consent is not a perfect solution. It can result in the continuation of a marriage if one party wants to ignore the costs imposed on the parties by the marriage. This can occur when a spouse, basing a decision on spite, is opposed to a divorce in any circumstances. However, people can be surprisingly rational even when dealing with emotional issues such as marriage and divorce. In most divorces, at least one spouse initially wanted the marriage to continue (Wallerstein and Kelly, 1980, p. 17) but, when the benefits for all affected parties – especially any children – from divorce exceed the costs, social welfare is increased by a divorce. In those circumstances, the spouses have incentives to construct an agreement that leaves them both better off. The large number of divorces based on mutual consent under the fault grounds illustrates the willingness of spouses to negotiate even under trying conditions.

Although mutual consent as a basis for divorce is unappealing to some people because it appears to lock people into unsuccessful and potentially abusive marriages, recognition is seldom given to the benefits of mutual consent that would flow to people willing to make a long-term commitment. The provisions for no-fault and fault grounds for divorce discussed below should address some of the concerns about unsuccessful marriages. Moreover, we need to recognize the limited ability of mutual consent to keep an antagonistic couple together. Either spouse can always leave the relationship, with the only restrictions being the response of others, any financial obligations imposed by law on the spouses to each other and their children, and – of course – the ability to marry anyone else.

In reaching their agreement to divorce, the couple could ignore any statutes except those that attempt to protect the interests of children. Still, it would be appropriate for there to be default statutes for the financial and custodial arrangements that would apply unless modified or rejected. The most important change from current statutes should be a more systematic recognition of the effect of marriage on the parties' income-earning capacities (Parkman, 1998–9).

No-fault divorce

No-fault divorce is still attractive during the early period of a marriage. Mutual consent divorce gives substantial power to spouses who do not want a divorce. To limit abuse of this power, it would appear to be attractive to permit no-fault divorce when the potential costs of divorce are likely to be low, as they tend to be early in a marriage and when there are no children. Early in marriage, a couple are still involved in an evaluation process. During this period of evaluation, no-fault divorce should continue to be the grounds for divorce, giving the parties incentives to investigate their commitment to their relationship.

Eventually, at least one spouse may make sacrifices based on a long-term commitment to the marriage and then the grounds for divorce should shift to mutual consent. These sacrifices will usually occur because a spouse is limiting a career or the couple are having a child. In our highly mobile society, it is common for a couple to relocate. Frequently in this process a spouse is forced to relinquish a desirable job so that the other spouse can take advantage of an employment opportunity that appears to be in the couple's long-term best interest. In addition, children usually require one parent to adjust his or her career to assist in child care. With these changes in the couple's circumstances, the grounds for divorce would shift to mutual consent. Since accommodations for the long-term benefit of the marriage may be subtle, setting a predetermined period, such as five years, as the basis for the shift from no-fault to mutual consent divorce would seem to be reasonable. Recognizing that the grounds for divorce are going to change in certain circumstances – a relocation, a child, or a specified time period – will force a couple to re-evaluate their commitment to each other. If they are uncomfortable with the restrictions that would accompany mutual consent divorce, they can mutually agree to maintain no-fault grounds for divorce.

With no-fault divorce, there would have to be laws to govern the financial arrangements. However, without career adjustments and children, the range of financial considerations should be limited.

Fault divorce

Fault divorce too can still have a role in dissolving marriages. Mutual consent can create problems when someone is "driven out" of a marriage rather than "wanting out." It is often difficult for anyone, including the spouses and judges, clearly to identify fault. Being driven out of a marriage raises concerns similar to those addressed with the fault divorce statutes. Under fault divorce, the "guilty" spouse did something that gave the "innocent" spouse a right to dissolve the marriage: the innocent spouse was driven out of the marriage. Mutual consent

68   *Allen M. Parkman*

would not provide a solution for the situation in which one spouse is the victim of acts such as cruelty or adultery but the "guilty" spouse does not want a divorce. Courts during the fault divorce era showed little skill, however, at making determinations in these cases (Rheinstein, 1972). Often the grounds given for fault divorce were hypocritical and the marriage had failed for other reasons. And, even when the fault grounds could be proven, the reasons a marriage failed were probably a great deal more complicated than just the acts that established the grounds. Nonetheless, fault divorce would appear to be appropriate when there is clear evidence of fault, such as abuse of a spouse or any children. Because abuse is socially unacceptable behavior and should be discouraged, it should also be the basis for an adjustment in the default financial and custodial arrangements at divorce.

4   Conclusion

Mutual consent as the grounds for the dissolution of most marriages is not a perfect solution to problems facing the family, but it is superior to the alternatives, especially no-fault divorce for all marriages. Mutual consent is attractive because it creates incentives for people to search diligently for a spouse and, during marriage, to make decisions based on the best interests of the family rather than taking a narrow focus on themselves. No-fault divorce early in marriages provides spouses with an opportunity to evaluate their commitment to each other at a fairly low cost. The potential for a fault divorce encourages spouses to avoid socially unacceptable behavior.

REFERENCES

Alexander, Gregory S. (1998), "The New Marriage Contract and the Limits of Private Ordering," *Indiana Law Journal*, 73, 503–10.
Amato, Paul R., and Alan Booth (1997), *A Generation at Risk*, Cambridge, MA: Harvard University Press.
Becker, Gary S. (1991), *A Treatise on the Family*, Cambridge, MA: Harvard University Press.
Becker, Gary S., Elisabeth M. Landes, and Robert T. Michael (1997), "An Economic Analysis of Marital Instability," *Journal of Political Economy*, 85, 1141–87.
Bix, Brian (1998), "Bargaining in the Shadow of Love: The Enforcement of Premarital Agreements and How We Think about Marriage," *William and Mary Law Review*, 40, 145–207.
Bradford, Laura (1997), "The Counterrevolution: A Critique of Recent Proposals to Reform No-Fault Divorce Laws," *Stanford Law Review*, 49, 607–36.
Cohen, Lloyd (1987), "Marriage, Divorce, and Quasi Rents; or, 'I Gave Him the Best Years of My Life,' " *Journal of Legal Studies*, 16, 267–303.
Coontz, Stephanie (1997), *The Way We Really Are: Coming to Terms with America's Changing Families*, New York: Basic Books.

Ellman, Ira Mark (1996), "The Place of Fault in a Modern Divorce Law," *Arizona State Law Journal*, 28, 773–836.

Ellman, Ira Mark and Sharon Lohr (1997), "Marriage as Contract, Opportunistic Violence, and Other Bad Arguments for Fault Divorce," *University of Illinois Law Review*, 3, 719–72.

Glenn, Norval D. (1996), "Values, Attitudes, and the State of American Marriage," in David Popenoe, Jean Bethke Elshtain, and David Blankenhorn (eds.), *Promises to Keep: Decline and Renewal of Marriage in America*, Lanham, MD: Rowman & Littlefield.

Gordon, Robert M. (1998), "The Limits of Limits on Divorce," *Yale Law Journal*, 107, 1435–65.

Kay, Herma Hill (1987), "An Appraisal of California's No-Fault Divorce Law," *California Law Review*, 75, 291–319.

Parkman, Allen (1998–9), "Bringing Consistency to the Financial Arrangements at Divorce," *Kentucky Law Review*, 87, 51–93.

(2000), *Good Intentions Gone Awry: No Fault Divorce and the American Family*, Lanham, MD: Rowman & Littlefield.

Posner, Richard A. (1992), *Economic Analysis of Law*, 4th edn, Boston, MA: Little, Brown.

Rheinstein, Max (1972), *Marriage Stability, Divorce, and the Law*, Chicago: University of Chicago Press.

Wallerstein, Judith S., and Joan Berlin Kelly (1980), *Surviving the Breakup*, New York: Basic Books.

5 An economic approach to adultery law

Eric Rasmusen

> Wilt thou have this Woman to thy wedded wife, to live together after God's
> ordinance in the holy estate of Matrimony? Wilt thou love her, comfort her,
> honour, and keep her in sickness and in health; and, forsaking all other, keep
> thee only unto her, so long as ye both shall live?
>
> (Book of Common Prayer, 1662)

1 Introduction

When two people marry, they promise fidelity. Adultery occurs when one of
them breaks this promise, and it is generally believed that breaking promises,
and breaking this promise in particular, is wrong. "Every wrong has its remedy,"
equity used to say. The subject of this paper is which of the myriad possible
remedies are suitable for adultery. In modern US law, the formal remedy is
that the wronged party can file for divorce and force a division of the assets.
This really is not a remedy, however, since under modern no-fault divorce laws
anyone can file for divorce anyway, no reason being required. To the extent that
divorce deters adultery, it does so simply as an extension of adultery's tendency
to displease the injured spouse. In the eyes of the law, adultery and complaining
about the other spouse's adultery are equally good reasons for divorce.

In the past, other remedies existed, of which vestiges continue today. These
include criminal penalties, tort actions, and self-help. This chapter discusses
remedies using the tools of law and economics. The approach will be to view
adultery law as a problem in efficient contracting, of setting up a legal regime
in which marriage is structured to maximize the net benefit of the husband and
wife, with attention where appropriate to spillovers onto third parties. When
such spillovers do not exist (the simplest case), efficiency requires adultery law
that replicates the marriage terms the husband and wife would choose if transactions costs were low. Adultery will be analyzed as a problem not of morals,

I would like to thank Antony Dnes, Lillian BeVier, Margaret Brinig, Kevin Kordana, Geoffrey
Manne, J. Mark Ramseyer, Mark Rushton, Jeffrey Stake and participants in seminars at the
Purdue University Economics Department, the Federalist Society of the University of Virginia,
and Northwestern University Law School for their comments.

order in society, patriarchal domination, or inalienable rights, but of the welfare of individuals as seen by individuals.

2   The model

Assumptions

It will be useful to set up a verbal formal model to clarify thinking on the costs and benefits of adultery. For simplicity, let us take the point of view of a Wife who is considering making an investment such as learning to love her Husband more, giving up her job, or moving to a different city, an investment that is useful only for the sake of the marriage and that she will regret making if her Husband turns out to be unfaithful.[1] We will call the husband's partner in adultery "the Other Woman." Assume that if the Wife does not invest in the marriage she would be willing to divorce the Husband upon catching him in adultery and that this threat would be sufficient to deter him.

If, however, she has invested in the marriage, her threat to divorce him would not be credible; she would have too much to lose. The Husband also receives a benefit from the Wife's investment if he remains faithful, but his most preferred outcome is for the Wife to invest and for himself to commit adultery. The Wife may exert monitoring effort to increase the probability that she detects adultery.[2] The Husband incurs a cost to find a woman with whom to commit adultery and to conceal it, a cost that depends on the Wife's precautions. With some probability depending on these efforts, the Wife detects the adultery if it exists. Such detection reduces the utility of the Husband and increases the utility of the Wife, though not so much that she would invest in an adulterous marriage just for the pleasure of catching the Husband. This detection disutility for the Husband is a penalty independent of the law and represents such things as his

---

[1] It should be understood that "Husband" in this model means "the spouse who is tempted by adultery," not "the male spouse." The conventional wisdom has it that men are more tempted than women, however, and this seems to be true in the thirty-nine Fairfax County, Virginia, cases examined in Allen and Brinig (1998). I am well aware that, in most times and cultures, adultery law has treated men and women asymmetrically. The reasons (evolutionary biology? the relative unimportance of adultery with prostitutes? the greater danger of violence from angry men?) are well worth exploring, which could be done using the framework of the present article. If in some cultures women do not mind the kind of adultery by husbands that occurs, then asymmetric laws would be efficient; if the laws simply ignore wives' harm from adultery, they are inefficient. I judged it best to focus on the United States here.

[2] I have implicitly assumed that this probability is positive even with zero effort, since the Husband is deterred from adultery by the threat of divorce if the Wife has not invested in the marriage. Lillian BeVier has suggested to me that the Wife's effort to prevent adultery could be socially useful, increasing the benefits to both parties from the investment if, for example, it consisted of being unusually attentive to the Husband's desires. If this effect is strong enough, adultery should be made fully legal so as to channel the Wife's efforts in this good direction, just as pedestrians could be made more careful by removing liability for the negligence of drivers.

embarrassment at being caught and the inconvenience of his Wife knowing the identity of the Other Woman. Many, perhaps most, men and women would be deterred from adultery by a high value for detection disutility combined with a low benefit from the adultery itself, just as shame and scruples deter most people from crimes such as burglary, but the law is concerned with those people for whom social norms are insufficient.[3]

In this model, undetected adultery hurts the Wife but she benefits from detecting it, given that it occurs. Why should this be so?[4] A partial answer is that the Wife can deduce that the Husband is committing adultery even if she fails to detect it through her monitoring. Why, however, do people try to learn the specifics of negative occurrences even if they know they will become unhappy? We will avoid the question by falling back on the economic idea of revealed preference and using the payoff function to represent willingness to expend resources to obtain particular outcomes, not to represent psychological well-being. Thus, the assumption that the Wife obtains a benefit from detecting the Husband's adultery is equivalent to her being willing to expend resources to detect it, rather than saying anything about whether she feels happier afterwards.

Analysis

Let us first consider what will happen in the absence of legal penalties. The Wife will look ahead and realize that she needs to monitor if she is to deter the Husband's adultery after her investment. Two things could happen. First, she might decide to make the investment and monitor carefully, in which case the Husband will not even try to find the Other Woman. Second, she might decide that deterrence is too expensive and abandon investment in the marriage.

In this simple model, adultery never happens, because it is deterred either by the Wife's precautions or by her credible threat of divorce when she has not invested in the marriage. There is, nonetheless, a welfare loss, and potentially a very large welfare loss. This loss is created by the deterrence itself, the Wife's precaution cost, or the loss to Husband and Wife if the Wife does not invest. If we relaxed the assumption that the Wife knows the Husband's degree of temptation precisely, adultery could occur in equilibrium when the Wife underestimates the precautions she needs to take. This would create two further costs, the direct

---

[3] By "independently of the law" I mean that the adultery penalty will take the same value if there is no law concerning adultery. We normally think of the law as increasing the penalty for adultery, but it is also conceivable to have a law protecting adulterous husbands by punishing wives who show their anger, in which case the law could actually reduce the private penalty. This sounds absurd, but no-fault divorce has some of this flavor, by allowing the adulterous husband to divorce his wife if she bothers him too much about his affairs.

[4] This issue arises in other contexts also, for example when a gynecologist rapes patients without their knowledge; *People v. Minkowski*, 204 Cal. App. 2d 832 (1962), where the court held that there was indeed criminal harm.

loss to the Wife and the transactions costs to the Husband of committing and concealing adultery.

Adding a legal penalty for adultery is adding a new penalty to the private detection embarrassment. To deter adultery efficiently, the penalty must be large enough that even if the Wife spends nothing on monitoring the Husband will find the expected payoff from adultery too low to justify its transactions costs. In that case, the Husband will be deterred, the Wife will feel secure in using her time investing in the marriage and not in monitoring, and social surplus will be maximized. Both parties would be happy to accept the possibility of extraordinary penalties for adultery, *ex ante*; the Husband would be willing because he knows that if the penalties are in place he will be deterred and not have to suffer them.[5]

It has often been noted regarding contracts generally and marriage in particular that long-term relationships are likely to break down without penalties for breach and that both parties will freely agree to become liable to punishment.[6] Indeed, that is the very idea of a contract. Adultery is just one more example. Viewing the situation *ex post*, however, it is easy for commentators to see such penalties as illegitimate infringement on the Husband's liberty (see, for example, Note, 1991).

Externalities

So far we have focused on the Husband and Wife, in analogy to contract law. Adultery has spillovers, however externalities in economic terminology. For the Other Woman, adultery is a beneficial spillover. For other people, it is harmful. Parents and children dislike adultery, other couples may be dismayed by the bad example, and many people dislike it in their community for reasons of religion, natural law, or aesthetics. Adultery interests outsiders just as much as pollution, racial discrimination, environmental destruction, and new building construction. Adultery law is like land-use law, regulation of how people live based on the idea that people in a community care about what their neighbors are

---

5 See, for example, Cohen (1987) and Dnes (1998). The present model can be modified to add non-deterrable adultery. If it is really true that some people could not prevent themselves from committing adultery even if they were sure to be caught and to receive the death penalty – something I doubt, but which others believe – that can be incorporated into the model as a fixed probability that adultery occurs beyond what is chosen by the husband. The model would not change much.

6 As Lillian BeVier pointed out to me, even in the absence of law, long-term relationships can survive based on mutual threats of retaliation for breach, something my own writing has discussed in chapter 5 of Rasmusen (1994). This requires sufficient interest by both parties in the future, however, and mutual vulnerability to breach, which is why courts are so useful. Mutual threats are more likely to work for minor offenses such as rude language that are instantly detectable and where the benefit from a single transgression is not worth risking later retaliation. This, together with the cost of adjudication relative to the alleged harm, is why the courts have always stayed out of minor household disputes.

doing. Just as land-use law varies dramatically among different communities, so we should expect adultery law to vary.

Using the model, if the sum of the benefits to the Husband and the Other Woman is exceeded by the cost to the Wife and other people, adultery will be inefficient. The Wife and the outsiders would be willing, were it feasible, to pay the Husband and the Other Woman enough that they would refrain from adultery. Transactions and organization costs prevent this, and so the adultery occurs. A law that prevented adultery would then increase social surplus by leading to the result to which all parties would agree if they could transact costlessly.

The point that other people's desires must enter a cost–benefit analysis is often resisted, so it is worth clarification. The ideas of economic efficiency, wealth maximization, and Pareto optimality all rely on taking people's preferences as given, without the analyst judging their moral worth. If consumers say they like chocolate, the chocolate-neutral analyst does not say that banning chocolate would create no harm. Suppose the Husband and the Other Woman would pay $50,000 and $40,000, respectively, for the right to commit adultery, and the Wife and 100 outsiders would pay $60,000 and $1,000 each, respectively, to prevent it. The adultery is then inefficient. There is no need to ask whether the outsiders have "really been damaged" or whether the externality "really exists." If people would pay $1,000 to prevent an act, the act causes them damage, and the economist does not ask about motivation.[7] Whether the outsiders' objections are religious or material, for example, matters as little as the motivations behind the Husband's and the Wife's desires.[8]

A common traditional position is that people should care about a society's virtue. A common modern position is that they should not – that people should not interfere in the private lives of others.[9] The present paper adopts

[7] The puzzle of undetected misbehavior's harm arises again here. If the Husband is unfaithful and the Wife sees this but the public does not, is the public hurt? If not, then sanctions on the Wife for publicizing the adultery might be appropriate. The same issue arises in cases of cruelty to animals; if the only harm is unhappiness from observed cruelty, the logical solution is to legalize discreet torture but to penalize anyone who brings it to public attention. Of course, in both cases it seems that people also dislike knowing that the behavior is occurring somewhere even if they do not actually observe it, merely deducing it from human nature and the absence of legal penalties.

[8] The economic approach is, of course, vulnerable to the standard anti-utilitarian criticism that some desires are illegitimate. It implies that, if there are enough sadists, then torture is socially good, for example. The burden of proof is rightly on those who criticize a given desire, however. In the present case, this says that the burden is on those who say that either the Husband's benefit or the Wife's and other people's disutility from adultery should be ignored. Ignoring either of these requires religious or philosophical considerations that take us outside of the economic approach to law. For further discussion of the general principle, see Rasmusen (1997).

[9] John Stuart Mill is an older proponent of this view, which is a major theme of *On Liberty* (Mill, 1859). He makes clear what modern legal treatments often do not, that he disapproves even of

a neutral position, in accordance with the economist's usual pluralistic procedure of taking tastes as given. The degree to which people care about adultery is a crucial empirical question, of course, which would be reflected in such things as their choices in living location, friends, and spouses, and their willingness in political logrolling to trade votes on adultery law for votes on tax policy.

3   Penalties

Features of penalties

Having established that efficiency requires some sort of penalty for adultery, let us consider the possibilities. A number of choices need to be made.

- **Who initiates punishment?** Someone has authority to make the decision to initiate the formal process. In a tort lawsuit, this is the plaintiff; in a criminal prosecution, it is the grand jury or prosecutor.
- **Is the penalty a fine, or does it destroy real resources?** The penalty might be a money transfer, involving no real resources, or it might be a penalty such as confinement that hurts the Husband without benefiting someone else by the same amount.
- **Who gets the fine or pays for inflicting the real-resource penalty?** If a fine is paid, someone receives the fine and benefits from the punishment. If the penalty destroys real resources, someone must pay for that destruction and bear a cost.
- **Is the penalty determined before the offense, or afterwards?** The penalty can be set *ex ante*, before the harm occurs, or *ex post*, once the damage is measured. This is the difference between liquidated and compensatory damages in contract and between fixed and discretionary sentencing in criminal law. *Ex ante* penalties help the Husband make a more informed decision and are cheaper to implement, but they may be far from the damage in a particular case.[10]

---

social disapproval of vice, much less of legal penalties. To be consistent, advocates of this view might wish to turn self-help on its head and make illegal behavior that is ordinarily legal, if it is done from bad motives. Landlords in the United States are forbidden to deny rental to a tenant because of his race, even though they are free to deny rental to him for other reasons. In the case of adultery, a regime that believed sexual behavior to be within a person's sphere of privacy should penalize the Wife if she tried to punish the Husband by what were ordinarily legal means – leaving him, refusing to cooperate in household finances or legal matters, and so forth.

[10] The *ex ante*/*ex post* distinction is similar to Robert Cooter's distinction between "prices" and "sanctions," that is, between penalties lacking in moral opprobrium and varying with the scale of the behavior and fixed, discontinuous penalties with moral opprobrium. Cooter (1984) argues that sanctions are appropriate when the law maker knows behavior is undesirable but cannot measure the harm easily, which would seem to be the case with adultery.

- **Can the wife alienate her rights, waiving the penalty?** It may be that the Wife can either stop the penalty from being imposed, or agree in advance to stop the penalty from being imposed. If the Wife initiates the penalty process, she certainly can stop the penalty from being imposed, simply by inaction. It is a different matter, however, for her to be able to make a binding agreement to stop the penalty, something she may wish to do in exchange for concessions from the Husband. Also, even if the Wife does not have the ability to initiate the penalty process, it may be that she can stop it – by being given the authority to veto criminal prosecutions, for example.
- **Who is punished: the Husband, the Other Woman, or both?** The penalty could be imposed on either or both of the two adulterers.

An adultery law could be constructed using any combination of these features. Since there are six of them, each with at least two alternatives, there are at least sixty-four types of law (two to the sixth power). Here, we will discuss just three representative laws: civil damages, criminal penalties, and self-help.

Civil damages

Under this legal regime, the Wife initiates punishment of a fine, which is paid to the Wife and is variable depending on the amount of damage. The Wife can alienate her right to initiate punishment, and it is the Other Woman who is punished.

Tort and contract law exist to provide recourse for private injuries, when one person inflicts damage on another. It would seem well suited to adultery: the Husband has breached his agreement with the Wife, and the Other Woman cooperated in his breach and took actions that harmed the Wife. The situation has elements of breach of contract, tortious interference with contract, and intentional tort generally. In the context of the model, one form of tort liability would be for the Other Woman to be liable to the Wife for compensatory damages. Let us assume that the Husband and the Other Woman can agree to cooperate in paying the penalty and other costs of adultery, and for the moment put aside the possibility of the Wife alienating her right to sue. The Wife might monitor either less or more than she would were tort damages not available. On the one hand, the possibility of compensation means that adultery causes her less harm on net. If the detection probability is relatively unresponsive to the Wife's effort, the Wife's main reason to monitor would be to raise the cost to the Husband of finding the Other Woman enough to forestall adultery, but that reason disappears if she is fully compensated. On the other hand, if adultery does occur and she detects it, she can collect damages. In either case, the Wife is more likely to invest in the marriage, because the Other Woman's liability reduces the loss to the Wife from investment followed by adultery.

One advantage of civil actions when the Wife can alienate her right to sue by agreeing to a settlement or by waiving her right in advance of the adultery is that if the Husband and Other Woman benefit more from adultery than the Wife loses they will make a deal. The Wife would sell her right to sue, and all parties would save on the transactions costs of detecting or concealing the adultery. This is a disadvantage, however, if spillovers on outside parties are large, since they are not part of the deal; in the example earlier, the Husband and the Other Woman would be willing to pay the Wife $61,000 for her permission, but that does nothing to compensate for the $100,000 loss to outsiders.

A key practical disadvantage is that the defendant may be judgment proof. If the Other Woman cannot afford to pay damages, the Wife's right to sue is irrelevant. Since many, perhaps most, people lack the wealth to pay damages substantial enough to compensate for a wrecked marriage, or perhaps even for the cost to the Wife of hiring a lawyer, civil suits may disappear as an effective penalty altogether. This is a standard economic argument for why civil damages and fines are not used for the various misbehaviors we call criminal (see Posner, 1998, section 7.2). A problem special to adultery is that the Husband and Wife are financially interdependent. Even if the Other Woman paid the entire penalty, much of its deterrent effect would be nullified if the Husband, as part of the household, were to receive half the penalty. Or, if the Husband aids the Other Woman in paying the judgment, the household ends up paying damages to itself.

Another general disadvantage of civil suits is the cost of determining the size of the damage. If plaintiffs give one-third of their judgment to compensate their lawyer, defendants spend about the same amount, and there is a competitive market for lawyers, then it must be that the cost of establishing and measuring liability is about two-thirds of the size of the damage itself. The measurement problem is particularly severe for an injury such as adultery whose damage is not monetary; for adultery, proof of liability may be relatively easy compared with typical tort and contract suits, but proof of damages is relatively difficult. It is not necessary that civil judgments be variable, of course. They could be fixed, like workmen's compensation for the loss of a particular body part. The problem would then arise of plaintiffs choosing to sue even if the true damages are small, knowing that the court has committed itself to positive error in the damage award (see Rasmusen, 1995).

Civil damages are, however, the remedy most often used in the area of commercial law closest to marriage: partnership. As Levmore (1995) nicely lays out using the property/liability framework of Calabresi and Melamed (1972), the common law remedy in partnership disputes has been dissolution of the partnership followed by civil litigation over prior misbehavior. He notes that the requirement of dissolving the partnership first creates difficulties, and has gradually been eroding in partnership law, but that in marriage law, to which he compares it, the requirement remains much stronger and the possibilities for later lawsuit are weaker. Note, too, that criminal penalties are also available for misbehavior in partnership if the violation of fiduciary duty is severe enough.

Criminal penalties

Under this legal regime, the state initiates punishment in the form of a real penalty, whose cost is paid by the state. The penalty is fixed, independent of the damage. The Wife can block the punishment and can alienate her right to do so, and both Husband and Other Woman are punished.

Criminal law is used for penalties for many kinds of intentional injuries. Punitive damages are used for the same purpose in civil suits, but punitive damages are never fixed *ex ante* and the person injured initiates the penalty process and receives its benefit. Criminal law is often used for offenses such as rape and robbery that are considered serious and have high mental costs to the victim even if the out-of-pocket costs are small. This suggests that criminal law might be suitable for adultery also.

One form a criminal law might take is for adultery to be prosecuted at the discretion of the county prosecutor, on complaint by the Wife, with a sentence of five years in the state prison. If this sentence is long enough, the Husband would be deterred even if the Wife did not exert special effort to monitor him and the Other Woman were willing to compensate him up to her own benefit from adultery. This achieves the efficient outcome: the Wife can safely invest in the marriage, and neither she nor the Husband incurs transactions costs.

Alienability becomes relevant if the adultery is efficient from the point of view of the three parties. If the criminal penalty is large, adultery will not occur even if it is efficient, unless the wife's right to veto prosecution is alienable. If it is alienable, however, then no harm results even if the state has set the penalty extremely high. The penalty will not be imposed anyway, because the Wife will veto it in exchange for compensation, and the penalty serves only as the starting point for bargaining between her and the Husband.[11]

Alienability does have two disadvantages. First, if there are externalities to the public, these will be ignored by the Wife when she accepts payment from the Husband and the Other Woman to tolerate the adultery. This problem shows up in many areas of criminal law. Victims prefer to free the criminal

---

[11] This perhaps helps explain why adultery prosecutions have never been common, despite the prevalence of adultery laws. The law may be important, but only as a threat the injured spouse could wield to extract concessions from the adulterous spouse. To the extent that the law served this purpose, its penalties would not need to be imposed.

to commit crimes against others rather than forgo extracting concessions; an employer, for example, would rather be reimbursed for embezzlement than stop a criminal employee stealing from a future employer. The second disadvantage is that alienability prevents strategic precommitment. The penalty is likely to be costly to the Wife as well as to the Husband, because of public shame or loss of the Husband's earning power. Thus, she might veto prosecution because it hurts the household. She might actually benefit from not being allowed to veto prosecution because then the threat of punishment becomes credible and the Husband would be deterred. This paradox is not merely theoretical; it is the justification for the "zero-tolerance" rules now common for spousal assault.[12] In many jurisdictions, if a wife calls the police for help when her husband hits her and if the police decide that he has indeed hit her, the criminal process will proceed even if the wife objects.

The Model Penal Code, proposed by the American Law Institute (ALI) in 1962 and a strong influence on US state criminal codes, deliberately decriminalized adultery, saying, "private immorality should be beyond the reach of the penal law" (Part II, Article 213, "Note on Adultery and Fornication"). It said that adultery laws were rarely enforced anyway, that it would be costly to enforce them, and that an act should not be illegal "simply because such behavior is widely thought to be immoral." Although recognizing that adultery laws were popular with voters and that the crime is not victimless, the ALI regarded these as unimportant points.

Non-enforcement is a red herring. Many crimes exist that are rarely prosecuted. A notorious example is the US "Brady Bill," which makes attempts by felons to buy guns illegal. This is much easier to prosecute than is adultery, since the government has in its hands written evidence that the felon broke the law. Yet in the two years or so of its existence, the government claimed to detect some 186,000 violations, of which it chose to prosecute just 7, about 1 in 20,000.[13] Even such an uncontroversial crime as burglary is rarely prosecuted. In 1994, only about 1.4 percent of burglaries in the United States led to conviction and 0.8 percent to incarceration.[14] There is, to be sure, a qualitative difference between the precisely 0 percent prosecution rate for adultery in many states and the 0.005 percent rate for Brady offenses, but it is not clear why that difference should matter. My impression is that the real problem for the ALI was

[12] Rorie Sherman, "Domestic Abuse Bills Gain Momentum in Legislatures," *National Law Journal*, 4 July 1994, p. A9.
[13] Seven prosecutions in 17 months: "Implementation of the Brady Handgun Violence Prevention Act," Report to the Committee on the Judiciary, US Senate, and the Committee on the Judiciary, US House of Representatives, GAO/GGD-96-22 Gun Control, January 1996. 186,000 illegal acts in the first 28 months: Ron Scherer, "Gun-Control Laws Scrutinized after Empire State Shooting," *Christian Science Monitor*, 27 February, 1997, p. 3.
[14] Langan and Farrington (1998, pp. 19 and 29). In England, 0.6 percent of burglaries led to conviction and 0.2 percent (1 in 500) to incarceration.

that its members did not think adultery was really immoral, since they offer no grounds to differentiate adultery from other criminal behavior. The same issue arises with respect to laws against cruelty to animals (see Beirne, 1999), which the Model Penal Code proposes at 250.11 "to prevent outrage to the sensibilities of the community." The ALI certainly did not consider the spillover argument explained in the present article, in keeping with the common position in the 1950s that tastes for retribution are barbarous and illegitimate.

Self-help

Under this legal regime, the Wife initiates punishment, a real penalty whose cost she pays and that is variable in magnitude. The Wife can alienate her right to inflict punishment and she can punish both the Husband and the Other Woman.

"Self-help" refers to a private person being allowed to take actions that the state ordinarily prohibits.[15] Ordinarily, one person cannot take away another person's furniture and sell it. A creditor, however, is allowed to do just that. In the case of adultery, self-help consists of the Wife being allowed to punish the adulterous Husband by actions that would ordinarily be illegal – by dissipating assets, leaving with the children, refusing to help support him financially, assaulting him, or even murder. The law can do this formally, by statute or case law, or informally, by non-prosecution or jury nullification. The right is alienable if the Wife loses her defense for the criminal act and is prosecuted as a normal defendant if it is shown that she agreed to the adultery.

Self-help combines features of tort and criminal law. Like tort law, it is initiated by the offended party and the penalty is variable. Like criminal law, the penalty is a real cost. Self-help can be seen as privatized criminal law. The Wife, not the state, initiates the punishment and bears its cost, but she is allowed to use violence, something the state ordinarily monopolizes.

Self-help has both advantages and disadvantages. An advantage is low transactions costs. Although it does not completely eliminate government costs, since the government still must determine whether self-help was justified, clear cases will avoid lawyers and courts altogether, and penalties can be variable without the need for a government factfinder to evaluate damage. Moreover, if the imposition cost is increasing in the size of the penalty, and the Wife's satisfaction from a greater penalty increases with the emotional damage of the adultery to her, then she will choose to inflict a larger penalty if the damage is greater. A Wife who did not really care about adultery

---

[15] More narrowly, self-help is used to refer to a private person being allowed immediately to take an action that otherwise requires going through a legal process, e.g. to repossess an automobile used as collateral without waiting for a court's order. I use the term to refer generally to taking actions that except for the special circumstances are illegal.

would not bother even scolding the Husband; a Wife who did care might kill him. This contrasts with civil damages, which have the disadvantage that even an indifferent Wife would pretend to be hurt in order to collect the damages.

Self-help also has disadvantages. If people are often mistaken, and more mistaken than courts, in evaluating whether their spouses are adulterous, self-help will move the amount of punishment further from the optimum. It puts the cost of mistakes and the cost of inflicting punishment on the victims, who may be ill prepared to bear those costs. "Self-help" carried out by unbiased committees rather than by victims would work rather better – the classic vigilante committees – but this starts to shade into criminal punishment, for what else are courts? In any case, even then self-help would have real costs, unlike civil damages. And self-help, like civil suits and alienable criminal penalties, takes no account of spillovers on the public.

Self-help is relevant to this discussion in one more way: as a motive for providing civil or criminal legal remedies to the victim. If these are not provided the victim may decide to punish the adulterer even if it is illegal, creating the possibility of mistakes and requiring the government to bear a cost of punishing the adultery victim. Smith (1998) has noted this kind of victim retaliation as a reason for the illegality of blackmail, and the argument carries over to much of criminal law. Indeed, it was explicitly cited as a reason for passing a criminal law against adultery by natives in Rhodesia in 1916. The native criminal law had been abolished by the British without replacement (though civil damages were still available in native courts), and numerous hut burnings were the result (Mittlebeeler, 1976, pp. 122–34, 183). This argument depends, of course, on a culture's level of honor and violence.

4   Adultery law in practice

Posner (1999, chapter 2) and Epstein (1999) have argued persuasively that theorizing about law without reflecting on any real cases or statutes is dangerous. This section responds to that warning. As one might expect when efficiency calls for a law, diverse nations and times have provided legal sanctions for adultery, from "Thou shalt not commit adultery" up to the present day.[16] Describing the law in any particular time and place is difficult because much of it has been unwritten, being embodied in prosecutorial discretion, the attitude of juries,

---

[16] The commandment is *Exodus* 20:14: "Thou shalt not commit adultery," with specifics in *Leviticus* 20:10: "And the man that committeth adultery with another man's wife, even he that committeth adultery with his neighbor's wife, the adulterer and the adulteress shall surely be put to death." Note that, if the death penalty was alienable, side payments might have resulted in it being rarely inflicted in Israel. Chapter 8 of Posner and Silbaugh (1996) is the best place to look for modern US state and federal law on adultery. See also Haggard (1999) and Weinstein (1986).

and the degree of self-help tolerated. Even more than usual, published cases are an unreliable guide to what actually happens; the shame of the offense to both victim and perpetrator makes quiet resolution attractive. What is easier, however, is to pick one jurisdiction and show how its law fits in the theoretical framework I have used. I will pick my own state of Indiana, not because Indiana law, Anglo-American law, or 1990s law are the most important laws to study, but simply because I have easy access to it and it is not unrepresentative of modern American law.

Civil damages

The English common law's remedy for adultery was a civil action for damages. Blackstone (1765) says,

> Adultery, or criminal conversation with a man's wife, though it is, as a public crime, left by our laws to the coercion of the spiritual courts; yet, considered as a civil injury (and surely there can be no greater,) the law gives a satisfaction to the husband for it by action of trespass *vi et armis* against the adulterer, wherein the damages recovered are usually very large and exemplary. But these are properly increased or diminished by circumstances; as the rank and fortune of the plaintiff and defendant; the relation or connection between them; the seduction or otherwise of the wife, founded on her previous behavior and character; and the husband's obligation by settlement or otherwise to provide for those children, which he cannot but suspect to be spurious.[17]

The common law has used two different causes of action for adultery: "alienation of affections" and "criminal conversation." *Restatement of Torts, Second* (1977), one of the American Law Institute's efforts to summarize the common law, describes the two actions thus:

> § 683 ALIENATION OF SPOUSE'S AFFECTIONS. One who purposely alienates one spouse's affections from the other spouse is subject to liability for the harm thus caused to any of the other spouse's legally protected marital interests.

> § 685 CRIMINAL CONVERSATION WITH A SPOUSE. One who has sexual intercourse with one spouse is subject to liability to the other spouse for the harm thus caused to any of the other spouse's legally protected marital interests.

---

[17] Book 3, chapter 8 of Blackstone's *Commentaries*. See also Book 4, chapter 34, where he discusses adultery in the context of criminal law. Blackstone is somewhat misleading, because the caveat about the spiritual courts is crucial. Until their jurisdiction was limited in 1640, these courts actively prosecuted adultery, imposing severe fines and jailing for nonpayment (Stephen, 1883, volume 2, chapter 25). It is noteworthy that Macaulay's Indian Penal Code made adultery a major crime, prosecutable only at the husband's request, even though England had recently rejected domestic criminalization. Macaulay was perhaps enough of a utilitarian to recognize the spillover problem; Section 298 of his code also criminalized deliberate insults against someone's religion (Stephen, 1883, volume 3, chapter 33).

The elements of the two actions are different. The wrong in alienation of affections is foreseen damage to the relationship between husband and wife, which requires the marriage not to have been in ruins before the outsider interfered.[18] On the other hand, the action does not require adultery, and even an interfering mother-in-law can be liable for breaking up a marriage.[19] Criminal conversation, on the other hand, is closer to strict liability. It is an intentional tort in the sense that the third party must intentionally be performing the sexual act, but he is liable even if he did not know the adulterous spouse was married.[20] A single act is sufficient (though perhaps with small damages), but a physical act is necessary.

Indiana abolished both actions in 1935, the first of several American states to do so in the 1930s in "[a]n Act to promote public morals, by abolishing civil causes of action for breach of promise to marry, alienation of affections."[21] The act was tested in 1937 when a suit argued that since Article 1, Section 12, of the Indiana Constitution said, "every man, for injury done to him in his person, property, or reputation, shall have remedy by due course of law," the abolition of alienation of affections was unconstitutional. The Indiana Supreme Court disagreed, saying that neither person, property, nor reputation was hurt and that marriage was a matter not of contract or property, but of a status that falls under the regulatory power of the state.[22]

---

[18] Comment h to §683: "Not only must the actor have caused a diminution of one spouse's affections for the other by acts, but the acts must have been done for the very purpose of accomplishing this result."

[19] For such a case, see *Beem v. Beem*, 193 Ind. 481 (1923). This case also illustrates the requirement of malice. The Indiana Supreme Court approves of the following jury instruction requested by the defense but rejected by the trial judge (§489, italics in original): "*were they [the defendant parents] impelled by a spirit of malice and ill will toward said plaintiff or were they acting in good faith and without malice and what they considered for the best interest of said Bruce. If the latter, your verdict should be for the defendants.*" Note, however, that an adulterous third party, unlike a mother-in-law, can rarely assert the defense that his motives in breaking up the marriage were disinterested.

[20] Comment f to §685: "Although knowledge or belief that a person is married is essential to liability for alienation of affections under the rule stated in §683, neither knowledge nor belief is necessary to liability under the rule stated in this Section. One who has sexual relations with a married person takes the risk that he or she is married to another. The fact that the spouse misrepresents the marital status is not a defense."

[21] As cited in *Pennington v. Stewart*, 212 Ind. 553; 554 (1937). Nolan (1951) describes how in the nineteenth century Indiana was a divorce-mill state for a time, to which people from New York traveled for easy divorces. In 1999, Indiana Code §34-12-2-1a still specifically eliminates the two actions, along with breach of promise and seduction.

[22] *Pennington v. Stewart*, 212 Ind. 553 (1937). That marriage is not a contract is a common finding in American courts. A more recent example is *In re the Marriage of Franks*, 189 Colo 499 (1975, en banc), which rejected the argument that a no-fault divorce law violated the contracts clause of the state constitution when it nullified existing marriage contracts. The *Pennington* court did rule unconstitutional a provision of the 1935 act that made the plaintiff liable to a criminal penalty of from one to five years of prison for even trying to bring an action for alienation of affections.

Alienation of affections has gone out of style as a tort, an exception to the general increase of tort liability in the United States.[23] Oddly enough, the similar action of tortious interference with contract is alive and well (see Landes and Posner, 1980; BeVier, 1990; McChesney, 1999). The *Restatement* says:

§ 766 INTENTIONAL INTERFERENCE WITH PERFORMANCE OF CONTRACT BY THIRD PERSON

One who intentionally and improperly interferes with the performance of a contract (except a contract to marry) between another and a third person by inducing or otherwise causing the third person not to perform the contract, is subject to liability to the other for the pecuniary loss resulting to the other from the failure of the third person to perform the contract.

Note the exception for marriage. As in so many areas of the law, marital agreements receive substantially less protection than do commercial agreements. Whether a prenuptial agreement executed as a commercial contract would expose a third party to liability for tortious interference is an interesting question, not yet tested in any court, to my knowledge. When people have brought suit against their spouses on general tort grounds such as fraud or intentional infliction of emotional distress, however, they have lost, with courts saying that, because of the abolition of torts such as criminal conversation, behavior that might otherwise have been tortious must now be ruled legal.[24] Thus, in some states the law has changed to the point where behavior that would otherwise be tortious is exempted from liability if it can be shown to be connected with adultery. Curiously enough, feminist scholarship has noted the same point, though with more attention to the distributional effects. Linda Hirshman and Jane Larson have proposed that adultery be restored in divorce settlements and in tort (Hirshman and Larson, 1998, pp. 283–86). Larson (1993, p. 471) comments:

it surprised me to learn in researching this Article that higher standards of honesty and fair dealing apply in commercial than in personal relationships. . . . One response to the dilemma of intimate responsibility has been to silence and devalue individuals who make stifling personal claims on the independence and mobility of those who possess privilege

---

[23] Like Indiana, many states abolished alienation of affections in the 1930s, and the topic was actively discussed in law reviews then (Weinstein, 1986, p. 220). England abolished criminal conversation by Stat. 20 & 21 Vict. Ch. 85, sched. 59 (1857) and enticement by Law Reform (Miscellaneous Provisions) Act 1970, sched. 5. Two states in which the tort is still alive are Illinois and North Carolina. Carol Sander, "Alienated-affections Case Ends in $11,667 verdict," *Chicago Daily Law Bulletin*, 28 July 1997, p. 3; "Personal Negligence: Alienation of Affection 90,001 Verdict: Emotional Distress," *Personal Injury Verdict Reviews*, 7, 22 (24 November 1999).

[24] *Doe v. Doe*, Court of Appeals of Maryland, Sept 1998, no. 99 (2000), http://pub.bna.com/fl/99a98.htm; *Weicker v. Weicker*, 22 N.Y.2d 8 (1968); *Koestler v. Pollard*, 162 Wis.2d 797 (1991); *Speer v. Dealy*, 242 Neb. 542 (1993). Note that the common law rule of interspousal immunity from suit had to be abolished before spouse could sue spouse on these grounds.

and power. Because of the gendered history of romantic and sexual relationships, it has tended to be men in our society who have sought relational freedom, and women whose interests have been compromised by reliance on intimate relationships.

Criminal penalties

Until 1976, adultery was a crime in Indiana, as it still is in some American states, but in that year the law was repealed.[25] The earlier law did not criminalize adultery per se. Rather, "[t]he offenses prohibited by the statute here involved (although sometimes inaccurately referred to as "adultery" and "fornication") are cohabiting with another in a state of adultery or fornication. . . . The design of this law is not to affix a penalty for the violation of the Seventh Commandment, but to punish those who, without lawful marriage, live together in the manner of husband and wife" (*Warner v. State,* 202 Ind. 479, 483 [1931]). Occasional, or even frequent, acts of adultery were not criminal by themselves; "cohabitation" was an essential element of the crime.

What this suggests is that criminalization was motivated not so much by the victimized spouse (who had, until 1935, civil damages and divorce-for-fault available) as by the public. Whether the ill consequence of public immorality was thought to be a direct offense to the feelings of the public or a tendency to corrupt is unclear, but damage to the non-adulterous spouse was not the main concern. If public feeling in Indiana changed by 1976, then it is possible that the criminal law was efficient earlier but became inefficient owing to change in tastes.[26]

---

[25] Indiana Code "§§ 35-1-82-1–35-1-82-3. [Repealed.] COMPILER'S NOTES. This chapter, concerning incest, cohabitation, and seduction, was repealed by Acts 1976, P.L. 148, § 24." Curiously, Indiana Code §34-15-5-1, on slander, still says, "Every charge of incest, homosexuality, bestiality, fornication, adultery, or whoredom falsely made against any person is actionable in the same manner as in the case of slanderous words charging a felony." Footnote 4 of Haggard (1999) gives cites for twenty-four state laws against adultery in 1998. In New York, Virginia, North Dakota, and Utah only the married adulterer is liable (Haggard, 1999, p. 474). In Minnesota and North Dakota, the injured spouse is explicitly authorized to block prosecution (Minn. Stat. Ann. 609.36; N.D. Cent. Code 12.1-20-09 (1997)). Adultery is still actively prosecuted in the US military. See *United States v. Green,* 39 M.J. 606 (A.C.M.R. 1994). It is also subject to federal law in the White-Slave Traffic (Mann) Act, ch. 395, 36 Stat. 825 (1910), *Caminetti v. United States,* 242 U.S. 470 (1916), *Whitt v. United States,* 261 F2d 907 (1959, CA6 Ky).

[26] A separate question is whether criminal (or other) laws against adultery somehow violate the state or federal constitution. At the federal level, various opinions have said in dicta that adultery is a legitimate subject for criminal law, but one never knows what the Supreme Court will do in the future. *Poe v. Ullman,* 367 U.S. 497, 546, 552 (1961) (Harlan, J., dissenting): "[L]aws forbidding adultery, fornication, and homosexual practices . . . form a pattern so deeply pressed into the substance of our social life that any Constitutional doctrine in this area must build upon that basis . . . . I would not suggest that adultery, homosexuality, fornication and incest are immune from criminal enquiry, however privately practiced." *Griswold v. Connecticut,* 381 U.S. 479, 498 (1965) (Goldberg, J., concurring): "The State of Connecticut does have statutes, the constitutionality of which is beyond doubt, which prohibit adultery and fornication." *Bowers*

Self-help

Adultery being grounds for divorce creates a penalty similar to self-help in the sense that adultery provides an excuse for the innocent spouse to do something that would otherwise be illegal: unilaterally to terminate the marriage. Such divorce is not self-help in its purest form, however, because it still requires petition to the courts. The innocent spouse cannot simply behave as if unmarried (for example, marrying someone else) and then plead the other spouse's adultery as an excuse when later prosecuted or sued. Self-help proper consists of imposing a penalty without the aid of the courts but with their acquiescence when the penalty would be an illegal act except for the justification of adultery. The most dramatic form is adultery as justification for killing someone.[27] Indiana has never formally allowed this, although whether juries would convict a wronged spouse for murder is uncertain. Their reluctance to convict is known as the "unwritten law," which is pervasive enough across time and culture to make the relevance of written laws suspect.[28] If prosecutors will not prosecute and juries will not convict, the written law's relevance is questionable. Jury instructions from Indiana judges, however, have always been to convict, as the case law amply shows. Adultery can reduce the charge from murder to manslaughter but cannot excuse the killing altogether, and the killing must have occurred immediately on discovery of the adultery for the charge to be reduced at all.

The mere fact that one person had sexual intercourse with another person's wife will not justify the taking of human life. Proof of this fact alone will be no defense in a

---

v. Hardwick, 478 U.S. 186, 208 (1986): "A State might define the contractual commitment necessary to become eligible for [marital] benefits to include a commitment of fidelity and then punish individuals for breaching that contract."

[27] Texas, Utah, New Mexico, and Georgia all allowed adultery as an excuse for killing adulterers caught *in flagrante delicto* up until the 1970s, Georgia by judicial interpretation and the other states by statute (Weinstein, 1986, p. 232). I am told that Grotius said the same for civil law, but have not found the reference. Interestingly, Texas did not allow castration to replace killing: *Sensobaugh v. State*, 92 Tex. Crim. 417 (1922). The first Georgia case on point makes an interesting argument from jury nullification and democratic common law: "Has an American jury ever convicted a husband or father of murder or manslaughter, for killing the seducer of his wife or daughter? And with this exceedingly broad and comprehensive enactment on our statute book, is it just to juries to brand them with perjury for rendering such verdicts in this State? Is it not their right to determine whether, in reason or justice, it is not as justifiable in the sight of Heaven and earth, to slay the murderer of the peace and respectability of a family, as one who forcibly attacks habitation and property?" *Biggs v. State*, 29 Ga. 723, 728 (1860).

[28] Three notorious examples are: (1) the 1952 acquittal of Yvonne Chevallier for shooting her husband, a cabinet minister and mayor of Orleans, upon his refusal to give up his mistress (Stanley Karnow, *Paris in the Fifties*, New York: Random House, 1997, pp. 127–31); (2) Lorena Bobbitt's acquittal after mutilating her husband (David Margolick, "Lorena Bobbitt Acquitted in Mutilation of Husband," *New York Times*, 22 January 1994, p. 1); and (3) the acquittal of Congressman Daniel Sickles for the murder of his wife's lover after a defense by attorney Edwin Stanton, later US Attorney General and Secretary of War (Daniel Rezneck, "It Didn't Start with O.J.; Like the Simpson Saga, the 1859 Murder Trial of Dan Sickles Gripped the Nation," *Washington Post*, 24 July 1994, p. C5).

prosecution for criminal homicide. The most it can do is, in certain cases, to reduce the grade of the crime from murder to manslaughter. If a man finds another in the act of sexual intercourse with his wife and kills him in a heat and transport of passion engendered thereby, the crime will be manslaughter only. (*Thrawley v. State*, 153 Ind. 375; 378 [1899])

Indeed, a plausible interpretation of this doctrine is not that Indiana is granting the killer a discount from his prison sentence because he was engaged in self-help, but that murderous passion is so typical of people who discover adultery that it is a waste of time to debate whether such a person has the state of mind that ordinarily qualifies a killing as manslaughter instead of murder.

Similarly, adultery has generally not been considered sufficient provocation to justify battery, and courts have held that the victims of such battery are legally entitled to damages, including punitive damages. This means that even if prosecutors use their discretion not to bring criminal charges against the angry spouse, adulterous third parties may sue on their own behalf. Whether the jury will be sympathetic is again questionable.[29]

Self help often comes up in less dramatic forms than murder and mayhem. One is for the injured spouse to be exempt from what would otherwise be marital duties. The Indiana statutes of 1933 said,

Whosoever deserts his wife, except for the cause of adultery or other vicious or immoral conduct, leaving her without reasonable means of support and continuing support, or whoever deserts his or her child or children and leaves them, or any of them, without reasonable means of support and continuing support, or a charge upon any county or township of this state, shall be deemed guilty of a felony, and, upon conviction thereof, shall be imprisoned in the state prison not less than one year nor more than three years, and be disfranchised and rendered incapable of holding any office of trust or profit for a period of three years.[30]

This is interesting not only for its disqualification of deadbeat dads as elected officials but for the extent of its excuse of marital duties. Not only may a man refuse to support his adulterous wife in the style to which she is accustomed; he may abandon her and their children entirely, to the extent that they must live on public charity. It is a clear example of self-help, and of one of

---

[29] Two cases show what can happen. *Hamilton v. Howard*, 234 Ky 321 (1930) involved appeal from erroneous jury instructions by a trial judge that, if the plaintiff victim of three gunshots in the legs had attempted to alienate the affections of the defendant's wife, defendant would not be liable. The appeals court reversed and remanded, but noted that the jury could take provocation into account in setting punitive damages, which were the bulk of the claim. *Chykirda v. Yanush*, 131 Conn 565 (1945) was an appeal from an award of $72 to a supposed alienator of affections who was the target of battery. The jury said the $72 included both compensatory and punitive damages, and the appellate court ruled that the jury was justified in considering provocation in the setting of the punitive damages.

[30] *Crumley v. State*, 204 Ind. 396; 399 (1933), citing "Section 2866 Burns 1926, Acts 1913, p. 956, ch. 358, §1."

the difficulties mentioned earlier in this paper: even if the husband were free to hurt the adulterous one, he might find it painful. The law allowed a man to impoverish his children, no doubt to the unhappiness of his wife, but this hurts the punisher as much as the punished – at least if they really are his children.[31]

Various legal disabilities created by commission of adultery are hard to classify as civil, criminal, or self-help, since the penalty is neither a cost borne by the state or the victim nor a property transfer. I have been able to find only one example currently in force in Indiana: elimination of any claim by an active and continual adulterer and deserter to the estate of an intestate spouse.[32] In the past, other disabilities have also existed, particularly in connection with divorce. Before Indiana adopted no-fault divorce in 1971, adultery could be considered in division of property, as well as being one of the grounds that made divorce available in the first place.[33] Moreover, under an "unclean hands" statute, which codified earlier case law, a spouse's adultery barred filing for divorce on the grounds of the other spouse's adultery.[34]

In summary, the law of one jurisdiction, Indiana, has almost no penalties for adultery, but in the past it has used tort law, criminal law, and self-help in different ways and to achieve different objectives. Tort law has deterrent and compensatory effects for the wealthy; self-help deters the judgment proof; and criminal law prevents open adultery from offending public feelings. The most important penalty may have been the status of adultery in divorce proceedings, which, like a criminal penalty, is not proportionate to damage but which, like a civil penalty, is imposed at the initiative and to the benefit of the injured spouse.

---

[31] If the husband's paternity was a legal presumption in Indiana at that time, one purpose of the desertion statute might have been to amend that presumption for practical purposes.

[32] Indiana Code § 29-1-2-14 says: "If either a husband or wife shall have left the other and shall be living at the time of his or her death in adultery, he or she as the case may be shall take no part of the estate of the deceased husband or wife." This came up in reported cases as recently as the early 1990s: *Oliver v. Estate of Oliver*, 554 N.E.2d. 8 (Ind. App. 1st', 1990) and *Estate of Calcutt v. Calcutt*, 6 N.E.2d 1288 (Ind. App. 5th, 1991).

[33] As discussed in *Clark v. Clark*, 578 N.E.2d 747 (Ind. App. 4th, 1991). The opinion starkly tells Mrs. Clark the current state of the law, at 750: "Wife also argues when it awarded attorney fees and litigation expenses, the trial court failed to consider that husband had taken another woman, that wife had not wanted the separation, and that it was solely husband's idea. Wife is wrong. The court may not consider such matters when dividing property in a dissolution of marriage action." In some states – Virginia, for example – adultery can still affect divorce settlements and alimony. See *L.C.S. vs. S.A.S.*, 453 S.E.2d 580 (Va. App. 1995) and Va. Code Ann. pp. 20–107.2–3.

[34] *O'Connor v. O'Connor*, 253 Ind. 295; 307 (1968) quotes the Indiana Code as saying (§ 3-1202) that "[d]ivorces shall not be granted for adultery in any of the following cases: . . . Third. When the party seeking the divorce has also been guilty of adultery under such circumstances as would have entitled the opposite party, if innocent, to a decree," and notes that "The statute was originally passed in 1873 (Acts 1873, ch. 43, § 9, p. 107) but the doctrine had already been recognized by case law."

5 Concluding remarks

Efficiency in marriage, as in partnership, requires that there be a legal remedy for adultery. Civil damages, criminal law, and self-help all have their advantages and disadvantages. The law need not restrict itself to one of these, and traditionally has not. Which laws are best depends heavily on empirical magnitudes such as the strength of public offense, the amount of damage to injured spouses, and the assets available for paying judgments. This article has not, of course, considered other objectives besides efficiency but, even for those people who consider other objectives more important, it will be useful to know when wealth is being sacrificed. The efficient laws may well violate a particular person's beliefs about what is necessary to achieve a free society or another's for a virtuous society, but it is useful to think about how much such societies cost.

One policy that seems clearly beneficial from the point of view of wealth maximization, and perhaps freedom and virtue as well, would be to allow people to opt into adultery penalties via prenuptial agreements. The law could be written to allow people to opt into tort, criminal, or self-help as they are now free to opt into certain kinds of financial arrangements. This would require specific statutes for criminal and self-help penalties, since they are not standardly available as penalties for breach of contract. For civil damages, it would merely require dependable government enforcement of premarital contracts, without judicial discretion to ignore them as marriage related. Such contracts are starting to appear and be tested.[35] The argument is the same as for contract enforceability in general: it permits intertemporal disjunction of performances and encourages reliance on future performance.[36] Some contracts, for example price-fixing or murder-for-hire, have negative spillovers onto third parties and should not be enforced; but, if spillovers are nonexistent or positive, court enforcement is a public good. Whether the law should go beyond this and include penalties for adultery as the default for every marriage contract, or even require marriage to include them, is a more difficult matter, depending on the size of spillovers.

[35] See Desa Philadelphia, "'Bad Boy' Clauses," *Time*, 19 February 2001, p. 14; Ian Brodie, "Suspicious Wife Tests Husband's Dirty Linen in Public," *The Times (London)*, 29 December 2000.

[36] For detailed discussion see Cohen (1987), Stake (1992), Rasmusen and Stake (1998), and Dnes (1998). The 1997 Louisiana "covenant marriage" law goes some way towards this, offering a choice of two marriage types. See 1997 La. House Bill 756 amending 9 Louisiana Revised Statutes sec 272–275 and 307–309. On the confused current state of the law on enforcing premarital agreements, see Graham (1993) and Haas (1988). Also see, however, Merrill and Smith (2000) for an objection from property law: allowing many forms of marriage increases the transactions cost of anyone, such as an employer, who wishes to categorize people by marital status. Merrill and Smith do not note the application to marriage law, but it is implicit in their argument.

REFERENCES

Allen, Douglas and Margaret Brinig (1998), "Sex, Property Rights, and Divorce," *European Journal of Law and Economics*, 5, 211–33.

American Law Institute (1962), *Model Penal Code and Commentaries*, Philadelphia: American Law Institute, 1980.

American Law Institute (1977), *Restatement of the Law, Second, Torts*, Philadelphia: American Law Institute.

Beirne, Piers (1999), "For a Nonspeciesist Criminology: Animal Abuse as an Object of Study," *Criminology*, 37, 117–48.

BeVier, Lillian (1990), "Reconsidering Inducement," *Virginia Law Review*, 76, 877–936.

Blackstone, William (1765), *Commentaries on the Laws of England*. New York: Garland, 1978.

Calabresi, Guido and A. Douglas Melamed (1972), "Property Rules, Liability Rules, and Inalienability: One View of the Cathedral," *Harvard Law Review*, 85, 1089–128.

Cohen, Lloyd (1987), "Marriage, Divorce, and Quasi Rents; or, 'I Gave Him the Best Years of My Life,'" *Journal of Legal Studies*, 16, 267–303.

Cooter, Robert (1984), "Prices and Sanctions," *Columbia Law Review*, 84, 1523–60.

Dnes, Antony (1998), "The Division of Marital Assets Following Divorce," *Journal of Law and Society*, 25, 336–64.

Epstein, Richard (1999), "Life Boats, Desert Islands, and the Poverty of Jurisprudence," *Mississippi Law Journal*, 68, 861–85.

Graham, Laura (1993), "The Uniform Premarital Agreement Act and Modern Social Policy: The Enforceability of Premarital Agreements Regulating the Ongoing Marriage," *Wake Forest Law Review*, 28, 1037–63.

Haas, Theodore (1988), "The Rationality and Enforceability of Contractual Restrictions on Divorce," *North Carolina Law Review*, 66, 879–930.

Haggard, Melissa (1999), "Note: Adultery: A Comparison of Military Law and State Law and the Controversy This Causes under Our Constitution and Criminal Justice System," *Brandeis Law Journal*, 37, 469–83.

Hirshman, Linda and Jane Larson (1998), *Hard Bargains: The Politics of Sex*, Oxford: Oxford University Press.

Landes, William and Richard Posner (1980), "Joint and Multiple Tortfeasors: An Economic Analysis," *Journal of Legal Studies*, 9, 517–56.

Langan, Patrick and David Farrington, (1998), *Crime and Justice in the United States and in England and Wales, 1981–96*, Bureau of Justice Statistics, NCJ 169284.

Larson, Jane (1993), "Women Understand So Little, They Call My Good Nature 'Deceit': A Feminist Rethinking of Seduction," *Columbia Law Review*, 93, 374–472.

Levmore, Saul (1995), "Love it or Leave it: Property Rules, Liability Rules, and Exclusivity of Remedies in Partnership and Marriage," *Law and Contemporary Problems*, 5, 221–49.

McChesney, Fred (1999), "Tortious Interference with Contract versus 'Efficient' Breach: Theory and Empirical Evidence," *Journal of Legal Studies*, 28, 131–86.

Merrill, Thomas and Henry Smith (2000), "Optimal Standardization in the Law of Property: The *Numerus Clausus* Principle," *Yale Law Journal*, 110, 1–70.

Mill, John Stuart (1859), *On Liberty*. New York: Norton, 1975.

Mittlebeeler, Emmet (1976), *African Custom and Western Law: The Development of the Rhodesian Criminal Law for Africans*, London: Holmes & Meier.

Nolan, Val (1951), "Indiana: Birthplace of Migratory Divorce," *Indiana Law Journal*, 26, 515–27.

Note, (1991), "Constitutional Barriers to Civil and Criminal Restrictions on Pre- and Extramarital Sex," *Harvard Law Review*, 104, 1660–79.

Posner, Richard (1998), *Economic Analysis of Law*, 5th ed, Boston: Little, Brown.

(1999), *The Problematics of Moral and Legal Theory*, Cambridge, MA: Harvard University Press.

Posner, Richard and Katharine Silbaugh (1996), *A Guide to America's Sex Laws*, Chicago: University of Chicago Press.

Rasmusen, Eric (1994), *Games and Information: An Introduction to Game Theory*, 2nd edn, Oxford: Blackwell.

(1995), "Predictable and Unpredictable Error in Tort Awards: The Effect of Plaintiff Self Selection and Signaling," *International Review of Law and Economics*, 15, 323–45.

(1997), "Of Sex and Drugs and Rock'n Roll: Law and Economics and Social Regulation," *Harvard Journal of Law and Public Policy*, 21, 71–81.

Rasmusen, Eric and Jeffrey Stake (1998), "Lifting the Veil of Ignorance: Personalizing the Marriage Contract," *Indiana Law Journal*, 73, 454–502.

Smith, Henry (1998), "The Harm in Blackmail," *Northwestern University Law Review*, 92, 862–915.

Stake, Jeffrey (1992), "Mandatory Planning for Divorce," *Vanderbilt Law Review*, 45, 397–454.

Stephen, James (1883), *A History of the Criminal Law of England*. New York: Franklin, 1964.

Weinstein, Jeremy (1986), "Note: Adultery, Law, and the State: A History," *Hastings Law Journal*, 38, 195–223.

6   Louisiana's covenant marriage law: recapturing the meaning of marriage for the sake of the children

Katherine Shaw Spaht

Though American divorce law was never intended in principle to be as unusual as it has turned out in fact, it nevertheless carries a powerful ideology, sending out distinctive messages about commitment, responsibility, and dependency. . . . The American story about marriage, as told in the law and in much popular literature, goes something like this: marriage is a relationship that exists primarily for the fulfillment of the individual spouses. If it ceases to perform this function, no one is to blame and either spouse may terminate it at will.

(Glendon, 1987, pp. 106, 108)

1   Introduction

The described redefinition of marriage "did not take place overnight in Western nations" (Glendon, 1987, p. 65). The process of change began well before the 1960s and 1970s, when "no-fault" divorce was generally adopted in the United States and other Western countries. In fact, divorce legislation in developed countries has proceeded for the past two hundred years in one general direction: it has become easier and easier for dissatisfied spouses to escape the marital relationship and, consequently, their familial responsibilities.

What has happened to alter so radically the American conception of marriage? Unquestionably, powerful social, economic, and cultural forces have been at work, eroding traditional notions of moral responsibility, and changes in the law have reflected such trends. The ideology of "no-fault" divorce conforms to fashionable theories that abhor objective value judgments[1] and promotes

---

[1] In the United States, the "no-fault" idea blended readily with the psychological jargon that already has such a strong influence on how Americans think about their personal relationships. It began to carry the suggestion that no one is ever to blame when a marriage ends: marriages just break down sometimes, people grow apart, and when this happens even parents have a right to pursue their own happiness. The no-fault terminology fits neatly into an increasingly popular mode of discourse in which values are treated as a matter of taste, feelings of guilt are regarded as unhealthy, and an individual's primary responsibility is assumed to be to him/herself. Above all, one is not supposed to be "judgmental" about the behavior and opinions of others. As Bellah (1985) points out, the ideology of psychotherapy not only refuses to take a moral stand, it actively promotes distrust of "morality" (Glendon, 1987, pp. 107–8).

an obsessive concentration on each individual's subjective self-fulfillment (Kramer, 1997; see also Glendon, 1987, p. 119; Gallagher, 1996, p. 265; Whitehead, 1997, p. 194). It is perhaps mere coincidence, as Professor Glendon suggests, that the label "no-fault" migrated into marriage law from tort law, where the innovative notion of "no-fault" automobile insurance had captured the legal and cultural imagination,[2] but the term effectively sums up the new attitudes Americans began to assume toward marriage and familial responsibility.[3]

It might well be asked, however, whether there is not something wrong with the story being told now by American law. *Should* marriage be reduced to "a relationship that exists primarily for the fulfillment of the individual spouses" (Glendon, 1987, p. 108; see also Popenoe and Whitehead, 1999a)? What about the individual spouses' joint commitment to children born of their union? What effect do "no-fault" assumptions have upon the creation of stable families, the first communities into which human beings are born?

Those questions lead to a further line of inquiry. How complete is the story told by current American law when it omits from its concluding pages any mention of the gurgling young characters introduced in the second chapter? Can the average American reader perhaps believe that this story has been unsatisfactorily abridged? Would she or he perhaps not yearn to rewrite the story, to supply it with a happy ending?

To some Americans, indeed, the story told by American marriage law has begun to take on the characteristics of a tale told by Poe, unfolding within a cultural landscape that equates to urban blight.[4] This horror story has important societal effects:

When divorce and illegitimacy become normal, when single parenthood begins first to compete with and then displace marriage, when not just a few, but many or most parents adopt a risky pattern of child rearing, the result is not just a bit more suffering for a few more children, but the impoverishment of society and the none-too-slow erosion of American civilization. (Gallagher, 1996, p. 4)

The prosperity of the United States and other Western countries – indeed perhaps their very survival – depends upon the health of their constituent

---

[2] "It seems to have been a legal coincidence that caused the move to breakdown grounds to be translated back into ordinary language as 'no-fault' divorce.... Once ['no-fault'] was established in tort law, it was practically inevitable that the 'no-fault' label should then migrate to the new divorce law, where proposed legal changes were similarly designed to eliminate litigation over issues of fault" (Glendon 1987, pp. 79–80).

[3] "Discontent with fault-based divorce seems to have been felt more acutely by mental-health professionals and academics than by the citizenry in general" (Glendon, 1987, p. 66).

[4] For a sampling of proposals to address the increasingly disturbing prevalence of divorce, see, e.g., Stanton (1997); Whitehead (1997); Gallagher (1996); Blankenhorn (1995); Glendon (1987); Gallagher and Blankenhorn (1997); Parkman (1993); Wardle (1991); Scott (1990); Younger (1981); Popenoe (1992). Even His Holiness, Pope John Paul II, has had occasion to describe the battle to destroy the family (Apostolic Exhortation of John Paul II, 1994).

families,[5] yet our laws presume to treat the existence of the central institution of family life as if it were merely a matter of individual personal preference, with no consequences for the children of the marriage or for society in general.[6]

How can legal reformers act to recapture the traditional meaning of marriage,[7] marriage understood as a permanent institution serving as a gateway to a stable and nurturing family life? Two American states, Louisiana[8] and then a year later Arizona,[9] chose to experiment with legislation, which creates a legal framework for reconceptualizing marriage. The legislation permits a husband and a wife to obligate themselves legally to a stronger, more enduring union: a "covenant marriage." The choice of a more binding, more permanent marriage by civil covenant encourages the participation of the church in premarital counseling and, it is anticipated, in pre-divorce counseling as well.[10] The idea of a choice offered to spouses is neither new nor unique to Louisiana: in 1945 renowned French law professor Léon Mazeaud proposed the choice of indissoluble marriage for French couples.[11] Because a covenant marriage is a choice made by the couple, the legislation offers the possibility of eventually changing the culture

---

5   Yankelovich (1992, p. 4) connects economics with the health of the family as follows: "There exists a deeply intuitive sense that the success of market-based economy depends on a highly developed social morality – trustworthiness, honesty, concern for future generations, an ethic of service to others, a humane society that takes care of those in need, frugality instead of greed, high standards of quality, and concern for community. These economically desirable social values, in turn, are seen as rooted in family values. Thus the link in public thinking between a healthy family and a robust economy, though indirect, is clear and firm."

6   "We are rightly accustomed to viewing our self-reliance and independence as sources of some of our greatest strengths. . . . We are less conscious, however, of the dangers that De Tocqueville warned us could flow from overemphasizing them. . . . [I]n the end, a people in a country where liberty has been severed from other republican virtues can paradoxically display both individualism and conformity, restlessness and huddling, rejection of authority and political impotence" (Glendon, 1987, p. 119).

7   "For marriage to thrive, and perhaps even to survive, we need to recapture our vision of the undertaking, to reimagine it as worthy for its own sake" (Gallagher, 1996, p. 264).

8   Louisiana Revised Statutes Annotated [La. Rev. Stat. Ann.], Sect. 9:272 (St. Paul, MN: West Supp., 1999) (as amended by 1999 Louisiana Acts [La. Acts] 1298, § 1). See Spaht (1998a).

9   Arizona Revised Statutes Annotated, Sect. 25-901-906 (St. Paul, MN: West Publishing Co., 1999).

10 La. Rev. Stat. Ann., Sect. 9:273(A)(2)(a) (as amended by 1999 La. Acts 1298, § 1): mandatory premarital counseling, which includes a discussion of the seriousness of marriage and the fact that a covenant marriage is a commitment for life, as well as the obligation to seek counseling in times of marital difficulties to be performed by a priest, minister, rabbi, any clergyman of any religious sect, or a professional marriage counselor.

11 See Léon Mazeaud, "Solution au Problème du Divorce," in *Recueil Dalloz, Jurisprudence*, 1945, pp. 11–12. Subsequently, Henri Mazeaud proposed the solution in *Contre-projet, Travaux de la Commission de Reforme du Code Civil* 498 (1947–48). In the same publication (pp. 499–511) is reprinted the discussion of the proposal by the Commission Plenière on 5 December, 1947. See also Mazeaud and Mazeaud, *Leçons de Droit Civil: Tome Premier*, 1318–1334 (3rd edn, Editions Montchrestien). I am indebted to Professor Cynthia Samuel of Tulane University Law School who discovered these materials (see also Wolfe, 1995).

for the following reasons.[12] First, to promote the selection of a stronger marital commitment, proponents of covenant marriage must convince each couple of the desirability of covenant marriage, which requires intensive missionary work, winning converts one couple at a time. Secondly, the results of research published in 1999 show that couples with more permissive attitudes about divorce are more likely to dissolve their marriages than are those who hold less permissive attitudes.[13] Thus, "[a] commitment to marital permanence as an ideal is an important safeguard to making marriage last. It's a matter of – if you believe in it – it may come" (Horn, 1999, p. 4). A covenant marriage contains just such a commitment, which is not dependent solely upon the continuing conviction (and affection) of the spouses but is *legally* binding.[14]

2   Why strengthen marriage? For the sake of the children

Despite increasing relativism during the 1970s and 1980s about family structure, the most recent empirical evidence now available establishes what is instinctively known – a child benefits measurably by having a married mother (a female) and father (a male) in the home (Fagan, 1999). The child benefits physically,[15] emotionally,[16] psychologically, and economically (Fagan, 1999). In their authoritative book on single-parent families, Sara McLanahan and Gary

[12] See Laconte (1998), in which the author refers to covenant marriage as a sleeping giant: "Covenant marriage uses both law and civil society to confront couples with the nature of their marriage commitment. Such confrontation could help rewrite our nation's most troubling cultural tale" (p. 34).

[13] The study was conducted and the results published by noted social scientists Paul Amato and Stacy Rogers at the University of Nebraska (see Amato and Rogers, 1999). "What they found was this: Couples who have more permissive attitudes toward divorce tended over time to experience declines in marital quality, whereas those who have less permissive attitudes toward divorce tended over time to experience improvements in marital quality. This pattern held for women as well as men, and for those in long term as well as short-term marriages. In summary, holding permissive attitudes toward divorce was dangerous to a couple's marital health" (Horn, 1999, p. 3).

[14] "Whether meant to or not, law, in addition to all the other things it does, tells stories about the culture that helped to shape it and which it in turn helps to shape: stories about who we are, where we came from, and where we are going" (Glendon, 1987, p. 7).

[15] The report compiled data drawn from Sedlak and Broadhurst (1996) and Whelan (1993). "There is strong evidence from the British research that the structure of the family is related directly to the safety of mothers and children. The most dangerous place for a woman and her child is in an environment in which she is cohabiting with a boyfriend who is not the father of her children. The rate of child abuse may be as much as 33 times higher. Even cohabiting with the children's father may lead to a rate of abuse as much as 20 times higher. *Marriage provides the safest environment for children.* It therefore truly makes a difference in advancing the safety and well-being of America's children" Fagan, FitzGerald, and Hanks (1997, p. 14).

[16] See Guidubaldi (1988), Demo and Acock (1988), and Kunz (1992). See also Brinig (1998) and Stanton (1997), which is one of the most recent of all the books written by authors who wish to emphasize the positive effects of marriage. Stanton compiles all of the sociological data to the date of publication on the detrimental effects of divorce.

Sandefur compared educational attainment, idleness/labor force attachment, and premarital child bearing of the children of single-parent and two-parent families (McLanahan and Sandefur, 1994). According to their study, "[t]he data clearly shows that children who live with only one parent are at much higher risk of dropping out of high school."[17] Furthermore, "young men from one-parent families are about 1.5 times as likely to be idle (out of school and not working) as young men from two-parent families" (McLanahan and Sandefur, 1994, pp. 48–9). Young women from single-parent homes fare little better.[18] When compared with a young woman from a two-parent home, a young woman from a single-parent home bears a far greater risk of giving birth to a child out of wedlock, a risk that significantly increases when her father is not around (McLanahan and Sandefur, 1994, p. 114). In addition to all of these factors, the children reared in single-parent homes experience more poverty than their counterparts in two-parent homes:[19]

The vast majority of children who are raised entirely in a two-parent home will never be poor during childhood. By contrast, the vast majority of children who spend time in a single-parent home will experience poverty. (Ellwood, 1988, p. 46; see also Fagan, 1999)

In addition to the comparisons made by McLanahan and Sandefur, other studies establish that children who live in single-parent homes "experience lower physical and mental health scores" (Stanton, 1997, p. 119; Larson, Swyers, and Larson, 1996). Not surprisingly, the two-parent family affords children access to the resources, economic and emotional, of two adults. Furthermore, the demonstrated benefits of a family in which the two parents are related to the child biologically recognize that the biological connection of parents to the child "increases the likelihood that the parents . . . identify with the child and [are] willing to sacrifice for that child, and . . . reduces the likelihood that either parent would abuse the child" (McLanahan and Sandefur, 1994, p. 38).[20] Of course, the category of children who live in single-parent homes includes illegitimate children whose biological parents were never married, as well as children who live with one parent after divorce. Maggie Gallagher in *The Abolition of Marriage* draws an interesting connection between divorce and illegitimacy: "There seems to be a tipping point at which marriage becomes so fragile and

---

[17] Stanton (1997, p. 105), summarizing the findings of McLanahan and Sandefur (1994) before quoting them as follows: "Regardless of which survey we look at, children from one-parent families are about twice as likely to drop out of school as children from two-parent families" (p. 41).

[18] Stanton (1997, p. 110), summarizing McLanahan and Sandefur (1994).

[19] "It is no exaggeration to say that a stable, two-parent family is an American child's best protection against poverty" (Kammack and Galston, 1990, p. 12); (see also Fagan, 1999).

[20] Their conclusions about likelihood of abuse have been confirmed by a study in Britain referred to in Fagan, FitzGerald, and Hanks (1997).

divorce so common that an increasing number of women decide it may be safer to dispense with marriage altogether: Illegitimacy surges in the wake of a surge in divorce" (Gallagher, 1996, p. 123; see also Fagan, 1999).

David Popenoe and Barbara Dafoe Whitehead, two names well known among social scientists and in the popular culture, completed a massive study of the increasing social phenomenon of cohabitation and issued a report (Popenoe and Whitehead, 1999b)[21] that among other findings concludes, "[c]ohabiting unions tend to weaken the institution of marriage and pose clear and present dangers to women and children."[22]

By comparison with children of intact first marriages, children of divorce suffer in virtually every measure of a child's well-being.[23] In 1985 Lenore Weitzman documented the devastating economic effect of divorce on children (Weitzman, 1985).[24] Mary Ann Glendon and Judith Younger, two law professors, had in the early 1980s offered different solutions to what each recognized as the problems created by the increasing incidence of divorce. Professor Glendon proposed dividing a couple's property at divorce subject to the "children-first" principle,[25] which required that the resources of both spouses first be used to satisfy the financial needs of the child. Professor Younger proposed a divorce law that did not permit a couple with minor children to obtain a divorce unless the couple could prove to the satisfaction of the court that the children would be better off after the divorce than before (Younger, 1981).[26] But it was Barbara Dafoe Whitehead's now famous 1993 article published in

[21] This comprehensive review of recent research is a part of the Next Generation Series (annual reports by Whitehead and Popenoe on attitudes of young people about cohabitation and marriage).

[22] Popenoe and Whitehead (1999a) place the cohabitating report in the context of declining marriage rates. See also Carlson (1998, p. 7): "The central error in the Swedish model lies at the very beginning: in the assumption that the human family is malleable, a *derivative* social construct ever adjusting to meet new economic conditions, rather than a system rooted in a relatively fixed human nature." These two representative studies essentially undercut Katharine T. Bartlett's notion of a "family-enabling model of reform" that treats all family structures as potentially desirable, including the cohabitation model, and suggests legal rules to govern such structures (gay and lesbian marriage, etc.) (Bartlett, 1998).

[23] See Stanton (1997), chapter 5, "Shattering the Myth: The Broken Promises of Divorce and Remarriage," pp. 123–58. See e.g., Kunz (1992). Waite and Gallagher (2000) document the same benefits of marriage for husbands and wives.

[24] Despite disagreements about Weitzman's calculations of the disparity between post-divorce income and standard of living for men and for women and children, few dispute that women and children suffer more economic hardship than men after divorce. See Hoffman and Duncan (1988); Stroup and Pollock (1994); Peterson (1996); also Fagan (1999).

[25] Glendon (1984); see also Glendon (1987). For a suggested implementation of the children-first principle, see Spaht (1999).

[26] See also Senate Bill No. 160 (1997 Regular Session, Louisiana Legislature), which amended the Louisiana Civil Code [La. Civ. Code], Arts. 102 and 103 (effective Jan. 1, 1991) and added a new article to prohibit couples with children under the age of 18 from obtaining a divorce without proof of fault. The bill failed to pass the Senate floor on a vote of 12 for, 25 against.

The Atlantic Monthly entitled, "Dan Quayle Was Right,"[27] which finally penetrated, and to some extent shattered, the widely popular public perception that divorce is a positive personal experience[28] and that children are resilient and suffer only short-term harm from their parents' divorce. Even before her most recent report, Judith Wallerstein in a book with Sandra Blakeslee wrote: "Divorce is a different experience for children and adults because the children lost something that is fundamental to their development – the family structure" (Wallerstein and Blakeslee, 1989, p. 11).

In June 1997 Judith Wallerstein announced the results of her most recent follow-up interviews with the children of divorce she had been tracking for twenty-five years.[29] The children had been between the ages of 2 and 6 at the time of the divorce.

Unlike the adult experience, the child's suffering does not reach its peak at the breakup and then level off. On the contrary. Divorce is a cumulative experience for the child. Its impact increases over time. At each developmental stage the impact is experienced anew and in different ways. . . . The impact of divorce gathers force as they reach young adolescence, when they are often insufficiently supervised and poorly protected, and when, additionally, they are required then (if not earlier) to adjust to new stepparents and stepsiblings. The impact gathers new strength again at late adolescence when they are financially barred from choosing a career or obtaining an education equivalent to that of their parents. And again, at young adulthood, when their fears that their own adult relationships will fail like those of their parents rise in crescendo. The effect of the parents' divorce is played and replayed throughout the first three decades of the children's lives. (Wallerstein, 1997)

Despite criticism of the sample of children she chose to use,[30] it is the only study of its kind based upon in-depth follow-up interviews over such a substantial period of time. Furthermore, most, but surely not all, subsequent studies have essentially confirmed her findings.[31] Even one of her most vocal critics, Andrew

---

[27] Whitehead (1993). Much that appeared in that article is now incorporated in Whitehead (1997). She discusses some of her conclusions in an excellent Public Broadcasting Service video entitled "Children of Divorce," a part of the National Desk Series. Judith Wallerstein appears in this video, too, along with children of divorce interviewed on camera.

[28] Thornton (1989); see also Ahrons (1985), which makes the case for divorce as a potential positive *personal* experience. In fact, one of the chapters in Stanton (1997) is entitled "Only a Piece of Paper: The Benefits of Marriage for Adults" (pp. 71–95), and in that chapter Stanton argues that first-time married adults, when compared with single, divorced or *remarried* adults, fare better in virtually every measurement of the quality of life. See also Waite and Gallagher (2000). Wallerstein and Blakeslee (1996) isolate what characteristics and qualities of a married couple lead to a rich and long marriage.

[29] Published in Wallerstein, Lewis, and Blakeslee (2000). The results of her interviews with these children at earlier points in time after their parents' divorce have been published in Wallerstein and Kelly (1980) and Wallerstein and Blakeslee (1989).

[30] The study sample included face-to-face interviews with 130 children and both parents. The children came from middle-class northern California homes and their parents were well educated.

[31] See the results of those studies in Stanton (1997), chapter 5, pp. 123–58.

Cherlin, co-authored a 1998 study that concluded: "[A] parental divorce during childhood or adolescence continues to have a negative effect when a person is in his or her 20s and early 30s" (Cherlin, Chase-Lansdale, and McRae, 1998 compare Cherlin et al., 1991; Cherlin, 1993).

In a culture of divorce, children are the most "unfree." Divorce abrogates children's rights to be reasonably free from adult cares and woes, to enjoy the association of both parents on a daily basis, to remain innocent of social services and therapy, and to spend family time in ways that are not dictated by the courts. . . . [D]ivorce involves a radical redistribution of hardship, from adults to children, and therefore cannot be viewed as a morally neutral act. (Whitehead, 1997, p. 184)

As intriguing as the Wallerstein and Cherlin reports are three recent studies[32] that "suggest . . . that if parents are experiencing not violence but unhappiness in their marriages, their children would be better off if they stayed married rather than if they divorced" (Horn, 1998, p. 25). As Dr. Wade E. Horn commented, "conventional wisdom tells us that it's better for the children if their parents divorce than if they stay in an unhappy marriage . . . Only trouble is, both conventional wisdom and the experts, it turns out, are wrong. Three new studies point to divorce – not marital conflict – as the problem" (Horn, 1998, p. 25). One of the studies to which Dr. Horn refers is included in a book entitled *A Generation at Risk* by Paul Amato and Alan Booth, who comment about the results of their study as follows:

Spending one-third of one's life living in a marriage that is less than satisfactory in order to benefit children – children that parents elected to bring into the world – is not an unreasonable expectation. (Amato and Booth, 1997, p. 238)

Among her other findings about the effect of divorce on children twenty-five years later, Judith Wallerstein's study concluded that the quality of the relationships between the divorced parents and the children varied often based upon with whom the children lived and spent the majority of their time. In her interviews with the children she "found that parent–child relationships that have been cut loose from their moorings to the marital bond within which they developed are inherently less stable than those in intact families" (Wallerstein, 1997). The relationship between the non-custodial father and his children was particularly precarious. Despite legal assumptions that the child of divorce can be expected to maintain a close relationship with the father if the mother does not interfere, the reality is far more complex. A divorced father's interest in his children varied according to his "sense of success or failure in the other parts of his life" and his remarriage (Wallerstein, 1997).

---

[32] The first study was conducted by Rex Forehand and colleagues, and the results are published in Forehand, Armistead, and David (1997), the second study is contained in Amato and Booth (1997); the third appears in Simons (1996), pp. 203–5.

David Blankenhorn in his seminal work *Fatherless America* (see Blankenhorn, 1995) marshals the evidence in chapter after chapter that the importance of the father's presence in the home cannot be overestimated: "In virtually all human societies, children's well-being depends decisively upon a relatively high level of paternal investment" (Blankenhorn, 1995, p. 25). A father in the home invests in the family and his children by providing physical protection, material resources, cultural transmission, and day-to-day nurturing; his paycheck in the form of child support is a poor substitute.[33] Blankenhorn observes that "the preconditions for effective fatherhood are twofold: coresidence with children and a *parental alliance with the mother*" (Blankenhorn, 1995, p. 18; emphasis added). Judith Wallerstein's study supports his observation about coresidency of the biological father with his children and a parental alliance with the mother.

All but three men in this sample remarried soon after the divorce. One third remarried three or more times while the child was growing up. Contact with the child also varied with the father's remarriage, with the attitude of the new wife and the presence of children within the new family. It varied again with the father's second divorce. Stepmothers, especially if they had children of their own, were often frank to say that they resented the children of the husband's first marriage and saw them as intruders. While some second wives grew to love the father's children, many did not. As one woman said, "I wanted the man. Not the kids." These attitudes were powerful influences. Understandably, the father was eager for the new marriage to succeed and gave it priority. Fathers who sent their stepchildren to college did not always provide financial support for their own. (Wallerstein, 1997)

If the only effective way to tie a father to his biological children is through an alliance with the mother, then the most effective way to tie the father to the mother and assure his critical presence in the home is through marriage (Blankenhorn, 1995, p. 223).

If a father and mother committed to each other through life-long marriage represent the ideal environment for the rearing of responsible, prosperous, and well-adjusted citizens,[34] can the law restore and strengthen the institution of marriage? With the prediction that almost half of all new marriages in the United States will end in divorce and most of those will involve minor children (Gallagher, 1996, p. 5), what can the law do to repair what it contributed to

---

[33] "From the child's perspective, child support payments even if fully paid, do not replace a father's economic provision. More fundamentally, they do not replace a father" (Blankenhorn, 1995, p. 127).

[34] See Institute for American Values (1998), which contained a recommendation that to renew American democracy morally the country should, first, increase the likelihood that more children will grow up with their two married parents. Specifically recommended is that state legislatures consider reforming no-fault divorce laws.

breaking?[35] How best to restore the ideal of eternal, self-sacrificial love is the urgent question.[36]

3   Louisiana's covenant marriage legislation

Citizens of Louisiana began their experiment[37] to recapture the meaning of marriage as life-long on 15 August 1997.[38] The legislation offers the opportunity to educate the citizenry about the importance and value of life-long marriage[39] and solicits the assistance of other "communities," principally the church,[40] an institution that possesses moral authority and is uniquely qualified to assist in preserving marriages. By encouraging the participation of other

[35] Friedberg (1998, p. 608) observes: "States that adopted divorce laws which were more strongly unilateral had greater increases in the divorce rate. Nevertheless, the evidence shows that adopting any type of unilateral divorce raised the divorce rate." To the same effect, see Brinig and Buckley (1998) (no-fault divorce significantly increased divorce rates because the costs of filing for divorce decreased; study isolated effect of legal variable from other demographic and social factors.) See also Wardle (1991) and Wolfe (1995), "On the other hand, even if [no-fault divorce law] is, to a considerable extent, an epiphenomenon of deeper cultural changes, once ensconced in the law, divorce becomes part of the 'moral ecology' of our culture and shapes the attitudes and expectations of many citizens about marriage."; also Teitelbaum (1996): "[T]he transformation of marriage itself from a legal relationship terminable only for serious cause to one increasingly terminable at will, amounted to a dejuridification of marriage." But see Ellman and Lohr (1997).

[36] See Scott and Scott (1998 p. 1227), "The Louisiana statute grows out of a widespread dissatisfaction with the current social and legal landscape of marriage and divorce, and a sense that marriage itself is threatened under no-fault divorce law."

[37] There are currently two separate empirical studies being conducted of Louisiana's experiment in divorce reform: (1) Professors Steve Nock of the University of Virginia and Jim Wright and Laura Sanchez of Tulane University under grants from the National Science Foundation, Brigham Young University's Center for the Family, and the Smith Richardson Foundation are conducting a five-year study and have already published two articles about their initial polling and focus group results; (2) Katherine Rozier of Louisiana State University is likewise studying Louisiana's covenant marriage (see Rozier, 1998).

[38] 1997 La. Acts, No. 1380. The legislation has been referred to in the *American Bar Association Journal* as "A Stealth Anti-Divorce Weapon" (Carter, 1997a).

[39] The covenant marriage law chooses to educate the citizenry for the first time by giving them information in pamphlet form, prepared by the Attorney General of Louisiana, about how a marriage can be terminated even before it is celebrated. The same pamphlet contains information about the ideal of marriage in the form of the covenant marriage. However, the educational efforts of the law do not cease with this information. To commit to the ideal of a covenant marriage, a couple must receive more in-depth information about the seriousness of marriage through mandatory premarital counseling, after which the couple and counselor sign notarized documents. The documents consist of a declaration of intent signed by the parties, a notarized affidavit by the parties that they have received the requisite counseling, and an attestation by the counselor that he/she provided the requisite counseling. La. Rev. Stat. Ann., Sect. 9:273 A (as amended by 1999 La. Acts, No. 1298,§ 1). Thus, the couple who commit to the ideal of a covenant marriage do so deliberately.

[40] La. Rev. Stat. Ann., Sect 9:273 A. (2)(a) (as amended by 1999 La. Acts, No. 1298, § 1).

"communities"[41] the legislation provides an opportunity to regenerate those "communities" to serve the purpose of supporting the institution of marriage and, consequently, the family.

As has been explained earlier, the legislation permits spouses to *choose* a more binding, more permanent marriage[42] by civil covenant. "Covenant marriage" ensconces in the law the ideal[43] that marriage is to be life-long[44] and incorporates legal obligations that constitute a more binding commitment by the spouses from the beginning of their marriage, by a declaration of intent, and throughout the duration of their marriage, by agreeing to take all necessary steps, including marriage counseling, if difficulties arise during the marriage.[45]

---

41 "Communities," the "seedbeds of civic virtue," include the family, which is the first community into which human beings are born; the church; the neighborhood; the school; and the myriad of voluntary associations and religious and charitable organizations that exist in the United States for the purpose of nourishing the social dimension of human beings. Glendon and Blankenhorn (1995) is a collection of essays about the "seedbeds" of civic virtue. In the Introduction, Glendon writes that all the contributing authors agree that " the simultaneous weakening of child-raising families and their surrounding and supporting institutions constitutes our culture's most serious long-term problem"(1995, p. 3). The reason a weakening of the family is so serious is because US society relies heavily on families to socialize its young citizens. It is from the family and its supporting institutions that children learn the liberal virtues. See also Glendon (1991).

42 La. Rev. Stat. Ann., Sect. 9:272 (as added by 1997 La. Acts 1380 § 3): "A. A covenant marriage is a marriage entered into by one male and one female who understand and agree that the marriage between them is a life-long relationship. . . . Only when there has been a complete and total breach of the marital covenant commitment may the non-breaching party seek a declaration that the marriage is no longer legally recognized. B. A man and woman *may contract* a covenant marriage by declaring their intent to do so on their application for a marriage license [La. Rev. Stat. Ann., Sect. 9:225, 234 (as added by 1997 La. Acts 1380 § 1)], as provided in R.S. 9:224(c), and executing a declaration of intent to contract a covenant marriage, as provided in R.S. 9:273." (emphasis added).

43 "Max Rheinstein, writing in 1972, was nearly alone among family law scholars in declining to condemn the status quo in which strict fault-based divorce laws were maintained on the books, while easy mutual consent divorce was available in practice. This dual approach to divorce was, he said, a 'democratic compromise,' which had 'resulted in the satisfaction of almost everyone concerned.' It was one way of accommodating the ideals of a large part of the population with the practices of those who could not live up to those ideals – even when, as is often the case, they supported them in principle" (Glendon, 1987, p. 66).

44 See also Wolfe (1995, pp. 37–8), who suggests an indissoluble marriage option: "some people might want to have that unbreakable, legally enforceable bond for themselves, on various grounds. It would provide very strong incentives for each person to make his or her own initial decision to marry carefully and reassure each person about the seriousness with which his or her prospective spouse makes that decision. It would provide similar incentives for each of them to exert the maximum effort to make the marriage work, and again, reassure each one that his or her spouse has the same incentives. This could be viewed as one 'strategy' for maximizing the likelihood of a successful marriage."

45 La. Rev. Stat. Ann., Sect. 9:273 (A)(1) (as amended by 1999 La. Acts, No. 1298, § 1): "A declaration of intent to contract a covenant marriage shall contain all of the following:
"A recitation by the parties to the following effects: 'A COVENANT MARRIAGE:
    'We do solemnly declare that marriage is a covenant between a man and a woman who agree to live together as husband and wife for so long as they both may live. We have chosen each other carefully and disclosed to one another everything which could adversely affect the decision to enter into this marriage. We have received premarital counseling on the nature, purposes, and

Covenant marriage adopts the notion of marriage as permanent, yet from the beginning recognizes realistically that difficulties will arise and that the couple may need assistance in resolving them. Furthermore, because the grounds for divorce are limited[46] and, but for one,[47] based on the fault of one spouse, the law restores broader notions of objective morality to conduct within the context of the marital relationship.[48] The law declares that at least in a covenant marriage, reflecting society's ideal, some behavior by a spouse toward the other is so reprehensible that despite society's interest in maintaining the marriage the offended spouse may terminate it. Thus, "fault" grounds for divorce represent society's collective condemnation of certain marital behavior, such as physical cruelty to a spouse or a child of one of the spouses.[49] Such collective social condemnation is altogether missing in pure "no-fault" divorce statutes, yet no one can deny its power.

In addition, the covenant marriage law restores the possibility of a legal separation,[50] which is particularly important for Catholics because their religious beliefs prohibit divorce. The same causes that justify divorce[51] also justify a separation, with the addition of two grounds: mental cruelty or habitual intemperance that render the spouses' life together insupportable. The latter are

responsibilities of marriage. We have read the Covenant Marriage Act, and we understand that a Covenant Marriage is for life. If we experience marital difficulties, we commit ourselves to take all reasonable efforts to preserve our marriage, including marital counseling.

'With full knowledge of what this commitment means, we do hereby declare that our marriage will be bound by Louisiana law on Covenant Marriage and we promise to love, honor, and care for one another as husband and wife for the rest of our lives.'"

[46] La. Rev. Stat. Ann., Sect. 9:307 (A) (as added by 1997 La. Acts, No. 1380, § 4). As originally introduced, House Bill No. 756 (1997 Regular Session, Louisiana Legislature), which contained the "covenant marriage" legislation, permitted immediate divorce for only two reasons: adultery and abandonment for one year. A legal separation could be obtained only for physical abuse of a spouse or physical or sexual abuse of a child of one of the spouses. The legislation as enacted contains six grounds for divorce. Obviously, the bill was amended significantly during the legislative process.

[47] La. Rev. Stat. Ann., Sect. 9:307 (A)(5) (as added by 1997 La. Acts, No. 1380, § 4). By comparison, in Louisiana in a marriage that is not a "covenant marriage" either spouse may obtain a divorce if the spouses have been living separately and apart for either 180 days after the filing of a petition for a divorce (La. Civ. Code, Art. 102) or six months before filing a petition for divorce (La. Civ. Code, Art. 103).

[48] Of course, there is fierce opposition from members of the legal profession, practitioners and academics, to a restoration of objective morality to the relationship of marriage. For a sampling, see e.g., Ellman and Lohr (1997); Oldham (1997); and selected essays in Sugarman and Kay (1991). See also Carter (1997b).

[49] The covenant marriage legislation, which includes physical and sexual abuse as grounds for immediate divorce, represents the first time in Louisiana that such behavior is a ground for divorce, but only in a covenant marriage.

[50] Separation from bed and board was repealed by the Louisiana legislature in 1990. See comment (c) to La. Civ. Code, Art. 101 (effective. Jan. 1, 1991). Thus, in a marriage that is not a covenant marriage legal separation is not possible, and the spouse who desires to alter his or her marital status has only the option of divorce.

[51] La. Rev. Stat. Ann., Sect. 9:307 (B) (as added by 1997 La. Acts 1380, § 4).

grounds only for a legal separation.[52] The Louisiana legislature considered neither offense to be as serious or compelling as adultery or physical or sexual abuse for terminating a marriage. Furthermore, the possibility of judicial expansion of "mental (or psychological) cruel treatment" to include any perceived disagreement or slight meant that a covenant marriage might be in effect terminable by immediate divorce, which is not even possible under Louisiana's "no-fault" divorce.[53]

4   Objectives of the covenant marriage legislation and how the legislation achieves those objectives

Strengthening marriage

The first and foremost objective[54] of the covenant marriage legislation is to strengthen the institution of marriage, an objective achieved by: (1) mandatory premarital counseling that stresses the seriousness of marriage and the expectation that the couple's marriage will be life-long;[55] (2) a *legally* binding agreement[56] in the declaration of intent that if difficulties arise during the marriage the spouses will take all reasonable steps to preserve the marriage, including marriage counseling;[57] and (3) limited grounds for divorce making termination of the marriage depend on either misconduct by a spouse within the marital relationship[58] that society collectively condemns, or a lengthy waiting period of two years living separately and apart.[59]

---

[52] La. Rev. Stat. Ann., Sect. 9:307 (B)(6) (as added by 1997 La. Acts 1380, § 4): "On account of habitual intemperance of the other spouse, or excesses, cruel treatment, or outrages of the other spouse, if such habitual intemperance, or such ill-treatment is of such a nature as to render their living together insupportable."

[53] See La. Civ. Code, Arts. 102 and 103 (1).

[54] For a detailed treatment of each of the objectives and how the legislation accomplishes those objectives, see Spaht (1998a).

[55] La. Rev. Stat. Ann., Sect. 9:273 (A)(2)(a) (as amended by 1999 La. Acts. 1298, § 1). The legislation provides the contours of premarital counseling; the counselors (mostly religious) can fill in the blanks.

[56] The agreement of husband and wife to take all reasonable steps to preserve the marriage, including marital counseling, is a legally binding contract permitted and sanctioned by the state as a limited exception to the fundamental principle that the personal obligations of the marriage contract may not be altered by the parties.

[57] La. Rev. Stat. Ann., Sect. 9:273 (A)(1) (as amended by 1999 La. Acts 1298, § 1). See also La. Rev. Stat. Ann., Sect. 9:273 A. (2)(a) (as amended by 1999 La. Acts 1298, § 1).

[58] La. Rev. Stat. Ann., Sect. 9:307(A) and (B) (as added by 1997 La. Acts 1380, § 1); such misconduct includes adultery, conviction of a felony and a sentence of imprisonment at hard labor or death, abandonment for one year, physical abuse of a spouse or a child of the parties, and a legal separation for cruel treatment (mental cruelty) or habitual intemperance that renders the life together insupportable plus an additional one year or one year and one hundred eighty days of living separately and apart (dependent upon minor children of marriage).

[59] La. Rev. Stat. Ann., Sect. 9:307 (A)(5) (as added by 1997 La. Acts 1380, § 1). This ground for divorce in a covenant marriage is considered to be an example of unilateral no-fault divorce. The

Mandatory premarital counseling is intended to impress upon the couple the seriousness of marriage, their commitment that the marriage be life-long, their obligation to seek counseling if difficulties arise during their marriage, and, for religious counselors, the spiritual dimension of marriage. Premarital counseling may, of course, involve retreats, seminars, premarital inventories, instruction in effective conflict resolution techniques, and a minimum number of sessions of specified length. Premarital counseling encourages seriousness, deliberation, reflection, and preparation by the couple for the undertaking of marriage.

The duty to take all "reasonable" steps to preserve the marriage if marital difficulties arise imposes a *legally* enforceable obligation. Under Louisiana law the obligation may not, in the ordinary case, be specifically enforced by compelling the resisting spouse to undergo counseling.[60] However, as in other breach of contract cases, the law entitles the aggrieved party to damages,[61] which are both pecuniary[62] and nonpecuniary[63] in nature. Pecuniary loss sustained may include, if causally related to the breach,[64] increased expenses for maintaining two households rather than one during the period of separation or expenses necessitated by attempts to obtain the other spouse's compliance with the obligation. Nonpecuniary damages consist of "damage of a moral nature which does not affect a 'material' or tangible part of a person's patrimony."[65] Examples of the type of loss suffered by the aggrieved covenant spouse if the other breaches his or her obligation to take reasonable steps to preserve the marriage include embarrassment, mental anguish, humiliation, and psychological damage. As to these damages, Louisiana law affords the court much discretion[66] and the award need not be nominal.[67] This obligation, furthermore, survives any attempt by a spouse to avoid the consequences of a covenant marriage by moving to another state and seeking a divorce there under that state's more liberal divorce laws (see Spaht, 1998a; Spaht and Symeonides, 1999).

If divorce is the enemy of marriage and inflicts the ultimate damage on the sacred institution, then limiting the grounds for divorce either to serious misconduct by a spouse or to a long waiting period can serve only to bolster

significant difference between unilateral no-fault divorce in a "standard" Louisiana marriage and that in a "covenant" marriage is the lengthier waiting period of an additional year and one-half in a "covenant" marriage. Thus, the two-year waiting period significantly slows down the process of divorcing when compared with the 180-day waiting period for divorce in a "standard" marriage. La. Civ. Code, Arts. 102, 103.

[60] La. Civ. Code, Art. 1986.
[61] La. Civ. Code, Arts. 1986, 1994–7.
[62] La. Civ. Code, Art. 1995.
[63] La. Civ. Code, Art. 1998.
[64] The breach by the covenant spouse could be proved by the particular response of the spouse to entreaties by the obligee to attend counseling sessions.
[65] La. Civ. Code, Art. 1998, cmt. (b).
[66] La. Civ. Code, Art. 1999: "When damages are insusceptible of precise measurement, much discretion shall be left to the court for the reasonable assessment of these damages."
[67] La. Civ. Code, Art. 1999, cmt. (b).

and strengthen marriage against assault. The story the law tells about covenant marriage is that the commitment made in the declaration of intent cannot be easily repudiated – a commitment that cannot be repudiated arguably even by moving to another state with a more relaxed attitude to marriage and divorce. For, in the declaration of intent, covenant spouses agree to be bound by the Louisiana law on covenant marriage, which under conflict of laws principles constitutes the equivalent of a choice of law clause in a contract (see Spaht and Symeonides, 1999).

If the past thirty years have taught Americans anything, it is that danger lies in making the conjugal bond too fragile (see Popenoe and Whitehead, 1999a). It is hoped that the three *legal* components of Louisiana's covenant marriage law working in combination will achieve the laudable goal of strengthening marriage.

Revitalizing mediating structures: inviting religion to assist in preserving marriages

Another less obvious objective of the legislation is to invite religion back "into the public square" (Neuhaus, 1984) for the purpose of performing a function for which religion is uniquely qualified – preserving marriages. A minister,[68] priest,[69] or rabbi may perform the mandatory premarital counseling, just as any of them may perform the ceremony.[70] Likewise, as in the case of performance of the ceremony,[71] the legislation provides a secular alternative, a professional marriage counselor.[72] Preventing bad marriages or identifying potential areas of disagreement through serious premarital counseling requires intensive one-on-one attention. Furthermore, the religious cleric has the opportunity to communicate in counseling sessions the religious view of marriage and the "community's"[73] expectation that the couple will devote serious effort to preserving the marriage.

Because the legislation "invites" religion back into the public square, the legislation is careful *not* to "dictate" the content of the counseling beyond its basic contours.[74] Furthermore, the legislature refused to dictate a fixed amount

---

[68] Generally, a minister is understood to be a clergyman in a church of Protestant denomination (Baptist, Methodist, Pentecostal).

[69] "Priest" clearly includes Catholic and Episcopalian clergymen.

[70] La. Rev. Stat. Ann., Sect. 9:202 (1). See also La. Civ. Code, Art. 91 and comments thereto.

[71] La. Rev. Stat. Ann., Sect. 9:202 (2). A state judge or justice of the peace is permitted to perform the marriage ceremony.

[72] 1999 La. Acts 1298, § 1.

[73] The "community" as used here refers not only to the congregation of the church or temple but also to the larger society in which the couple live, including their neighborhood, social circle, or city.

[74] The basic contours consist of an emphasis on the seriousness of marriage, and the intention of the couple that it be life-long. Although the counselor was originally required to explain the

of time for the premarital counseling, the reason being that to do so would be unnecessarily intrusive into religion's sphere. Many religious denominations already have extensive premarital counseling programs in place, such as the Catholic Church's Pre-Canaa, the Prep Course, and the Prepare or Foccus Inventory. The last two premarital counseling programs are attracting increased attention, particularly in those communities that have adopted a "Community Marriage Policy," such as Modesta, California (Milbank, 1996), Austin, Texas, and Grand Rapids, Michigan,[75] With the creation of the nascent national or ganization Marriage Savers,[76] such serious, extensive premarital counseling programs will increasingly be initiated by religious denominations.

If difficulties arise during the marriage, the couple in a covenant marriage agrees to further education in some form, such as counseling, in an attempt to resolve their differences and preserve the marriage. By inviting not only secular counselors but also the church[77] to participate in strengthening marriage through counseling when the couple encounter difficulties, the covenant marriage law permits religion to serve people of faith and the larger community in which those people live by coming to the assistance of troubled couples. Ministers, priests, and rabbis are uniquely qualified to offer assistance to the couple in preserving their marriage through the use of mentoring couples, church-based counseling centers, or couple retreats, such as the remarkably successful Catholic Retrouvaille. Religious counseling, unlike that of a secular counselor, focuses on preserving the marriage rather than the individual's psyche or personal self-fulfillment (see Doherty, 1997; Kramer, 1997).

Restoration of bargaining power to the "innocent" spouse

The covenant marriage legislation seeks to restore some bargaining power, or leverage, to "innocent" spouses who have kept their promises and desire

differing grounds for divorce in a covenant marriage, the requirement was removed in 1999 La. Acts 1298, § 1. An official explanation of the different grounds for divorce is contained in the Attorney General's pamphlet entitled "The Covenant Marriage Act."

[75] Sider (1998) describes the Grand Rapids' community marriage policy.

[76] Marriage Savers is headed by President, Mike McManus, 8500 Michael's Court, Bethesda, MD 20817. Michael McManus, the architect of the community marriage policy concept, points out that churches and synagogues are foundational to the policy's success. Because at least 75 percent of US weddings take place in churches, US clergy and congregations have both a special responsibility and a special opportunity to revitalize marriage.

[77] La. Rev. Stat. Ann., Sect. 9:273 (A) (2)(a) (as amended by 1999 La. Acts 1298, § 1): "An affidavit by the parties that they have received premarital counseling from [a priest, minister, rabbi, clerk of the Religious Society of Friends, any clergyman of any religious sect, or] *a professional marriage counselor*, which counseling shall include a discussion of the seriousness of covenant marriage, communication of the fact that a covenant marriage is a commitment for life, a discussion of the obligation to seek marital counseling in times of marital difficulties, and a discussion of the exclusive grounds for legally terminating a covenant marriage by divorce or by divorce after a judgment of separation from bed and board" (emphasis added).

to preserve the marriage.[78] Unilateral no-fault divorce deprives the "innocent" spouse who desires a continuation of the marriage of any defense to an action for divorce by the spouse who "broke up" the family.[79] Even Herma Hill Kay, Dean of the law school at the University of California, Berkeley, who continues to be an advocate of no-fault divorce law, observed that *unilateral* no-fault divorce is "closer to desertion than to mutual separation" (Kay, 1990, p. 8). By lengthening the period of time for a no-fault divorce to two years, the covenant marriage legislation empowers "innocent" spouses by granting them the exclusive right to a divorce during the same period on the basis of the other spouse's fault.

"Innocent" spouses' bargaining power[80] can be exercised to insist upon serious counseling in an effort to preserve the marriage or, barring counseling's success, to demand financial advantages for themselves[81] or for their children.[82] The right to receive for *two years* an interim allowance,[83] which is ordinarily a larger sum than final support,[84] serves only to enhance their already considerable

[78] "Divorce was also known to have had a greater negative economic effect on women than on men, one reason being that no-fault divorce took away the bargaining power that the innocent spouse, usually the wife, had under the fault system to agree to divorce only in exchange for adequate alimony, child support, and property.... By 1997 those who were frustrated in their attempt to better the economic situation of divorced women and those who were newly alarmed over the effect of divorce on children joined forces with those who objected to easy divorce on religious or moral grounds. They united in an effort to try a different approach" (Samuel, 1997, p. 189). For an example of the result of no-fault on the spouse who desires to preserve the marriage, see Spaht (1998b).

[79] "The fault doctrine may have served to lend emotional vindication to the rejected spouse, as well as a measure of financial protection and status as the preferred custodian of children. If so, greater justification may be required in those cases for eliminating that doctrine from the related core areas of support, property distribution, and child custody.... But if fault is withdrawn, the party formerly able to invoke that doctrine may be left in a vulnerable position both when negotiating a dissolution agreement and when litigating the matter in court" (Kay, 1990, p. 8). Later in the same article, Kay adds: "A no-fault, no-responsibility divorce law does harm by favoring the economically independent party over the dependent party, creating incentives to distort the law of property in search of just solutions" (p. 36).

[80] The phenomenon is described in Mnookin and Kornhauser (1979), see also Kay (1990).

[81] Such as a greater proportion of the community or marital property or a larger sum in final spousal support than that to which they would be entitled.

[82] This is particularly true when the "innocent" spouse is not employed or earns less than the other spouse and the children are approaching majority, the time when children are the most expensive. In Louisiana, the obligation to pay support for children 18 years or older is governed by the provisions of La. Civ. Code, Art. 229. Unlike child support for minor children, support for major children does not include a sum for education (i.e. college education). Furthermore, support is limited under Article 229 to food, clothing, and shelter, but only if the claimant is unable to support him/herself. Thus, the "innocent" spouse could exercise her/his bargaining power to entice the other spouse to agree to support the children during college (i.e. creation of a trust) in exchange for her/his initiation of divorce proceedings for legitimate grounds before the two-year period elapses.

[83] La. Civ. Code, Art. 113. This interim allowance may be claimed from the moment that the spouses begin living separately and apart before any divorce or separation action is instituted. See La. Rev. Stat. Ann., Sect. 9:291.

[84] La. Civ. Code, Arts. 111, 112. Compare the criteria of an interim allowance and those of final periodic support.

bargaining power. In addition to the interim allowance, the "innocent" spouse may also have a claim for damages should the other spouse refuse to comply with the obligation to take all reasonable steps to preserve the marriage.

Spouses who by their own fault have "broken up" the family unit must wait two years to seek their own divorce. While they wait, they will be paying a significantly higher sum in spousal support than they will pay after the divorce. They also may be obligated to pay damages for breach of the legal obligation to seek counseling. In addition, if they want to remarry, they will be the especially vulnerable target of this shift in divorce law policy. Even a critic of the covenant marriage legislation acknowledges these advantages in a footnote:

The delay offers two possible advantages to divorcing spouses: First, it permits an economically weaker spouse more time to make financial adjustments by prolonging the support obligation of marriage; and second, it may facilitate reconciliation if the partners' marital difficulties are not irremediable. (Carriere, 1998, p. 1720, n118)

Precisely.

Restoration of moral discourse to divorce law and the protection of the "innocent" spouse

Articulated motivations for no-fault divorce, consistent with the opinions espoused by the therapeutic culture,[85] included reducing the acrimony in divorce proceedings so as to spare the children their parents' conflict, avoiding the "impossible" determination of whose behavior caused the breakdown of the marriage, and removing punishment from marital dissolution. Acrimony in divorce has never been eliminated, and at least in Louisiana now takes the truly venal form of allegations of sexual abuse of a child in a custody dispute.[86] Is it not preferable for one spouse to accuse the other of abandonment for one year, or even of adultery, than of sexually abusing their child? After all, such allegations necessitate a physician's intimate examination of the child. Acrimony on account of divorce can never be eliminated unless both parties are in agreement that their relationship is "dead," for otherwise one spouse has been guilty of a violation of trust or a loss of romantic interest in the context of the most intimate of all human relationships. Furthermore, even if the two spouses agree that their relationship is "dead," what about the interests of the children, most of whom desire that their parents remain together? Does it matter if the interests of the children conflict with the desires of the two parents?

---

[85] See Glendon (1987, pp. 107–8) and note 1 above.
[86] La. Rev. Stat. Ann., Sect. 9:364 in essence makes allegations of sexual abuse of a child the "atomic bomb" of divorce proceedings. If such sexual abuse can be proven, then the abuser's custody and visitation rights are terminated.

Restoration of "moral discourse" to divorce law (Schneider, 1985) troubles most critics of the covenant marriage law more than any other aspect of the legislation.[87] The "moral discourse" consists of society's collective condemnation of certain conduct within the marital relationship. Returning to objective moral judgments about a spouse's conduct threatens the notion that morality cannot be legislated.[88] Congress and legislatures do it every day. Only when the morals to be legislated have the potential of impeding the affected person's "liberty"[89] to leave his or her family when he or she so chooses and be considered legally "a single person" do we hear objections. In matters of breach of contract, no one has objected to assigning *blame* for failure to perform a contract, requiring that contracts be performed in good faith, and assessing damages based upon whether the party breached the contract in good faith or bad faith. If principles of contract law involve moral judgments in the context of a relationship between strangers, why should the law hesitate to make a moral judgment about spouses who have been married for thirty years and have three children?

Another argument against the restoration of fault to divorce law is the assertion that fault cannot be proven, thus, those who desire a divorce will be relegated to perjury, allegedly a widespread practice prior to no-fault divorce. Fault in the nature of adultery or physical abuse sufficient for an immediate divorce may be proven by a mere preponderance of the evidence (more likely than not), and that evidence need only be circumstantial, not direct. Surely, it is no more difficult to prove adultery by a spouse than to prove which driver's fault, and the degree of that fault expressed in a percentage, caused a car accident. As a response to the expressed concern about widespread perjury, the answer is that

[87] See, e.g., Carriere (1998, p. 1723): "However, relatively few actions within the family are so violative of social norms that the relational context makes no difference to the question of blameworthiness. Western literature is replete with evidence for the proposition that even one party's adultery, while a clear breach of the marital obligation and never a good idea, can occur in a context in which culpability for the breach must be shared by the spouses." Professor Ira Ellman is particularly vehement about the restoration of fault to divorce proceedings for any purpose (see, e.g., Ellman, 1996, 1997). Professor Ellman is the chief reporter of the American Law Institute's project, on Principles of the Law of Family Dissolution. His strong aversion to fault explains why the project does not include fault as a relevant factor for purposes of marital property distribution or compensation payments at divorce.

[88] Or, "[a] good marriage cannot be legislated, because '[a]lmost all couples who marry believe their love is forever and their commitment is for a lifetime. *But things sometimes change and people sometimes change* [emphasis added]. And sometimes, no amount of work or commitment will make a marriage successful'" (Lindsay, 1998, n 120, quoting from "Difficult Divorces May Add to Misery," *The Advocate*, 13 June 1997, 10 B). Compare the language used in this newspaper editorial with that of Stackhouse (1997, p. 159): "Through covenant they become interlocked structures by which our human propensities to egoism, selfishness, short-sightedness, and carelessness are constrained and the possibilities of altruism, generosity, long-range vision, and engagement are evoked."

[89] "[F]amily standardizing reform [traditional family anchored by husband and wife] threatens the very diversity and *notions of individual freedom* on which more robust notions of the community and family depend" (Bartlett, 1998, p. 818, emphasis added).

the judiciary and attorneys bear responsibility.[90] Even though perjury should surely be condemned, the fraud upon the court did at least require *cooperation of both spouses* and precluded the current practice of legalized desertion by one spouse.

Since covenant marriage legislation indisputably restores broader notions of fault to divorce proceedings, the very existence of a covenant marriage and the strength of the spouses' commitment should have greater bearing upon incidental relief, such as spousal support and child custody. If no-fault divorce was motivated by a desire to remove the punitive function of fault from such questions as alimony and child custody, it is logical to argue that a partial repudiation of no-fault should restore a consideration of fault to such core issues of divorce.

An interim allowance awarded to an "innocent" spouse based upon his or her needs, the other spouse's ability to pay, and their standard of living during the marriage serves the purpose of maintaining the status quo.[91] In a covenant marriage, at the option of the "innocent" spouse, the status quo as married and the obligation to take steps to preserve the marriage may last as long as two years. "Innocent" spouses who are in need should be awarded a sum to maintain them as nearly as possible at the level of the marital standard of living throughout the entire two-year period. The purpose of the interim period in a covenant marriage is to assure that there is an opportunity to take all reasonable steps designed to preserve the marriage. Maintaining the status quo during the "interim" period in hopes of preserving the marriage guarantees the optimum climate for the serious work of reconciliation. Protection against traumatic economic dislocation to the extent possible, particularly for the "innocent" spouse, is justified because covenant spouses solemnly and *deliberately* promise a more binding commitment. The existence of a covenant marriage justifies a generous interim allowance for the maximum time allowable.

For final periodic support in Louisiana, the court must consider the factor of fault of the claimant prior to the filing of a proceeding to terminate the marriage.[92] The promises of the covenant couple made after counseling and reflection should be treated as extremely serious; and if one spouse breaches those promises, he or she should suffer the consequences. Thus, if one spouse proves the other engaged in conduct constituting grounds for divorce or legal separation in a covenant marriage, the other spouse should be denied final

---

[90] See Samuel (1997, p. 193): "Some of these problems festered in part due to the lenient attitude of lawyers and judges toward divorce at a time when the legislation was strict as to all couples. But when a couple has voluntarily chosen a strict regime of divorce after premarital counseling on the subject, there is no justification for the lawyer or judge to manipulate or allow manipulation of the law or evidence to effect a divorce for such a couple." The "problem" of perjured testimony is one that addresses itself to the lawyers and the judges.

[91] La. Civ. Code, Art. 113.

[92] La. Civ. Code, Art. 111.

support. Furthermore, the spouse who proves that the other committed such an offense should be entitled to a presumption of "innocence" that the other spouse must overcome by clear and convincing evidence.[93]

Fault of a covenant spouse that constitutes grounds for a separation or divorce should also be considered relevant in decisions relating to child custody, particularly the factor of *moral* fitness.[94] The purpose of covenant marriage after all was to strengthen marriage, and one of the means to accomplish that objective is society's collective judgment about unacceptable conduct within the marital relationship. The covenant marriage law offers spouses the opportunity to bind themselves to a stronger commitment than the law is willing to impose. By voluntarily undertaking this commitment, permitted because it is in the interest of children to be born of the union, covenant spouses accept society's judgment about their behavior during the marriage. They should also expect consequences should their behavior breach the obligations they solemnly undertook, especially consequences as to their relationship with their children.

Permitting one spouse in effect to destroy a family unit of five persons, particularly if he or she is the morally guilty party, without good reason and without significant consequences, has had a corrosive effect on US society. As evidence mounts of the social destruction in the wake of surging divorce rates and now surging cohabitation rates, responsible policy makers can no longer simply wring their hands in despair and helplessness. Action is required. Covenant marriage legislation, it is to be hoped, is only the beginning of the resurgence of interest in and protection of the institution of marriage – the foundation upon which the "family" is built.

5   Conclusion

The Western tradition has learned, through centuries of experience, to balance the norms of marital formation, maintenance, and dissolution. . . . The lesson in this is that rules governing marriage formation and dissolution must be comparable in their stringency. . . . Loose formation rules demand loose dissolution rules, as we see today. To fix "the modern problem of divorce" will require reforms of rules at both ends of the marital process. (Witte, 1997, pp. 217–18).

Covenant marriage legislation accomplishes the balancing of norms of formation, maintenance, and dissolution. It more stringently regulates the formation of marriage by mandating premarital counseling and the execution and filing of documents that require the participation of the counselor and a notary public.[95] By virtue of the contractual provisions in the declaration of intent, covenant

---

[93] See Spaht (1998a), pp. 127–9.
[94] La. Civ. Code, Arts. 131, 134 (6).
[95] La. Rev. Stat. Ann., Sect. 9:273 (A)(as amended by 1999 La. Acts 1298, § 1) and (B) (as amended by 1997 La. Acts 1380, § 3).

marriage legislation imposes the duty upon spouses to maintain their marriage, if possible, by taking reasonable steps to preserve it.[96] Last, but surely not least, covenant marriage legislation contains more stringent rules of dissolution by divorce.[97]

Marriage has been described by Maggie Gallagher as the only truly heroic act most of us can attempt.[98] Easy divorce denies us that opportunity for heroism. Covenant marriage extends the invitation to Louisianans to be heroic, to make a choice that represents a measure of self-sacrifice. Furthermore,

[a]t the present juncture in history, what may really matter is that the Louisiana legislature has recognized the harm done by the tide of no-fault divorce in America, and by a large majority has voted to begin the process of reversing this tide. . . . Having been to the brink with marital instability, Americans are now starting to address the basic legal framework which has helped to undermine the institution of marriage. Britain and other European countries could follow this example, rather than wait until things get as bad as they are in America. (Rowthorn, 1999, p. 688)

And, to think, Louisiana started the retreat from the precipice.

REFERENCES

Ahrons, Constance (1985), *The Good Divorce: Keeping Your Family Together When Your Marriage Comes Apart*, New York: HarperCollins.
Amato, Paul and Stacy Rogers (1999), "Do Attitudes toward Divorce Affect Marital Quality?" *Journal of Family Issues*, 20, 69–86.
Amato, Paul and Alan Booth (1997), *A Generation at Risk*, Cambridge, MA: Harvard University Press.
Bartlett, Katharine T. (1998), "Saving the Family from the Reformers," *University of California at Davis Law Review*, 31, 809–35.
Bellah, Robert (1985), *Habits of the Heart*, Berkeley: University of California Press.
Blankenhorn, David (1995), *Fatherless America*, New York: Harper Perennial.
Brinig, Margaret F. (1998), "Economics, Law and Covenant Marriage," *Gender Issues*, 16, 4–34.
Brinig, Margaret F. and F.H. Buckley (1998), "No-Fault Law and at Fault People," *International Review of Law and Economics*, 18, 235–325.
Carlson, Allan (1998),"The Family, Public Policy & Democracy: Lessons from the Swedish Experiment," *The Family in America* (Newsletter of the Howard Center for Family, Religion & Society), 12, 7.
Carriere, Jeanne (1998), "It's Deja Vu All Over Again: The Covenant Marriage Act in Popular Cultural Perception and Legal Reality," *Tulane Law Review*, 72, 1701–48.
Carter, Terry (1997a), "Stealth Anti-Divorce Weapon," *American Bar Association Journal*, 28.

---

[96] Ibid., § 273 (A) (1).
[97] Ibid., § 307.
[98] Gallagher (1996, p. 265): "To dare to pledge our whole selves to a single love is the most remarkable thing most of us will ever do. With the abolition of marriage that last possibility for heroism has been taken from us."

Carter, Terry (1997b), "End No-Fault Divorce? Yes: Maggie Gallagher; No: Barbara Dafoe Whitehead," *First Things*, August/September, 24.

Cherlin, Andrew J. (1993), "Nostalgia as Family Policy," *The Public Interest*, 110, 1–8.

Cherlin, Andrew J., P. Lindsay Chase-Lansdale, and Christine McRae (1998),"Effects of Parental Divorce on Mental Health through the Life Course," *American Sociological Review*, 63, 239–49.

Cherlin, Andrew J., Frank F. Furstenberg, Jr., P. Lindsay Chase-Lansdale, Kathleen E. Kiernan, Philip K. Robins, Donna Ruane Morrison, and Julien O. Teitler (1991), "Longitudinal Studies of Effects of Divorce on Children in Great Britain and the United States," *Science*, 252, 1386–89.

Demo, David and Alan Acock (1988), "The Impact of Divorce on Children: An Assessment of Recent Evidence," *Journal of Marriage and Family*, 50, 619–22.

Doherty, William J. (1997), "How Therapists Threaten Marriages," *The Responsive Community*, 7, 31–42.

Ellman, Ira Mark (1996), "The Place of Fault in a Modern Divorce Law," *Arizona State Law Journal*, 28, 773–838.

(1997), "The Misguided Movement to Revive Fault Divorce, and Why Reformers Should Look Instead to the American Law Institute," *International Journal of Law Policy and Family*, 11, 216–45.

Ellman, Ira Mark and Sharon Lohr (1997), "Marriage as Contract, Opportunistic Violence, and Other Bad Arguments for Fault Divorce," *University of Illinois Law Review*, 3, 719–72.

Ellwood, David (1988), *Poor Support: Poverty in the American Family*, New York: Basic Books.

Fagan, Patrick F. (1999), "How Broken Families Rob Children of Their Chances for Future Prosperity," *Heritage Foundation*, 11 June.

Fagan, Patrick F., William H.G. FitzGerald, Sr., and Dorothy B. Hanks (1997), "The Child Abuse Crisis: The Disintegration of Marriage, Family, and the American Community," Roe Background No. 1115, *Heritage Foundation*, 15 May.

Forehand, Rex, Lisa Armistead, and Corinne David (1997), "Is Adolescent Adjustment Following Parental Divorce a Function of Predivorce Adjustment?" *Journal of Abnormal Child Psychology*, 25, 157–64.

Friedberg, Leora (1998), "Did Unilateral Divorce Raise Divorce Rates? Evidence from Panel Data," *American Economic Review*, 88, 608–27.

Gallagher, Maggie (1996), *The Abolition of Marriage: How We Destroy Lasting Love*, Washington DC: Regnery.

Gallagher, Maggie and David Blankenhorn (1997), "Family Feud," *The American Project*, pp. 12–15.

Glendon, Mary Ann (1984), "Family Law in the 1980s," *Louisiana Law Review*, 44, 1553–74.

(1987), *Divorce and Abortion in Western Law*, Cambridge, MA: Harvard University Press.

(1991), *The Missing Dimension of Sociality, Rights Talk: The Impoverishment of Political Discourse*, New York: Free Press, 109–44.

Glendon, Mary Ann and David Blankenhorn (eds.) (1995), *Seedbeds of Virtue: Sources of Competence, Character, and Citizenship in American Society*, Lanham, MD: Madison Books.

Guidubaldi, John (1988), "Differences in Children's Divorce Adjustment across Grade Level and Gender: A Report from NASP-Kent State Nationwide Project," in Sharlene A. Wolchik and Paul Karoly (eds.), *Children of Divorce: Empirical Perspectives on Divorce*, New York: Gardner Press.

Hoffman, Saul and Greg Duncan (1988), "What Are the Economic Consequences of Divorce?," *Demography*, 25, 641–5.

Horn, Wade E. (1998), "Strong Case for Staying Together Despite Discord," *Washington Times*, National Weekly Edition, 18 January, p. 25.

(1999), "Divorce – If You Believe in It...It May Come," *Fatherhood Today*, 4, 3–4.

Institute for American Values (1998), "Call to a Civil Society," Council on Civil Society and University of Chicago Divinity School, 28 May.

Kammack, E. and W. Galston (1990), *Putting Children First: A Progressive Family Policy for the 1990s*, Washington DC: Progressive Policy Institute.

Kay, Herma Hill (1990), "Beyond No-Fault: New Directions in Divorce Reform," in Stephen Sugarman and Herma Hill Kay (eds.), *Divorce Reform at the Crossroads*, New Haven, CT: Yale University Press.

Kramer, Peter (1997), "Divorce and Our National Values," *New York Times*, 29 August.

Kunz, Jenifer (1992), "The Effects of Divorce on Children," in Stephen Bahr (ed.), *Family Research: A Sixty Year Review, 1930–1990*, New York: Lexington Books, 325–76.

Laconte, Joe (1998), "I'll Stand Bayou," *Policy Review*, 89, 30–3.

Larson, David B., James B. Swyers, and Susan S. Larson (1996), *The Costly Consequences of Divorce: Assessing the Clinical, Economic, and Public Health Impact of Marital Disruption in the United States*, Rockville, IL: National Institute for Healthcare Research.

Lindsay, Nicole D. (1998), "Marriage and Divorce; Degrees of 'I Do' An Analysis of the Ever-Changing Paradigm of Divorce," *University of Florida Journal of Law and Public Policy*, 9, 265–86.

McLanahan, Sara S. and Gary Sandefur (1994), *Growing up with a Single-Parent: What Hurts, What Helps*, Cambridge, MA: Harvard University Press.

Milbank, Dana (1996), "Demographics: More Get Marriage Counseling before Marriage," *Wall Street Journal*, B1, 6 February.

Mnookin, Robert and Lewis Kornhauser (1979), "Bargaining in the Shadow of the Law: The Case of Divorce," *Yale Law Journal*, 88, 950–97.

Neuhaus, Richard John (1984), *The Naked Public Square: Religion and Democracy in America*, Grand Rapids, MI: Eerdmans.

Oldham, J. Thomas (1997), "ALI Principles of Family Dissolution: Some Comments," *University of Illinois Law Review*, 1997, 801–31.

Parkman, Allen M. (1993), "Reform of the Divorce Provisions of the Marriage Contract," *Brigham Young University Journal of Public Law*, 8, 91–106.

Peterson, Richard R. (1996), "A Re-Evaluation of the Economic Consequences of Divorce," *American Sociological Review*, 61, 528–36.

Pope John Paul II (1994), Apostolic Exhortation: *The Role of the Christian Family in the Modern World*, Washington, D.C.: US Catholic Conference.

Popenoe, David (1992), "Fostering the New Familism," *The Responsive Community*, 2, 31–4.

Popenoe, David and Barbara Dafoe Whitehead (1999a), "The State of Our Unions," *National Marriage Project*, Rutgers, State University of New Jersey, July.

(1999b), "Should We Live Together? What Young Adults Need to Know about Cohabitation before Marriage," *National Marriage Project*, Rutgers, State University of New Jersey, February.

Rowthorn, Robert (1999), "Marriage and Trust: Some Lessons from Economics," *Cambridge Journal of Economics*, 23, 661–91.

Rozier, Katherine (1998), "No Honeymoon for Covenant Marriage," *Wall Street Journal*, 17 August.

Samuel, Cynthia S. (1997), "Letter from Louisiana: An Obituary for Forced Heirship and a Birth Announcement for Covenant Marriage," *Tulane European and Civil Law Forum*, 12, 189–90.

Schneider, Carl E. (1985), "Moral Discourse and the Transformation of American Family Law," *Michigan Law Review*, 83, 1803–40.

Scott, Elizabeth S. (1990), "Rational Decisionmaking about Marriage and Divorce," *Virginia Law Review*, 76, 9–94.

Scott, Elizabeth S. and Robert E. Scott (1998), "Marriage as a Relational Contract," *Virginia Law Review*, 84, 1225–334.

Sedlak, Andrea J. and Diane Broadhurst (1996), "The Third National Incidence Study of Child Abuse and Neglect" (NIS-3): Final Report, *U.S. Department of Health and Human Services, National Center on Child Abuse and Neglect*, Washington DC, September.

Sider, Roger (1998), "Grand Rapids (Michigan) Erects a Civic Tent for Marriage," *Policy Review*, 78, 6–7.

Simons, Ronald L. (1996), *Understanding Differences between Divorced and Intact Families: Stress Interaction, and Child Outcome*, Thousand Oaks, CA: Sage Publications.

Spaht, Katherine Shaw (1998a), "Louisiana's Covenant Marriage: Social Analysis and Legal Implications," *Louisiana Law Review*, 59, 63–130.

(1998b), "Why Covenant Marriage? A Change in the Culture for the Sake of the Children," *Louisiana Bar Journal*, 46, 116–21.

(1999), *The Family as Community Act*, a position paper of the Communitarian Network, New York: Rowman & Littlefield.

Spaht, Katherine Shaw and Symeon Symeonides (1999), "Covenant Marriage and Conflict of Laws," *Creighton Law Review*, 32, 1085–120.

Stackhouse, Max L. (1997), *Covenant & Commitments: Faith, Family, and Economic Life*, Louisville, KY: Westminster John Knox Press.

Stanton, Glenn S. (1997), *Why Marriage Matters: Reasons to Believe in Marriage in Post-Modern Society*, Colorado Springs, CO: Pinon.

Stroup, Atlee L. and Gene E. Pollock (1994), "Economic Consequences of Marital Dissolution," *Journal of Divorce and Remarriage*, 22, 37–54.

Sugarman, Stephen D. and Herma Hill Kay (eds.) (1991), *Divorce Reform at the Crossroads*, New Haven, CT: Yale University Press.

Teitelbaum, Lee E. (1996), "The Last Decade(s) of American Family Law," *Journal of Legal Education*, 46, 546–8.

Thornton, A. (1989), "Changing Views towards Family Issues in the United States," *Journal of Marriage and the Family*, 51, 873–93.

Waite, Linda S. and Maggie Gallagher (2000), *The Case for Marriage*, New York: Doubleday.

Wallerstein, Judith (1997), unpublished paper presented at the Association of Family and Conciliation Courts conference, San Francisco, June 6.

Wallerstein, Judith and Sandra Blakeslee (1989), *Second Chances: Men, Women, and Children a Decade after Divorce*, Boston: Houghton Mifflin.

(1996), *The Good Marriage: How and Why Love Lasts*, New York: Houghton Mifflin.

Wallerstein, Judith and Joan Berlin Kelly (1980), *Surviving the Breakup: How Children and Parents Cope With Divorce*. New York: Basic Books.

Wallerstein, Judith S., Julia Lewis, and Sandra Blakeslee (2000), *The Unexpected Legacy of Divorce: A 25-Year Landmark Study*, New York: Hyperion.

Wardle, Lynn D. (1991), "No-Fault Divorce and the Divorce Conundrum," *Brigham Young University Law Review*, 79, 79–142.

Weitzman, Lenore (1985), *The Divorce Revolution: The Unintended Social and Economic Consequences on Women and Children in America*, New York: Free Press.

Whelan, Robert (1993), *Broken Homes & Battered Children: A Study of the Relationship between Child Abuse and Family Type*, London: Family Education Trust.

Whitehead, Barbara Dafoe (1993), "Dan Quayle Was Right," *The Atlantic Monthly*, 271, 47–82.

(1997), *The Divorce Culture*, New York: Knopf.

Witte, Jr., John (1997), *From Sacrament to Contract: Marriage, Religion and Law in the Western Tradition*, Louisville, KY: Westminster John Knox Press.

Wolfe, Christopher (1995), "The Marriage of Your Choice," *First Things*, February, 37–41.

Yankelovich, Daniel (1992), "Foreign Policy after the Election," *Foreign Affairs*, 7 (1), 3 4.

Younger, Judith T. (1981), "Marital Regimes: A Story of Compromise and Demoralization, together with Criticism and Suggestions for Reform," *Cornell Law Review*, 67, 45–102.

7   Cohabitation and marriage

Antony W. Dnes

1   Introduction

Simple cohabitation occurs when a man and woman live together as though married but without completing any recognized marriage ceremony or meeting the requirements for common law marriage, where this exists. This least formal relationship has been growing in significance over recent decades. Such a quasi-married state carries fewer of the legal obligations that characterize marriage. In England there has been no legal recognition of common law marriage since an Act of Parliament of 1753. Among other things, this implies that one, home-owning, cohabiting party could eject another from a shared home without there being any claim on its value or services, although this position is currently under review by the Law Commission. In other countries, for example in some American states and in continental Europe, greater legal recognition of cohabitation is nonetheless usually limited compared with marriage. Where US states have recognized cohabitation contracts (for example, awarding "palimony" upon separation) as in *Marvin v. Marvin* (1976),[1] they have done so under contract rather than family law.

Several questions are of great interest. Why would some men and women deliberately seek a set of lesser obligations towards each other? Is the trend towards cohabitation in some sense therefore supportive of the welfare of these couples? In that case, the trend might be judged to be efficient. Alternatively, are there barriers to marriage that could be removed to everybody's benefit? Finally, what is an appropriate response for the state, given the growth in cohabitation?

I wish to thank the Leverhulme Foundation for the Study Abroad Fellowship that provided support for this work.

[1] 18 Cal. 3d 660 (Cal. 1976). Michelle Marvin enforced an oral agreement with Lee Marvin that during the time they lived together they would combine their efforts and earnings and share property. Michelle would act as companion, housekeeper, and cook, and give up her career as an entertainer and singer, and Lee Marvin would provide financial support for the rest of her life. Later Lee Marvin forced her to leave his household, and refused to pay any further support or share property rights. The court held the terms of the contract did not rest upon any unlawful consideration, and that it furnished a suitable basis upon which the trial court could render declaratory relief.

2 Cohabitation trends

The move towards cohabitation represents a hugely significant shift in social behavior during the post-war period. The trends for the 1960–2000 period are similar across many European countries and North America.[2] Taking England as an example, first marriages fell from approximately 70 per 1,000 to 30 per 1,000 of the male population. The age at which first marriages occur has typically risen; for example, in England men and women wait an extra three years. Births outside of marriage have increased from 5 percent to 35 percent of all births. In addition, the proportion of cohabiting women between the ages of 20 and 50 has trebled. Finally in this regard, we know that divorce rates have risen dramatically over the past thirty years.

The trends illustrate a move away from marriage that is different from earlier time periods. The significant change is that marriage rates are falling and cohabitation rates are rising. People are not simply cohabiting as a prelude to marriage, as may have been the case in eighteenth-century Britain. Although cohabiting people often state that cohabitation is a matter of "trying out" prior to marriage (Lewis, Datte, and Sarre, 1999), this claim can be true only in the sense that weaker potential marriages may be filtered out, as subsequent marriage appears not to be the typical result. Furthermore, cohabitation is even less stable than marriage has become after the post-1970 increases in divorce rates. The reality is that many people either have substituted cohabitation for marriage or have been "trying out" but dissolving their relationships relatively quickly. A puzzling aspect of the substitution is that cohabitation is against the interests of many women. Marriage is potentially a good mechanism for supporting long-term family investments, in which without marriage women may be vulnerable to opportunistic behavior, defined as "self seeking with guile" (Williamson, 1985).

3 Cohabitation in relation to marriage

To analyze cohabitation one must study it in relation to marriage. A useful *starting point* is to regard marriage as a contract between two parties, although it should be noted that marriage originated as a status relationship pre-dating the development of contract. Another caution arises because there are many restrictions on freedom of contract that apply to marriage, for example in terms of entering and dissolving the marriage. Also, such commercial analogies tend to lead eventually to a focus on covenants or relationships of trust in law (Brinig, 2000). A contractual starting point is useful because contractual elements are present in marriage, albeit in a bounded sense.

---

[2] Figures that follow are for England and are summarized from *Population Trends* 89 (HMSO, 1999).

A contractual approach is capable of considerable sophistication, particularly if one draws in elements of the study of relational contracts (Scott and Scott, 1998) and regards the marriage as evolving over time within a surrounding set of social norms. It is unhelpful to dismiss the contractual approach out of hand, especially where inherently economic issues such as asset division upon dissolution are at stake. Economic analysis regards both marriage and cohabitation as the result of rational purposeful behavior, with the parties seeking gains from action that are a mixture of financial and other, typically psychic, benefits and costs. A contractual approach is a particularly good method of analysis in looking at pecuniary issues in marriage and divorce, including those attached to the maintenance of children, although the approach need not be limited to pecuniary issues. As a matter of fact, the pecuniary elements do come to dominate discussions of long-term relationships, in the sense that public policy and the courts are typically asked to address pecuniary rather than emotional concerns.[3]

Writers opposed to economic approaches to the family are often hostile to Becker's (1991) pioneering work. In fact, Becker's model of the family is imbued with considerable altruistic elements, but many modern institutional economists would reject it anyway as too limited in its scope (Lundberg and Pollak, 1996). Becker sees marriage as the culmination of a search and matching process, which establishes a household production function allowing efficient division of labor to take place and, in particular, delivering shared marital "goods" such as children.[4] Search may be extensive if focused on the marriage market, or intensive if aimed at the socialization occurring after a relation has been formed (Oppenheimer, 1988). Divorce results from search in a remarriage market and is therefore a result of inefficient first-partner searching (Becker, Landes, and Michael, 1977). Becker's model of the family actually has little to say about incentives to cohabit or about non-cooperative marriages existing in the shadow of divorce.

Becker, along with other "traditionalists," regards marriage as an exchange of domestic services, typically by the female, in return for long-term financial support (Carbone and Brinig, 1991). Marital "output" comprises shared marital "goods" such as children and other aspects of joint lifestyle, as well as private benefits for the parties, for example a reciprocal insurance function covering old age and sickness. There is generally some "surplus," i.e. a set of net benefits that must be divided between the parties in a marriage, and many of the "investments" (such as time spent raising children) are long term in nature

---

[3] As is well recognized in the (American) case *Piper v. Hoard*, 107 N.Y. 73, 13 N.E. 626 (1887) (courts have little to do with sentiment but focus on the business side of marriage).

[4] A shared (strictly a "public") good is one that is not mutually exclusive in consumption; i.e. two or more people can share units. Both parents enjoy the same children and "two can live as cheaply as one."

and marriage specific (becoming unrecoverable "sunk costs"). Becker's view of marriage would raise major concerns in relation to legal environments that allow easy divorce, or cohabitation, without the tying of post-separation support obligations to findings of substantial breach of contract. In particular, if husbands can abandon wives easily there may be poor incentives for investment (by the wife) in domestic production, and this incentive problem would follow through even more strongly in the case of cohabitation.

Recently, economists have focused on less consensual, bargaining models of the family, which give powerful insights. In these approaches, people can behave selfishly and opportunistically. Lloyd Cohen (chapter 2 in this volume) has given opportunistic behavior within the family considerable prominence in his work. Both marriage and cohabitation require the parties to exchange promises of mutual support, where the value of the support is crucially dependent on the attitude with which it is delivered.[5] In a traditional marriage, many of the domestic services provided by the wife occur early in the marriage, whereas the support offered by the male will grow in value over the longer term as his career develops. The economic and marriage-market opportunities of the parties may change (supposing passionate love to lessen in an older relationship) so that one of them might have an incentive to breach the contract. Separation or, in the case of marriage, divorce imposes costs on both parties, equal to at least the cost of finding a replacement partner of equivalent value. Cohen has argued in chapter 2 that the risks and costs of being an unwilling party to divorce are asymmetrically distributed. The husband might be tempted to take the wife's early services and dispense with her to enjoy his later income without her, perhaps also taking a younger spouse, the "greener-grass" effect (Dnes, 1998). Older divorced women, particularly with children, experience difficulty in remarrying compared with males of similar age, being approximately half as likely to remarry than their male counterparts in the 45–54 age group.

In the case of cohabitation, the parties must rely largely on natural "hostages" that emerge in the relationship to limit the kind of opportunism described above. Such hostages may be provided by the presence of children, with whom a parent may wish to maintain easy contact. Also, the search costs of finding a new partner, or the social stigma that can be attached to living alone, may act to hold people together over a long period of time. In the case of marriage, the hostages will typically be bolstered by legal obligations between the ex-spouses to pay child and possibly spousal maintenance and to divide marital property according to statute and case law. As far as obligations for the maintenance of children are concerned, there is little difference between the

---

[5] Married couples are usually subject to a legal requirement for mutual support, which has replaced the old common law duty of a husband to support his wife in relation to the necessaries of life.

dissolution of cohabitation and marriage in countries that have some form of child support legislation. Nonetheless, it is clear that it would be rational to choose to cohabit if the parties actually wished to avoid, or perhaps in some jurisdictions just to lessen, the legal obligations towards each other in the event of termination.

At first sight and temporarily leaving aside the issue of greener-grass opportunism, there are similar psychic and instrumental benefits to cohabitation and marriage. The willingness of someone to commit to another is evidence of worthiness of such love that applies in both cases. However, the signal will be stronger in the case of marriage because of the greater costs of its dissolution; and that is a very valuable differential signal for those trying to assess the intensity of the feelings professed by a potential long-term partner. On the instrumental side, marriage provides insurance: a husband gives up his freedom to seek new partners if his prospects improve in exchange for a similar commitment from his wife. However, both cohabitation and marriage are capable of providing mutual support as partners age, experience illness, or go through other life changes – although, at the start, marriage is a stronger commitment. Both marriage and cohabitation are capable of supporting the genetic imperatives considered by Posner (1992).

4   Optimal cohabitation

The "wrong" judicial approach to obligations such as long-term support can lead to too much or too little divorce, marriage, and cohabitation. This observation brings in the idea of an optimal level of divorce, which might be broadly encapsulated in a rule such as "let them divorce when the breaching party (i.e. the one who wants to leave, or who has committed a 'marital offense') can compensate the victim of breach" (Dnes, 1998, p. 343). Similarly, one can think of an optimal level of cohabitation and marriage.

What would optimal cohabitation look like? Cohabitation is optimal, from the point of view of a couple, when both parties are as fully informed as possible about each other, and when they prefer not to incur the long-term legal obligations of marriage. It is not optimal in a case of fraud, for example when one party claims falsely to be unable to marry. Nor is it optimal in cases where a party believes wrongly that common law marriage exists and carries long-term obligations over property division upon dissolution, which is not the case in England or in most American states, although many suppose the obligations to exist. Empirical work on cohabitation in the UK (e.g. Lewis, Datte, and Sarre, 1999) typically avoids the crucial question "Do you realize that cohabitation does not amount to common law marriage?" Consequently, evidence on the extent of misinformation is largely anecdotal. The impression of many British and American women with whom I have discussed this issue is that it is common to believe wrongly that cohabitation equals common law marriage and carries obligations over property. There are also occasional press reports of high-profile relationships breaking up, where the former cohabiting sexual partner is surprised to find herself turned out of a property. Therefore, in terms borrowed from contract law, at least some cohabitation occurs based on mistake and cannot be optimal for the parties.

Cohabitation is likely to be optimal in cases where it is very clear that both parties understand that they are deliberately avoiding marital law and feel it to be in their best interests to do so. The following very different illustrative cases show that this could be so for quite different reasons. In all cases, assume that the parties properly understand the difference between marriage and cohabitation.

Case 1 – James and Anne
James met Anne when both were teaching at the Optimistic High School for Dangerous Children in Camden Town, London, England. Both were on a similar career grade and intended from the start to maintain their careers. They agreed that if Anne needed to take time off to have children it would be kept to a short period with paid maternity leave. Anne has never felt that she would be disadvantaged, compared with James and relative to her own plans, should they separate later in life – although she is fully aware that a traditional wife could be left with few options in similar circumstances. James and Anne have agreed to finance and own their property jointly, which determines the property division that would apply in the event of separation. They both understand that, in the case of separation, the Child Support Agency would determine child support payments. They believe in their own equality and prefer to cohabit instead of creating asymmetrical obligations.

Case 2 – Nancy and Doug
Nancy is extremely rich and has no wish ever to dilute this family wealth through marriage. She inherited her wealth from her mother, a successful engineer in the USA. Nancy is not a particularly romantic person but welcomes male company and enjoys the social benefits of having a companion at parties and similar events. Doug was a tennis instructor in upstate New York before he met her and is quite clear in his own mind that the main attraction was the immediate increase in standard of living available to him through living with Nancy. He is in effect a self-confessed "gold-digger." They have agreed upon a modest property settlement to be paid to Doug if their cohabitation ends. Doug knows he would never substantially share in Nancy's property or income, either during or after cohabitation, but is happy that he is much better off than he could be under any other option he may have had.

Case 3 – Travis and Laura
As Case 2 but with the wealth levels of the sexes reversed so that Laura cohabits with the wealthy Travis.

Case 4 – Neil and Germaine
Neil and Germaine are part of an alternative culture. Neither has any wealth or significant income. They live simply together with their dog, relying on social security

payments and the proceeds from selling a homeless persons' magazine on the streets of Nottingham, England. Both share a belief that they do not wish to marry. Formalizing their cohabitation would not alter the view they take of each other.

Case 5 – Noël and Gertrude
Two high-profile London show-business personalities cohabit as a try-out before possible marriage. Realizing that they have made a big mistake, they separate, deciding not to marry.

In all of the above cases, unless it was argued that one or both parties were contractually incapable in some way, cohabitation is presumptively optimal. It would seem that they know the facts and are clear, *ex ante*, that they are better off in a cohabiting rather than a married state. The only other possible way to undermine the optimality of cohabitation in these cases would be to find evidence of a harmful external effect imposed onto a third party sufficient to outweigh the benefits to the couples of their freedom of action. The obvious area of possible externality is in relation to children. The social stigma of illegitimacy no longer seems to be strong, and harmful effects on children from the separation of their parents would appear to apply to both dissolved marriage and cohabitation (Popenoe, 1996). Therefore, the external effect would have to be pecuniary and would probably be related to post-dissolution support obligations. However, under the rules applied by modern Child Support Agencies, there is typically no difference between the child support obligations affecting separated former cohabiting parents and divorced parents. It would seem correct to focus largely on the benefits of cohabitation to the couple.

A preliminary conclusion is that cohabitation does not have to be a prelude to marriage to have a perfectly healthy function from an individually rational perspective. It simply needs to be the case that, for a variety of possible reasons, individuals are choosing to avoid marriage and are opting for a form of association that they prefer and therefore deliberately choose.

5   Cohabitation as a response to changed economic conditions

An issue related to the question of optimality concerns whether the growth in cohabitation might simply be a rational response to changed social conditions. The two changed conditions that stand out in this respect, leaving aside for the moment the question of legal change, are women's increased economic independence and the reduced economic fortunes of young men. As noted by Oppenheimer (1988), both the later transition of young men to economic maturity and the improved economic fortunes of independent young women are likely to increase the age at which people marry and make cohabitation more attractive.

Young men's median earnings have declined relative to the median of older men, comparing say 25 and 45 year olds, since the 1960s. Oppenheimer (1988) notes that *absolute* median earnings fell for younger American males, by approximately 20 percent, between 1950 and 1970. Thus, younger men may be taking longer to achieve economic maturity and be less attractive to women as marriage partners simply because unemployment has increased and well-paid employment has decreased for them. Modern careers appear to require greater human capital investment than was the case in earlier decades. Oppenheimer argues that men's economic fortune has always been an important factor driving demographic change, as shown by the statistical link between wars or trade cycles and marriage rates.

Over the same period, roughly since the 1950s, the labor force participation rate of women relative to men, between the ages of 25 and 40, has risen from around 40 percent to 80 percent. Female real wages have also been rising over the period, although these remain lower than male wages. Thus, women are embarking on careers and may not be able fully to predict how the value of these will turn out.

Both the increase in female economic independence and the slower transition to economic maturity for males are likely to increase the uncertainty attached to the value of early marriage. Two responses can be predicted, consistent with Becker's search-theory view of courtship. First, marriage may be delayed as people take more care over extensive search for a long-term sexual partner. The second rational response might be to evaluate a potential partner much more intensively; that is, cohabitation could be a useful mechanism for reducing uncertainty. Risks of unwanted pregnancy that once would have been attached to experimentation have been much reduced by modern contraception. An implication is that, even if cohabitation experiments fail, they were likely useful in avoiding a failed marriage.

If cohabitation is indeed a rational method of reducing uncertainty, public policy aimed at turning cohabitation into marriage is extremely misguided. It could conceivably increase the divorce rate if more people undertook marriages that they would otherwise learn sooner to avoid. The world is very different now compared with the 1930s, and we should not be surprised to find that cohabitation and marriage patterns have altered.

6   Judicial impacts

An alternative, less desirable reason for avoiding marriage and choosing cohabitation is that marital law might be dysfunctional and lead to unintended behavioral consequences. Marriage is optimal if the parties share the largest joint net benefit on their activities in a married state. Remaining married is not optimal for the parties if their joint surplus has become negative, that is, if the value of the sum of psychic and instrumental benefits shows a net cost. It is worth examining some alternative bases for divorce law to see how these could influence the incentives to cohabit.

Consider a case where at least one of the spouses wishes to divorce in a world where divorce can occur only by mutual consent. In such a case, if both parties experienced net costs from marriage, they would simply agree to divorce. If, however, one experienced a net gain while the other had a loss, the one with the loss would have to compensate the other to obtain consent to the divorce. In such a system, we could be sure that no one would be divorced against his or her will and be left worse off than in the marriage. A person unilaterally benefiting from a marriage would have to be bought out, which has two important implications. First, at least those benefits would have to be paid by the spouse wanting the divorce. Secondly, the divorce would not occur unless the joint surplus were really negative, so that the spouse experiencing net costs could buy out the one with net benefits and still feel better off after the change. One could say that only "efficient" divorces would occur and "inefficient" marriages would end, with both parties left better off after the divorce.

In practice, bargaining costs are unlikely to be so high in a general way that they might prevent a system of divorce law requiring mutual consent from working. We have a classic two-person bargaining case, where the parties know each other and communication should not be highly costly. In such cases, economics of law favors bargaining solutions reached from well-defined property rights (Calabresi and Melamed, 1972). Bargaining might be difficult if there are indivisibilities in a marriage, of which child custody may be the best example (Zelder, 1993). It might also be difficult if the law limits bargaining over some assets accrued during the marriage (Dnes, 1998), or if people behave strategically and hold out for more compensation than they really require. These difficulties are not central to the inquiry in this chapter and are not pursued here. The only required point is that a mutual consent system gives a good base line for thinking about efficient dissolution: if people voluntarily accept compensation then they become better off in their own assessment.

If marital law were to impose upon a would-be divorcee the obligation of compensating the other spouse fully for loss of the marriage, then a system of expectation damages like that in contract law would operate (Dnes, 1998). This system would also ensure that only efficient divorces occurred, and the court supervision might better safeguard the interests of children as well as administering a compensation package in a way that limits holding out by spouses. Any other system, for example based on the discretionary adjustment by courts of the spouses' assets and incomes to meet perceived needs, or based on restitution or reliance-based transfers (Trebilcock, 1993), would result in inefficient levels of divorce (and/or marriage). Suppose, for example, that a wife and mother wishes to leave a marriage that has a net cost to her. If the only asset is a house and the rule is to allocate this to the mother, then, under a needs-based system of settling up, the husband has nothing with which to bargain. He cannot persuade her to stay regardless of the level of net surplus that he experiences from continuation of the marriage. The law has in effect sealed off his bargaining possibilities. Prior knowledge of this legal regime could cause men to avoid marriage (or at least to avoid holding, e.g., housing assets in certain ways). Examples can also be given showing that restitution and reliance approaches to settling up are simply inadequate (Dnes, 1998) and create an incentive for avoiding marriage.

A reliance approach to settling up is often suggested by writers emphasizing the opportunity costs incurred by women on entering marriage, and there are elements of this in many systems of family law (although rejected by the Law Commission in England in 1980 as involving excessive speculation). Opportunity cost comprises the value of alternative prospects she gave up. In contract terms, this amounts to awarding reliance damages – the opportunity cost has become akin to wasted expenditure and the suggested rule seeks to put her in the position she would have been in had the marriage never taken place (the *status quo ante*). The implications of the loss of career opportunities for many women either on entering marriage or in stopping work to have children are well covered in Scott and Scott (1998). However, note that an economically strong woman (or one very weak before marriage) leaving a marriage might receive nothing under a reliance approach, as she could be shown to have lost nothing through marriage.

Unless it turns out to be identical to expectation damages, the use of a reliance standard for settling up will tend to make divorce too "cheap." Assuming the woman expected marriage to improve her life, expectation generally exceeds reliance.[6] Some men would divorce their wives, when imposing a requirement to compensate fully for lost promised lifestyle would stop them. Knowing this, women would tend to discount the value of promises and would be less willing to enter marriage. It would be hard for a man to make credible promises. Restitution would give a minimum protection for marriage-specific investments by the woman; she would be compensated for the cost of, for example, giving up a career to have children.

Carbone and Brinig (1991) identify a modern development in divorce law that they describe as a restitution approach, which is distinct from reliance. Courts have increasingly emphasized settlements that repay a wife's domestic support of her husband and children during periods that allowed for the development of business capital, and other contributions to a spouse's career. Although the

---

[6] The sexes could be interchanged in the examples used in this chapter. It would seem typically to be the case that women improve their economic well-being by marriage.

restitution approach is often thought of in relation to American law, one can detect restitution elements in English case law, for example *Gojkovic v. Gojkovic* (1992),[7] and §25(f) of the Matrimonial and Family Proceedings Act 1984 draw attention to the value of a contribution of domestic services. The canonical example would be where the wife undertakes child care so that her husband can develop his professional or business life. Restitution is often cited as an appropriate remedy in contract law when not returning money paid out by the victim of breach would lead to unjust enrichment of the breaching party. Restitution is ideologically acceptable to cultural feminists who wish to emphasize the *repayment* of sacrifices.

Under a restitution approach, compensation is in the form of a share in the market gain supported by the (typically) wife's supportive career choice, for example a share in the returns to a medical degree or a share of the business. Restitution is therefore possible only where *measurable market gains* have resulted from the "sacrifice." The reliance approach, in contrast, is based on measuring the value of the opportunity forgone, for example estimating the value of continuing with a career instead of leaving work to raise children – an input rather than output measure. However, like reliance, restitution undercompensates a wife for loss of a marriage. It is reasonable to assume that expectation exceeds restitution, unless the career investment was in some sense a poor investment. Therefore, similar comments apply: a restitution standard in settling up tends to make divorce cheap and could destabilize entry into marriage.

Separate from consideration of the standard to be used in settling up at divorce is the issue of when it is applied. In contract law, breach leads to compensation under the expectation-damages standard. It is a standard result that this leads to efficient breach (when the gainer can more than compensate the loser) only (Dnes, 1996). Compensation is paid only if there is breach of contract. Under English marital law, there is no necessary connection between breach (not necessarily the same thing as fault) and compensation. It is possible for a husband to leave a wife for another (even wealthy) woman and be expected to pay only the wife's housing needs (plus child maintenance) if she has children. It is also possible for a wife (in some low–medium wealth groups) to abandon her husband and still receive the majority of the assets of the marriage, if these are judged necessary to meet her needs. English law long ago gave up any attempt to ascertain fault in marital failure, which is related to the concept of breach (different because no-fault divorce can still represent breach). The failure to connect breach with damages must completely destabilize any

---

[7] [1992] Fam 40: "Equally important as financial need is . . . the contribution made . . . to the welfare of the family." See also the recent cases of *Cowan v. Cowan*, Court of Appeal, May 17, 2001, and *White v. White* (2000) WLR 1571 (restitution as a reason for a rebuttable presumption of equal division).

contractual elements in marriage. Surely no one believes there are absolutely no contractual elements in marriage, on which assumption the failure is of great concern.

The legal environment surrounding marital dissolution can easily create an adverse incentive structure. People with financial assets, or those likely to accumulate them, may feel that they cannot enter marriage in a way that will protect their long-term wealth relative to the promises they are happy freely to make (bear in mind that prenuptial agreements are still illegal in some jurisdictions, for example England). More importantly, the institution of marriage may become unstable if it is impossible to signal commitment. The signaling is at the very least diluted owing to the mixture of needs-based, restitution, and expectations standards used in settling up after divorce, and given the failure of the law to deal with fault/breach. In this sense, the growth in cohabitation may be nothing more than a rational response to rather messy marital laws.

7   Conclusions

An analysis of the interaction between marital law and individuals' incentive structures suggests that cohabitation is potentially a highly rational state chosen deliberately by people who wish to limit the commitments they assume towards each other, possibly as part of a pattern of careful search for a marriage partner. In that sense it would be counterproductive to turn cohabitation into a form of marriage. This is unfortunately precisely the drift of current legal reforms in several jurisdictions, including England where the Law Commission is expected to propose that cohabitation law may come to resemble marital law fairly closely. Such reform will not encourage marriage, and may even discourage it owing to a reduced scope for managing uncertainty between potential marriage partners. Cohabitation is in need of protection, it would seem, either as a genuine alternative to marriage or as a "try-out."

In order to deflect the criticism that cohabitees, particularly female ones (Barlow and Lind, 1999), do not know what they are doing in entering relationships, it would be useful to require a pre-cohabitation agreement. This could in fact be part of a wider requirement for enforceable prenuptial agreements aimed at encouraging the use of party-designed settling-up remedies when relationships break down. An appropriate role for the state might be to offer models that people could use, perhaps insisting on a standard model if they were unable to construct their own agreements. There seems to be growing general acceptance of the potential value of prenuptial agreements, subject to procedural safeguards (Thorpe, 1998).

At present much cohabitation may be simply a defensive response to marital laws that ignore standard principles of expectation damages used for breach of contract elsewhere in the law. It is enormously puzzling that many people worry about growing divorce rates, increased cohabitation, and the postponement of bearing children but do not ask the obvious question of whether our changed post-war marital law could have played a role in these changes. Cohabitation might well be reduced if marital law were placed on a more rational footing, paying attention to compensation for lost expectation and avoiding as far as possible the reward of breach of contract. Marriage would then become a more reliable institution that could well be attractive to more people. Cohabitation would then be a clear choice of preference and possibly a try-out mechanism. Men may well be avoiding marriage, given the impact of present rules over settling up after divorce and the ease with which no-fault divorce can occur. Many women may not be presented with the opportunity to marry and enjoy stronger safeguards for long-term relationship-specific investments. These are unintended, perverse consequences of irrational marital law.

REFERENCES

Barlow, J. and C. Lind (1999), "A Matter of Trust: The Allocation of Rights in the Family Home," *Legal Studies*, 19, 468–89.
Becker, G. (1991), *A Treatise on the Family*, 2nd edn, Cambridge, MA: Harvard University Press.
Becker, G., E. Landes, and R. Michael (1977), "An Economic Analysis of Marital Instability," *Journal of Political Economy*, 85, 1141–87.
Brinig, M.F. (2000), *From Contract to Covenant*, Cambridge, MA: Harvard University Press.
Calabresi, G. and A.D. Melamed (1972), "Property Rules, Liability Rules and Inalienability: One View of the Cathedral," *Harvard Law Review*, 85, 1089–28.
Carbone, J. and M.F. Brinig (1991), "Rethinking Marriage: Feminist Ideology, Economic Change, and Divorce Reform," *Tulane Law Review*, 65, 954–1010.
Dnes, A.W. (1996), *The Economics of Law*, London: International Thomson Business Press.
   (1998), "The Division of Marital Assets Following Divorce," *Journal of Law and Society*, 25, 336–64.
Lewis, J., J. Datta, and S. Sarre (1999), *Individualism and Commitment in Marriage and Cohabitation*, Research Paper 8/99, London: Lord Chancellor's Department.
Lundberg, S. and R.A. Pollak (1996), "Bargaining and Distribution in Marriage," *Journal of Economic Perspectives*, 10, 139–58.
Oppenheimer, V. (1988), "A Theory of Marriage Timing," *American Journal of Sociology*, 94, 563–91.
Popenoe, D. (1996), *Life without Father*, New York: Free Press.
Posner, R.A. (1992), *Sex and Reason*, Cambridge, MA: Harvard University Press.
Scott, E.S. and R.E. Scott (1998), "Marriage as a Relational Contract," *Virginia Law Review*, 84, 1225–332.
Thorpe, A. (1998), *Report to the Lord Chancellor by the Ancillary Relief Advisory Group*, London: Lord Chancellor's Department.

Trebilcock, M.J. (1993), *The Limits to Freedom of Contract*, Cambridge, MA: Harvard University Press.

Williamson, O.E. (1985), *The Economic Institutions of Capitalism*, New York: Free Press.

Zelder, M. (1993), "Inefficient Dissolutions as a Consequence of Public Goods," *Journal of Legal Studies*, 22, 503–20.

8   Marriage as a signal

Robert Rowthorn

1   Introduction

In Western countries, marriage is an institution for establishing a permanent and sexually exclusive union between a man and a woman, and for helping individuals to signal to each other and to the outside world their desire for such a union. The contractual aspects of marriage have been extensively analyzed in recent years from a law and economics perspective. There has been a prolonged debate about what type of contract is optimal and about the implications of various types of contract for marital behavior and divorce. However, apart from a brilliant, but neglected, paper by William Bishop and a handful of recent articles, the law and economics literature has been largely silent on the role of marriage as a signal.[1]

The structure of this chapter is as follows. There is a brief discussion of the contractual basis of marriage and of some of the current proposals for reform in this area. There is then a section on the role of marriage as a signal. This includes a short exposition of the economic theory of signaling and an application of signaling theory to marriage. The chapter concludes by examining the implications for government policy towards cohabitation and same sex marriage.

2   Marriage as a contract

The original emphasis in the law and economics literature was on the "traditional" family, in which a mother stays at home to look after the children while the father earns money outside to support his dependants. Gary Becker argued that such a division of labor may be efficient because it exploits the comparative advantage of the partners and allows them to develop specialized skills (Becker, 1976 and 1991). However, it can also make the woman extremely vulnerable

I should like to thank Antony Dnes, Allen Parkman, Carlos Rodriguez, and Elaine Tan for their helpful comments on earlier drafts of this paper.

[1] Bishop (1984), Buckley (1999), Posner (1999), Scott and Scott (1999), and Trebilcock (1999). This chapter draws heavily on these writings, especially the excellent papers by Bishop and Trebilcock, which anticipate most of the theoretical arguments presented here.

to family breakdown, since her prospect of finding a decent job may be poor if the relationship ends and she has to earn a living. The purpose of the marriage contract in this context is to deter the man from abandoning the woman and to force him to continue supporting her if he does so (see Landes, 1978; Ellman, 1989). Such an arrangement is efficient because it gives the woman the security required to invest in the family by becoming a specialized homemaker. Although the traditional family is no longer so widespread, the same issues still arise in most families with children. The majority of mothers have a job nowadays, but many of them work only part time and they are still vulnerable to family breakdown. It is often difficult for a part-time worker to transfer to a good full-time job, and in consequence the decision to work part time for the sake of the children may involve a significant financial risk for a woman. Thus, many women still need legal protection to offset the risks arising from specialization, and the traditional justification for marriage continues to apply, albeit with less force than in the past when full-time homemaking was the norm.

Raising children is not the only justification for marriage. Couples derive mutual benefits from living together, including economies of scale in the use of property, financial support in times of hardship, care in times of sickness or infirmity, companionship, and a regular sex life. To reap such benefits the partners must invest resources in their relationship and also turn away from otherwise attractive opportunities. A man may spend years nursing a sick woman back to health, a woman may work to put a man through college, or one of them may spurn an advance from a desirable suitor. Such behavior may involve a great expenditure of time and energy or a significant narrowing of future possibilities for the individual concerned. If individuals feel secure in their relationship, they may willingly engage in such acts of love or commitment, but their willingness may be greatly reduced if they feel the other person is likely to take advantage of them. And if they do engage in such acts, they may suffer a serious loss if the other person does eventually abandon or mistreat them. This explains why there is often such bitterness when a relationship breaks down. One of the partners may have made a huge sacrifice out of love or duty, only to be cast aside or betrayed by the other partner later on. Thus, even in the absence of children, there is a role for marriage as a device for reducing the risk that individuals may be exploited by their partners. From a contractual point of view, marriage can achieve this result by imposing constraints on the future behavior of the partners and ensuring an appropriate settlement in the case of divorce.

Apart from domestic violence, rape, and child abuse, the law rarely intervenes directly in ongoing marriages, and the main legal sanction available to a spouse is the threat of divorce. It is for this reason that divorce figures so prominently in the law and economics literature on marriage. So long as the marriage is expected to continue, the relationship between the partners is governed by social norms in which the main sanctions for misbehavior are the withdrawal of affection and a refusal to cooperate with the other partner. Social norms may also be internalized so that behavior is governed by individual conscience, or else such norms may be enforced by relatives and the wider community. Given the importance of social norms and the ongoing nature of the relationship, marriage is sometimes described as a relational contract (Scott and Scott, 1998). This is an apt description, although it does not imply that the legal framework is irrelevant to marriage. Social norms do not operate in a vacuum. The bargaining power of husband and wife within a marriage, and their incentive for give and take, depend on the legal constraints under which they operate and hence on the legal conditions governing divorce.

The law also performs an important expressive function in the context of marriage. It specifies in general terms how spouses should behave towards each other and the extent to which certain forms of behavior will be penalized in the case of divorce. These legal formulations do not merely reflect current social norms, but also help to shape them. This is a reason why communitarians are often hostile to no-fault divorce. They argue that divorce law should have a moral dimension, not just to ensure justice for injured parties but also to strengthen the moral understanding and commitment of those who get married. Under no-fault divorce, no one is penalized for misconduct or desertion, and the implicit message is that no specific individual is ever primarily responsible for the breakdown of a marriage.

There is evidence that modern legal reforms have led to a number of harmful consequences that were neither intended nor envisaged.[2] They have been a factor behind the massive increase in divorce rates and they have made many divorced women financially poorer than would have been the case under the old fault regime. They have also altered behavior within marriage, causing mothers to overwork and, on one account, causing husbands to become more violent.[3] Scholars in the law and economics tradition accept most of these findings, but there is little agreement about what can be done to reverse the damage. Some, including myself, believe that fault should be an integral part of divorce law, so that the availability and terms of divorce, including the financial settlement and possibly the custody of children, should depend on marital conduct.[4] Others reject this approach entirely, but argue for an effective alimony system (Ellman, 1989) or a prolonged waiting period between the application for divorce and the final termination of the marriage (Scott, 1990; Scott and

---

[2] The evidence regarding the impact of no-fault divorce is summarized in chapter 5 of Parkman (2000).

[3] The impact of no-fault divorce on domestic violence is examined in Brinig and Crafton (1994). For an opposing view, see Ellman and Lohr (1997).

[4] Amongst the many authors who have advocated some role for fault in divorce are Brinig (1999), Dnes (1998), Morse (1996), Rowthorn (1999), and Woodhouse (1994). See also chapter 6 by Katherine Spaht in this volume.

Scott, 1999). In chapter 4 of this volume, Allen Parkman argues that unilateral divorce should be allowed unconditionally in the first five years of marriage if no children are involved. After five years, or when there are children, divorce should be permitted only if one spouse commits a gross breach of the marital contract or if both spouses consent to dissolve the marriage. It is not my intention to discuss divorce law in detail, and I mention these proposals only to point out that all involve some constraint on future behavior and all provide some degree of protection for partners who invest in their marriage. These aspects of the marriage contract are central to the role of marriage as a signal.

3   Marriage as a signal

The intentions of other people are impossible to observe directly and can be only inferred from indirect evidence. Thus, individuals who are seeking a committed relationship must find some credible way of signaling this intention to each other. One such signal is the willingness of a person to get married. Marriage may also be a signal to the rest of the world about the intentions of a couple and the strength of their commitment. Before discussing the role of marriage as a signal, it may be useful to make a digression into the economic theory of signaling.

The theory of signaling

In his pioneering work on the subject, Michael Spence defines market signals as "activities or attributes of individuals in a market which, by design or accident, alter the belief of, or convey information to, other individuals in the market" (Spence, 1974, p. 1).[5] Attributes may be alterable or unalterable. An example of the latter is age. Suppose that older people are not on average very good at mastering a new technology. Then it may be rational for an employer who is seeking workers with this ability to discriminate in favor of younger applicants. Such behavior may have harmful social implications and seem unfair to those older workers who happen to be good with the new technology, but from the employer's point of view it may be perfectly rational if it avoids the need for a costly screening program to evaluate individual applicants.

In the case of alterable attributes, economists distinguish between two kinds of signal: those for which the cost of acquiring a specific attribute is irrelevant to the receiver, and those for which this cost is important because it conveys information about the sender. Signals of the former type are known as "cheap

---

[5] For a good exposition of the theory of signaling see Gibbons (1992).

talk." They are used when it is common knowledge that the sender has no incentive to mislead the receiver in a serious fashion. For example, someone advertising for a holiday companion is likely to give a fairly accurate picture of the intended holiday, since serious misrepresentation might result in a totally unsuitable companion and a miserable time for all concerned. The advertiser may exaggerate the attraction of the holiday a bit, but too much exaggeration is likely to be counterproductive. This will be assumed by anyone scanning the advertisements, so there is no need for the advertiser to make a great effort to convince people that what is said about the holiday is true.

Most signals in economic life are not of the cheap talk variety. In many situations signals are only credible if they involve a significant cost to the sender. For example, an employer may desire workers of above average intelligence and be willing to pay a wage premium of, say, £5 an hour to workers of this type. How can this employer identify such people? If applicants are known to respond truthfully, the employer can simply ask them whether they possess the required attribute. Failing this, a screening program can be set up to weed out undesirable applicants. However, such a program may be expensive or time consuming, so the employer may use some alternative attribute as a proxy for intelligence. An obvious proxy is education. Suppose that intelligent students find it relatively easy to obtain a BA degree and are willing to undertake this modest effort in return for an expected wage premium of £5 an hour. Suppose also that less intelligent students consider such a premium inadequate recompense for the much greater effort they must expend to obtain the required degree. In this case, it will be worthwhile for an employer to offer a £5 premium to anyone with a BA since only intelligent applicants will have bothered to acquire this qualification. Such behavior will be rational for the employer even if the knowledge and experience gained in acquiring a BA are irrelevant to the job in question. This is an example of a "separating equilibrium." The alternative is a "pooling equilibrium" in which all applicants find it profitable to acquire a BA, so that employers can no longer use this qualification as a proxy for intelligence. In this case, the employer may seek an alternative proxy such as a PhD degree.

In the above example a BA degree is an effective signal because it is more costly or difficult to acquire for certain types of individual than for others. This is an illustration of the principle that "honest signals are costly." In the theory of sexual selection in biology this is sometimes known as the "handicap principle," because animals can signal the quality of their genes to potential mates by handicapping themselves in some way. The peacock's tail is a handicap because it makes it more difficult to escape from predators. Thus, if a peahen observes a peacock with an unduly large tail, she can infer that this peacock must be very strong since otherwise it would not have survived. Because strength is a desirable attribute, it is rational for her to seek a mate with a large tail even though tail-size may not in itself be of direct interest. Tail-size acts as an effective signal because acquiring and supporting a large tail imposes a survival cost that only strong birds can afford to pay.[6]

The notion of cost in the context of signaling must be interpreted widely. The cost of transmitting a signal may be either an up-front expenditure of resources, as in the education example, or a constraint on future behavior, such as a legally enforceable guarantee to make good any defect in a product. Constraints on future behavior are often contingent in the sense that they involve a real cost or limitation only if something goes wrong. In the above education example, workers could in theory signal their intelligence and ability by guaranteeing to reimburse employers if they turned out not to have these personal attributes. Provided such a guarantee was enforceable, this might be a more efficient way to signal than spending a great deal of time and effort to acquire a university degree of questionable use in future employment. This illustrates the general point that the voluntary acceptance of enforceable constraints on future behavior can be an efficient way of signaling private information to others. It may be cheaper and more accurate than alternative signals that involve large up-front expenditures of time and money.

Marriage

Marriage can function as a signal in several ways. When an individual offers to marry another person, or accepts such an offer, this is normally taken as an indication of commitment and of desire for an enduring relationship. When a person is married, this normally signifies that he or she is in a committed relationship and is not sexually available to outsiders. The fact that a person is married may be an indication to potential employers or the government about his or her personal characteristics such as health, reliability, or ambition. The fact that a couple is married may be a good indicator of the likely stability of their relationship.

The effectiveness of marriage as a signal frequently depends on its having a significant cost attached. For example, the wedding ceremony may be extremely expensive, or the bride and groom may have to undergo prolonged counseling and other forms of initiation before they get married. The presumption is that only individuals who are serious about marriage will be prepared to shoulder these costs. Alternatively, the mere fact that someone is willing to get legally married may be a good indication of how they view their future relationship. This will be the case if the marriage contract imposes significant constraints on their future behavior, for only someone who is serious will accept such constraints.

It is not always the case that to function as an effective signal marriage must involve substantial costs. Consider a population that consists of only two

---

[6] The "handicap principle" is due to Zahavi (1975).

types of people: those wanting a committed, exclusive sexual relationship and those wanting a casual and open relationship. Suppose that each type would be unhappy with a partner of the other type and that committed individuals never change their preferences. Then individuals have no incentive to mislead each other and there is no need for their signals to be costly. Under these conditions, marriage can function as an effective signal, without the need for it to be accompanied by legal constraints, social sanctions, or large financial expenditures. It is sufficient to make a public manifestation that the individuals concerned are now married. This may be indicated by the exchange of rings for permanent display. By such means these individuals can signal to each other and to the rest of the world that they are now a committed couple and should be treated as such. Outsiders can now regard their relationship as stable and the individuals concerned as sexually unavailable.[7] Those who choose not to get married are presumed not to satisfy these conditions. In this way, a separating equilibrium is established in which the committed couples are married and the uncommitted are not.

The above is an example of signaling through "cheap talk." The example itself is highly simplified, but it mirrors quite well the situation amongst cohabiting couples in some countries. British evidence indicates that cohabiting couples typically break up or eventually get married. Using life history data from the British Household Panel Study, John Ermisch and Marco Francesconi (2000) estimate that about three in five cohabitations turn into marriage and 35 percent dissolve within ten years. Various reasons are given by cohabiting couples as their motive for getting married, such as legal security or pressure from parents, but one of the most frequent is the desire to make a public commitment. In her study of cohabiting mothers in Britain, Susan McRae (1993) found that 53–57 percent of those who had eventually married their partner cited commitment as a primary reason. Thus, where individuals know each other well and their preferences are well aligned, marriage may serve the purely symbolic function of formalizing their commitment and signaling it to the outside world. For this purpose, legal marriage is not important and any socially recognized manifestation of commitment, such as the exchange of rings, would do just as well.

This is the vision that informs much liberal thinking on marriage. According to this vision, marriage should be little more than a costless, non-binding declaration of commitment without either sanctions or constraints. It is not surprising that people with such a viewpoint often regard legal marriage as an unnecessary institution. However, this perspective ignores some of the crucial problems that people face when choosing their partners and shaping their life together. What individuals say about themselves is not always accurate, and to gauge the degree

---

[7] Bishop (1984) called this the "Omar Sharif effect."

of commitment of a potential partner something more than mere words may be required. For example, a man may be looking for a permanent relationship with a woman, perhaps with a view to having children or maybe simply for love and companionship. Some of his potential partners may have a similar aspiration, but there may be others who want a more casual relationship or who are unsure what they feel about him. If he is certain that all potential partners will answer him fully and truthfully, he can discover their feelings simply by asking them. However, he may fear that some of them may deliberately misrepresent what they feel or conceal their doubts. In this case, something more than a mere declaration will be required to convince him. One obvious signal is the willingness of a potential partner to get married. Such a signal is credible only if marriage involves a "cost" that unsuitable partners are unwilling to pay. Provided the cost is great enough, the fact that a potential partner is willing to pay such a cost will be a credible signal of her intentions. Marriage will then act as a signal that establishes a separating equilibrium in which those desiring commitment signal their type by making or accepting an offer to get married, whereas the others avoid such action.

A second problem arises from the fact that individuals and circumstances change. A couple may truthfully say to each other that they want a committed relationship and intend to spend the rest of their life as faithful and loving companions, but one of them may subsequently find this promise more difficult to honor than anticipated. This person may find out unexpected things about family life, his or her feelings and interests may change in an unexpected fashion, or the person concerned may become infatuated with someone else. The existence of a legally binding contract reduces the risk that a marriage will be destroyed by such eventualities. It encourages the partners to invest in their marriage and to avoid behavior that will undermine this relationship. At the same time it helps to shield individuals against the effects of an unprovoked breakdown. Thus, the marriage contract is like a product guarantee. The contract itself shields the other party against risk, and the fact that someone is willing to sign such a contract provides information about this person's intentions and expectations.

The amount of information that is conveyed by the act of marriage depends on the nature of the marriage contract and hence on the laws governing divorce. It also depends on the extent to which married couples have rights and responsibilities that differ from those of the unmarried. During the modern era, divorce has become easier and the penalties for misconduct or unilateral termination have diminished or disappeared altogether. In addition, new rights and responsibilities have been extended to, or imposed on, parents and partners who are not married. In particular, the financial responsibilities of fathers towards their non-marital children have been extended and more vigorously enforced, and in many jurisdictions fathers have acquired new legal rights of access or custody with respect to such children. Opinions may differ as to the desirability of some of these developments, but there is no doubt that their collective effect has been to undermine the value of marriage as a signal.

At one time marriage was a package. If a married woman had a child by her husband, she could normally rely on him to remain with her and provide both financial and practical support for her and the child. If an unmarried woman had a child there was a high probability that the father would abandon her and cause her and her children great hardship. The ability and manifest willingness to get married were thus a clear and valued signal of a man's intention to provide comprehensive long-term support for the woman and any children that might arise from their union. Conversely a woman would stick by her husband, providing him with a secure home and family. These responsibilities were understood by all concerned, and offers of marriage and the acceptance of such offers were unambiguous and reliable signals of commitment. Someone who refused to get married, or was unable to do so because they were already married, was not to be trusted.

Changes in the sphere of public policy and social life have transformed this picture. It has become more difficult for men and women to signal their commitment by getting married, since marriage commits the partners to less than used to be the case. They can walk out of a marriage more easily than in the past, and the financial responsibilities involved in marriage are less clearly differentiated from those of unmarried parents and partners. Yet even in the most liberal jurisdictions there still remain some psychic and practical obstacles to divorce, and marriage still involves certain rights and responsibilities that do not apply to the unmarried. These "costs" ensure that marriage retains some of its former credibility as a signal of commitment. Moreover, recent changes in divorce law may have strengthened certain aspects of the signaling role. In many jurisdictions, a divorced wife has gained new rights to share in the pension or future earnings of her former husband. To the extent that these rights are not extended to unmarried sexual partners, this change makes it more costly for a man to terminate his marriage and hence makes his decision to get married a more credible signal of commitment. Conversely, the same development reduces the cost to a woman of terminating her marriage, thereby reducing her ability to signal her commitment by getting married. Thus, the impact of recent changes on the signaling function of marriage has been ambiguous. This does not alter the overall conclusion that marriage has become a less effective signal of commitment in the modern era.

Standard form

In most jurisdictions, there is a standard form of marriage contract that specifies in general terms the responsibilities of the spouses to each other, the conditions on which the marriage can be terminated, and the principles that govern the divorce settlement. Standard forms vary across jurisdictions, but within each jurisdiction there is normally only one such form. The states of Arizona and Louisiana are unusual because they now have two standard form contracts, one for ordinary, easy-to-dissolve marriage and the other for fault-based covenant marriage. Many jurisdictions permit parties to contract around the standard form, so that certain provisions can be modified through pre- or post-nuptial agreements. However, the scope for such bargaining is normally limited and certain features of the standard form are compulsory.

The following questions arise with regard to standard form marriage contracts. Why are such contracts required? How do they relate to the signaling function of marriage? How many different standard forms should there be? What elements should they have in common? And what elements should be compulsory for all marriage contracts?

Standard form marriage contracts have a number of advantages. They reduce transactions costs by providing the parties with a template that has already been honed to shape by experience, thereby reducing the need to invent everything from scratch. They safeguard individuals from making catastrophic blunders. And they facilitate signaling by ensuring that all marriages within a given jurisdiction share certain basic features, so that people have a common understanding of what it means to get married or to be married. This is of central importance to the role of marriage as a signal. If every couple were to write their own marriage contract from scratch, without external guidance, the result would be chaos. There would be such a huge diversity of contracts that the informational content of knowing someone is married would be virtually nil.

It can be argued that modifications to the standard form contract should be forbidden on the grounds that prenuptial bargaining is harmful to marriage. Such bargaining encourages an egocentric and calculating approach to marriage and may result in misleading signals regarding the partners' degree of commitment and their belief in the likely durability of their marriage. If modifications were forbidden, it would also be easier for the outside world to understand what it means for a couple to be married, since the legal basis of everybody's marriage would be the same and hence common knowledge. However, this is rather an extreme position. There are certain details of the marriage contract, such as the precise allocation of property in the case of divorce, which are not of great significance to outsiders, and some variation in these areas is feasible without seriously damaging the signaling function of marriage. The outside world is mainly concerned with how committed the members of a couple are to each other, the fact that they will support each other during their marriage, and how sexually exclusive is their relationship. The fact that they are married is mainly of interest because it provides information on these matters. For example, an adoption agency may give preference to married couples because it is interested in the stability of the family unit into which its children are placed. An individual who is seeking a sexual partner is interested in whether a particular person is married because this provides information about this person's availability. As far as the outside world is concerned, the main signaling function of marriage is to convey the message that the members of a couple have a sexually exclusive, life-long commitment of mutual support. Contractual modifications that seriously inhibit this function should be forbidden.[8]

Signals have externalities. The effectiveness of any given marriage as a sig-nal depends on the nature of other marital contracts and on the behavior of people in other marriages. Suppose it became a common practice to delete from the marriage contract the vows of fidelity, permanence, and mutual sup-port. Who would then know that my contract still contained such promises? If adultery and divorce are widespread, who is to know that my marriage is different? If I wish to signal that my own marriage is a permanent and sexually exclusive commitment, then I have an interest in having such a commitment included as a compulsory part of all marriage contracts. I also have an inter-est in the existence of social and legal mechanisms that induce other married couples to stay together and remain sexually exclusive. Every act of adultery reduces the credibility of marriage as a signal of sexual exclusivity. Every time someone abandons a spouse it undermines the credibility of marriage as a signal of commitment. Every time a family dissolves it undermines the faith of children in other families that their own parents will stay together. If there are no children involved and the adults concerned are agreed, it may ap-pear that divorce is a purely private affair that harms no one. But this is not correct. Every divorce, even by mutual consent, increases the perceived risk that other marriages will dissolve and reduces the credibility of marriage as a signal of permanence. Marriage is like a professional qualification, whose value as a signal depends crucially on its reputation. Competent professionals and their potential clients have a common interest in maintaining the stan-dard of professional examinations and discouraging behavior that undermines public confidence in their qualifications. Likewise, committed couples and so-ciety at large have a common interest in discouraging modifications to the marriage contract or forms of behavior that undermine the reputation of marriage.

---

[8] There are also non-signaling reasons for restricting modifications to the marriage contract. Many jurisdictions ban modifications that significantly increase the probability that one of the spouses or their children will become a claimant on the welfare state. For example, it is normally forbidden to remove the standard provisions that spouses have the legal responsibility to support each other in times of misfortune while they are married or to provide for children under a certain age following divorce.

Covenant marriage

As mentioned above, the states of Arizona and Louisiana now have two forms of marriage, one is the ordinary, easy-to-dissolve type and the other is fault-based covenant marriage.[9] Couples can convert from ordinary to covenant marriage, but the reverse transition is not allowed. How will the existence of such a choice affect the signaling function of marriage? The answer partly depends on the experience of those who opt for covenant marriage. If only strongly committed couples choose covenant marriage, then this form of marriage will become associated with a low divorce rate and a high degree of marital satisfaction. Covenant marriage will then be widely interpreted as a signal of serious commitment. This is an argument for not forcing the pace by pressuring unsuitable couples into covenant marriage, because many of them might later divorce and undermine the reputation of this form of marriage. Such a danger was recognized by the initiators of covenant marriage, and it helps to explain why couples contemplating such a marriage are required to undergo premarital counseling to make clear the responsibilities and constraints involved.

How will the two forms of marriage coexist in practice? How will the existence of covenant marriage affect the signaling function of ordinary marriage? There are several conceivable scenarios, depending on the future popularity of covenant marriage. It may be that covenant marriage never really takes off, so that only a small percentage of couples, mostly of a strong religious persuasion, choose this type of marriage and the rest, including many highly committed couples, choose ordinary marriage. In this case, the social meaning of ordinary marriage will be largely unaffected and this type of marriage will retain its present role as a moderately credible signal of commitment. An alternative scenario is that all highly committed couples eventually choose covenant marriage, some immediately and others after a period of ordinary marriage. In this case, the average degree of commitment amongst those in ordinary marriages will decline significantly and ordinary marriage will lose much of its present credibility as a signal. Ordinary marriage will then become little more than a form of registered cohabitation.

Such a situation would give rise to interesting signaling issues. Would the same terminology continue to be used for both types of marriage? Would the words "husband" and "wife" be used for both types of spouse? Would people in covenant marriages develop a distinctive terminology so as to signal clearly their high level of commitment? Or would they seek to downgrade the terminology applied to people in ordinary marriages. One strategy would be to have ordinary marriages reclassified as domestic partnerships and the individuals involved legally defined as partners rather than husband and wife. If covenant

---

[9] Katherine Spaht in chapter 6 in this volume describes Louisiana covenant marriage.

marriage eventually takes off, there is likely to be a linguistic tussle between covenant and ordinary marriage, just as there is today between ordinary marriage and cohabitation. It is common in liberal circles to use the term "partners" indiscriminately to describe both married and unmarried couples. Many married couples resent this practice because they do not wish to be conflated with cohabiting couples, whose degree of commitment is ambiguous and is on average well below that of married couples. They wish to signal their commitment by using distinctive terms such as "husband," "wife," or "spouse," and they desire others to acknowledge this distinction by also using these terms. Likewise, couples in covenant marriages may come to resent having to share the use of terms such as "husband" and "wife" with couples in ordinary marriages, where the degree of commitment is ambiguous and is on average well below that in the typical covenant marriage.

Attitudes and behavior

This chapter has argued that two central notions should be a compulsory part of any marriage contract: commitment and sexual exclusivity. This is not just an arbitrary choice, but is in conformity with popular conceptions of what marriage should be. There is widespread support for the idea of marriage as a union for life. Despite the high rate of divorce, this is still an aspiration for most people and the outcome for many. For example, in 1994 the British Lord Chancellor's Department commissioned a survey into attitudes towards marriage (MORI, 1994). Of those questioned, 72 percent agreed that "marriage should be forever," a significant increase compared with three years previously (58 percent). Disagreement was registered by only 14 percent. Surveys also show that adultery is widely regarded as a serious betrayal of trust, and in practice extramarital affairs are rather uncommon. According to the British National Survey of Sexual Attitudes and Lifestyles, extramarital sex is considered always or mostly wrong by 79 percent of men and 84 percent of women (Wellings et al., 1994, p. 249). For 16–24 year olds, the figures are 82 percent and 87 percent, respectively. The picture is similar in the United States. In their study of sexual practices, Edward Laumann and his colleagues report that about 90 percent of American adults believe that extramarital sex is always wrong or almost always wrong (Laumann et al., 1994, table B4). For males aged 18–34 the figure is also around 90 percent, indicating that such views are widely held across the entire age spectrum and are not just a hangover from the past.

Not everyone lives up to their beliefs, so it is not surprising that some people who believe that adultery is wrong have had an extramarital affair. Even so, most married people claim to have been faithful to their spouse. In the American survey referred to above, 25 percent of husbands and 15 percent of wives, including those now divorced, admitted to having had an extramarital affair at some time in their married lives (Laumann et al., 1994, table 5.15). These figures are presumably an underestimate, since there must have been some respondents who were ashamed to admit to their adultery. But, given their apparent willingness to answer a wide range of other intimate questions about sexual behavior, it seems unlikely that there were many respondents who were too embarrassed to confess to an extramarital affair. Even though adultery is fairly common, it is reasonable to assume that most married people remain faithful to their spouse, and where a spouse does have an extramarital affair this is mostly an isolated lapse rather than a continuing pattern.

Despite more liberal attitudes towards sex and higher divorce rates, it is clear that most people continue to regard marriage as a sexually exclusive union for life and a large number of them still manage to achieve this ideal. Thus, even today marriage remains a moderately credible signal of sexual exclusivity.

4   Cohabitation

Communitarians and other supporters of marriage frequently argue that the current legal distinction between marriage and cohabitation should be retained, even strengthened.[10] Moreover, public policy should explicitly regard marriage as a signal of commitment and stability, and for this reason the institution should be given a privileged status as compared with cohabitation. In my own country, Britain, such views are normally greeted with a chorus of objections: "Why be so intolerant?" "People should not have to get married if they do not want to." "A cohabiting couple can be just as committed to each other as a married couple." "It's wrong to discriminate against cohabitation." "Why cannot we be treated just like a married couple?" In evaluating such objections, a distinction should be drawn between homosexuals and heterosexuals. At present, homosexuals cannot get legally married and their failure to do so indicates nothing about the nature of their relationship or intentions. However, the situation is quite different for heterosexuals, for whom marriage is legally possible. If heterosexuals choose to cohabit instead of getting married this indicates something about the likely stability of their relationship. There is evidence from many countries that marriages are on average more durable than cohabiting unions.[11] This applies whether or not there are children present. In the case of Britain, Kathleen Kiernan has estimated that 8 percent of couples who get married before their first child is born split up within five years of the birth (Kiernan, 1999, table 11). The figure is 25 percent for cohabiting couples who marry after their baby is born, and 52 percent for those cohabiting couples who never marry. Thus, even for those couples who are cohabiting when their first child is born,

[10] For a clear statement of this viewpoint, see Deech (1980).
[11] Chapter 2 of Morgan (2000) contains a good survey of the evidence regarding the instability of cohabiting relationships.

subsequent marriage is an indicator of stability. Using a different data source, John Ermisch estimates that, for those cohabiting couples who never marry, around five out of six unions will break up within ten years of the birth of their first child (Ermisch, 1997, p. 128). A similar pattern can be observed elsewhere in most Western countries, although the contrasts are not usually as extreme as in Britain.[12] Even in Sweden, where cohabitation has been common for many years, cohabiting couples with a young child are almost four times more likely to break up than are their married counterparts (Kiernan, 1999, table 11). The instability of cohabiting unions is not surprising since it is normally the premise of cohabitation that there is no life-long commitment and the option of breaking up is consciously preserved. People who view themselves as two separate individuals are more likely to leave a relationship than are those who view themselves as two halves of a permanent couple. Despite the high divorce rate, the best statistical predictor of whether or not a couple will stay together is whether or not they are married. It is therefore reasonable to regard marriage as a signal of commitment and stability.

Marriage is also a marker for many other outcomes.[13] Sexual fidelity tends to be higher amongst married couples than amongst those who cohabit. Married people are, on average, physically healthier and have lower mortality rates than single, cohabiting, divorced, or separated people. They suffer from less anxiety, depression, and other mental ailments. They report higher rates of sexual satisfaction. They live more regular lives and engage in less substance abuse and other harmful activities. Married men are on average better employees than other men and this is reflected in their superior earnings and more rapid progression up the promotion ladder. Married couples are on average less violent to each other than other couples, and there is less physical and sexual abuse of children when their parents are married (Stets and Straus, 1995). One of the riskiest situations for a child is to live in a stepfamily (Daly and Wilson, 1998). However, there is evidence to suggest that the incidence of abuse in stepfamilies is much lower if the adults concerned are married than if they are merely cohabiting (Whelan, 1994).

Correlation and causation are not the same thing. The observed correlations between marriage and attributes such as stability and health are partly due to selection bias. The fact that married couples split up less often than cohabiting couples is not simply because marriage adds stability to a relationship. The couples who get married are on average more committed than those who cohabit, and for this reason alone we should expect their unions to be more durable. Likewise, marriage rates may be higher amongst people who are healthier than average, or more reliable or less prone to violence or child abuse. But this is surely not the whole story. It is implausible to believe that the observed

[12] For evidence on Western Europe see Kiernan (1999, table 11).
[13] Stanton (1997) and Waite and Gallagher (2000) provide extensive surveys of this topic.

correlations are entirely due to selection bias and that marriage has no effect on behavior. In a book devoted to the subject of men, the American sociologist, Steve Nock, shows how their behavior changes significantly when they get married (Nock, 1998).[14] Marriage alters both the incentives that men face and their preferences. When they get married, men become subject to conventional rules and social expectations that make them more reliable and more committed partners. They take on the social role of husband. As husbands they are expected to be more reliable than other men, and they internalize these expectations by starting to think and act like husbands. Similar changes may also occur when women get married, although the effects may be weaker, because they tend to be more reliable than men in the first place.

A number of other studies reach similar conclusions regarding the causal impact of marriage on behavior and relationships. Writing in the *Journal of Marriage and the Family*, Catherine Ross states,

The positive effect of marriage on well-being is strong and consistent, and the selection of the psychologically healthy into marriage or the psychologically unhealthy out of marriage cannot explain the effect.[15]

In an interesting econometric analysis, George Akerlof (1998) finds that marriage has a causal impact on the behavior of men, but his results suggest that this effect may be diminishing through time. This may reflect the fact that marriage has been undermined by legal and cultural change and the institution is no longer taken so seriously as in the past. Even so, despite some decline in its influence, marriage is still correlated with positive outcomes and it still has a significant behavioral impact.

To the extent that marriage has socially beneficial effects on behavior, it is reasonable for society to encourage couples to marry rather than to cohabit. But, even if marriage did not affect behavior, it might still play an important role as a signal. If we have close personal knowledge of a couple, then we can assess the likely stability of their relationship irrespective of whether or not they are married. In the absence of such personal knowledge about the couple, we must rely on more accessible indicators such as their marital status. Knowing whether or not a couple is married conveys valuable information to outsiders about the likely stability of their relationship, their capacity as parents, and other personal attributes such as health or reliability. Such information is of a probabilistic nature, since not every married couple or cohabiting couple will conform to their stereotypes. Even so, probabilities are important and much of what we do in life is based on statistical information rather than detailed knowledge of individual cases. The world at large cannot look into a person's

---

[14] Waite (1995) and Akerlof (1998) survey the role of selection bias in the context of marriage.
[15] Ross (1995, p. 129) cited in Waite (1995).

heart or investigate his or her life in detail. It must rely on simple indicators or signals – of which marital status is one of the most reliable and readily available. It would be an even more reliable signal if the marriage contract were more binding than at present.

How should governments respond to the signal of marriage? Should they give special financial support to married couples that is not available to the unmarried? This was theoretically the position in Britain until the Labor government recently abolished the married couples' tax allowance. Certain other European countries also give tax privileges to couples who are married. These are often attacked on the grounds that they discriminate unfairly against people who are not married. But why is it unfair to give special tax treatment to an institution that benefits society in terms of greater stability, better health, and lower criminality? Insurance companies offer reduced premiums to customers who fit locks on their windows or who do not smoke. By the same logic, it is legitimate for the state to support a form of life that is beneficial to the rest of society and reduces future claims on the public purse. However, there is a potential moral hazard here. If the subsidy to marriage is too great, then many uncommitted people may be induced into marriage and their subsequent behavior may bring the institution into disrepute and hence undermine its value as a signal.

Although theoretically interesting, the issue of subsidizing marriage is not of great practical importance at the present time. In most countries, the few overt subsidies to marriage that currently exist are more than offset by the hidden bias against marriage elsewhere in the tax and benefit system. The relevant question is not whether to privilege marriage but how to eliminate the present bias against this institution. Welfare benefits based on "need" discriminate against marriage by supporting lone parents and financing some of the costs of separation or failure to marry. They may also indirectly subsidize cohabitation because some of these "lone" parents may have an undeclared partner living somewhere (Smart and Stevens, 2000). America's Earned Income Tax Credit and its British equivalent also discriminate against marriage and encourage lone parenthood, since they typically provide greater subsidies to working lone parents than to married couples.[16] It would be a major task merely to remove such distortions and establish a tax and benefit system that is genuinely neutral with respect to marriage. It is not clear how this could be done without impoverishing still further the vast number of lone parents who are already poor and

---

[16] The Working Families Tax Credit in the UK is modeled on the American Earned Income Tax Credit (EITC). Statistical analysis by Eissa and Hoynes (1999) suggests that the EITC has encouraged divorce and extramarital child bearing amongst certain sections of the US population. This effect comes about because lone parents who work in a low-paid job get a large tax credit that is not available if they are living with a spouse whose income is sufficient to lift them out of poverty. The Working Families Tax Credit in the UK operates in a similar fashion.

heavily dependent on welfare benefits or tax credits. Thus, although it might be theoretically desirable to support marriage through the tax and benefit system, this goal seems unattainable at present. It would be hard enough to eliminate the current fiscal bias against marriage.

Quite apart from the tax and benefit system, there are other areas where marriage might be used as a criterion for favorable treatment. In some jurisdictions only married people are allowed to bring their partners into the country, or adopt children, or get public finance for fertility treatment. These practices have been attacked as unfair and have been partially or entirely abandoned in many jurisdictions. Such attacks are mostly misplaced. To give permission for the immigration of a partner or the adoption of a child, or to authorize payment for fertility treatment, the public authorities need a credible signal of commitment from the couple concerned. Marriage can provide such a signal. If the partners concerned are legally able to get married, and fail to do so, it is reasonable to infer that they lack the required degree of commitment. This may not be true in every case, but policy must be based on information that is easily available to the authorities, not on private knowledge that is hidden from them.

5   Same sex marriage

For a heterosexual couple, marital status conveys valuable information about the likely stability of their relationship. If they reject marriage, it is rational for the world at large to question the strength of their commitment. Such an argument does not usually apply to homosexual couples, since legal marriage is not at present an option for them in most jurisdictions. Should legal marriage therefore be extended to same-sex couples? Alternatively, should they be provided with some legal equivalent to marriage such as a Vermont-style civil union? Same-sex couples wishing to signal and reinforce their commitment would clearly benefit from an established institution that gave their relationship public recognition and legal backing. This could also be of benefit to outsiders wishing to evaluate the degree of commitment of same-sex couples.[17]

However, there are also many objections. Some are based on the view that homosexuality is a curable disorder or that homosexual practice is a sin that should not be condoned by official recognition. There is also the argument that marriage is intended for the raising of children and is not therefore appropriate for homosexuals.[18] Many opponents, such as Frank Buckley (1999), believe that

---

[17] Jonathan Rauch (1996) makes these points in a powerful article in *The New Republic* advocating same-sex marriage.

[18] These issues are discussed at length in Sullivan (1996). An extensive collection of writings on same-sex marriage, including the previously cited article by Rauch, is contained in Sullivan (1997). See also Wald (1999).

same-sex marriage is the slippery slope. Once this kind of marriage is permitted, what is there to stop polygamy or marriage between siblings or even between parents and their children? There is also the impact on children to consider. Practically all children currently raised by same-sex couples are biologically related to one of the partners and are usually children from a previous hetero-sexual relationship. In most jurisdictions, the adoption of unrelated children by same-sex couples is either very difficult or illegal. If same-sex marriages were legalized, such restrictions would probably be relaxed and it would become more common for same-sex couples to raise unrelated children. Opponents of same-sex marriage claim that this would be damaging to the children concerned, whereas supporters deny this claim.[19]

Yet another objection, which is more relevant to the main theme of this chapter, concerns the signaling function of marriage. Western society places a high premium on marriage as a life-long, sexually exclusive union and the opponents of same-sex marriage believe that homosexual couples would not subscribe to, or abide by, these rules. They would reject the ideal of life-long monogamy. They would divorce and remarry even more frequently than heterosexuals do at present and they would be highly promiscuous while married. Such attitudes and behavior, it is claimed, would bring the institution of marriage as a whole into disrepute and undermine its value for heterosexual couples and society in general.

In evaluating these claims, it should be borne in mind that, as a proportion of the total population, the number of homosexuals likely to get married is extremely small. Modern estimates suggest that about 2 percent of the population are homosexual and only a modest fraction of these would get married.[20] The likely scale of same-sex marriages can be gauged from the Danish experience. In 1989 Denmark introduced a legal arrangement known as "registered domestic partnership," which apart from adoption rights gave same-sex couples most of the legal recognition associated with heterosexual marriage. Since then about 5,000 gays and lesbians have registered their partnerships, of which 700 have subsequently broken up (Egerton, 2000). Given that Denmark has 5 million inhabitants, these figures imply that 1 person in 1,200 is currently living in a registered same-sex partnership, and 1 person in 7,000 is an ex-member of

---

[19] Research on the subject of unrelated adoptions is sparse, so it is difficult to make an informed judgment on the issue. Chapter 7 of Sullivan (1997) contains a number of articles that survey the research on children raised by homosexuals. In one of these articles, Belcastro and his colleagues point out that most of the research in this area is seriously defective. Moreover, this research is mainly concerned with children brought up by lesbian mothers and provides little evidence about what happens to children brought up by gay fathers. The surveys say nothing about what happens to children raised by same-sex couples to whom they are not biologically related – which is not surprising since this is still a rare event.

[20] Laumann et al. (1994, fig. 8.1) report that around 1.4 percent of females and 2.8 percent of males have a "same-gender" sexual identity. Black et al. (2000) provide a careful discussion of the likely accuracy of such classifications.

such a partnership. No matter how they behaved, it is difficult to believe that the activities of such a tiny, clearly differentiated minority could have a decisive impact on public perceptions of heterosexual marriage. However, given the weakened state of this institution, even a small blow might be quite damaging. Thus, despite the small number of people involved, there is a legitimate public interest in the likely behavior of same-sex couples following marriage.

How would married same-sex couples behave? There are many homosexuals who reject the idea of monogamy and life-long commitment, but most of these also reject the idea of getting married. There are also homosexuals who do believe in life-long commitment and who support same-sex marriage because it would help them to signal their commitment to the outside world and reinforce their bond with their partner. The Danish experience with registered partnerships suggests that it would be mostly homosexuals of the latter type who would choose to get married. Registered same-sex partnerships have proved to be fairly stable and only one-seventh of the partnerships formed since 1989 have so far dissolved.

What about extramarital sex? Would same-sex couples play by the conventional rules? One of the best-known advocates of same-sex marriage, Andrew Sullivan, takes quite a stern view of adultery (Sullivan, 1997, pp. 280–1). Others, such as Evan Davies and Jonathan Rauch, support a life long commitment to mutual care and support, but believe that gay men are rather promiscuous and that marriage based on sexual exclusivity is inappropriate for them (Rauch, 1996; Davies and Phillips, 1999). This is consistent with the view that men in general are by nature promiscuous and it is only women who restrain them. American and British surveys provide the following evidence about promiscuity amongst homosexuals.[21] The average gay man has two to three times as many sexual partners as his heterosexual counterpart.[22] However, the high overall average for gay men reflects the activities of a promiscuous subgroup; there are many homosexual males who appear to be monogamous. In the British survey, over 40 percent of gay men reported only one sexual partner in the previous five years, whereas a quarter reported more than ten sexual partners over this time span (Wellings et al., 1994, fig. 5.14). The same survey confirms the stereotype that lesbian couples form strong and exclusive bonds. More than 60 percent of lesbians reported only one sexual partner over the previous five years and only a handful reported more than ten sexual partners during the period. However, the equivalent American survey found that lesbians average three to five times as many sexual partners as do heterosexual women (Laumann et al., 1994, table 8.4). As in the case of gay men, the high average may reflect the activities of a promiscuous subgroup.

---

[21] The evidence is taken from Laumann et al. (1994) and Wellings et al. (1994).

[22] Laumann et al. (1994, table 8.4) and Wellings et al. (1994, table 5.10).

Although many homosexuals are promiscuous or have very unstable partnerships, the significance of this for same-sex marriage is unclear. Many promiscuous homosexuals would probably reject the option of marriage, and others might behave differently once they got married. If it once became the norm for same-sex marriages to endure and to be sexually exclusive, then marriage would be the ideal institution for homosexuals who wanted such a union. By getting married they could signal their intentions to each other and to the outside world, just as in the case of heterosexual marriage. To establish such a norm, the main problem would be to ensure that marriage was reserved for homosexuals who were suitably committed. If divorce or promiscuity became the norm in same-sex marriages, then marriage would no longer be of much use to homosexuals wishing to signal or reinforce their exclusive commitment.

The only jurisdiction to establish full same-sex marriage is the Netherlands, which has recently extended the existing marriage law for heterosexuals to include same-sex couples. However, following the lead of Denmark, a number of European and other jurisdictions now register domestic partnerships and extend to registered couples many of the rights and responsibilities traditionally associated with marriage. In some cases, both heterosexual and homosexual couples can register their partnerships, and these partnerships are really just a form of recognized cohabitation. Such an arrangement does not satisfy those homosexuals who desire the kind of public recognition that is traditionally associated with marriage. They are much happier with the recent initiative in Vermont, where a same-sex couple can now form an officially recognized "civil union" that involves the same vows and most of the same legal rights and responsibilities as in a heterosexual marriage. Unlike Denmark and most other European countries, which still restrict the right of same-sex couples to adopt unrelated children, the parties to a civil union in Vermont will have the same adoption rights as married heterosexual couples. Civil unions are not available to heterosexuals and they are in effect same-sex marriage by another name.

Although they welcome Vermont-style civil union and similar arrangements, many activists see them as merely a transitional phase in the struggle for full same-sex marriage. They reject the "separate but equal" philosophy that underlies the new Vermont law and their ultimate objective is to obliterate any legal distinction between same- and opposite-sex marriage. Their ideal law would merely refer to marriage between two "persons" without reference to their sex. Although comprehensible from a psychological or political standpoint, this approach ignores the question of signaling. Suppose there is on average a major difference in the attitudes of homosexual and heterosexual couples towards external sexual activity. Then pooling the two types of couple within the same institution called "marriage" may not be in the interests of either. Homosexual couples may find themselves under pressure to conform to a dominant norm of sexual fidelity that does not suit them, whereas heterosexual couples may feel that their own type of marriage is undermined by the adulterous behavior of married homosexual couples. This problem could be minimized by having distinct legal institutions for the two types of couple – marriage for heterosexuals and civil union or registered partnership for homosexuals. Both institutions might involve a similar degree of commitment in terms of permanence and caring, but their expectations with regard to sexual behavior would be different.

6   Conclusions

Signaling plays a central role in economic and social life. Cooperation of any kind requires communication and this in turn requires a means of transmitting information. Marriage functions as a signal on at least two levels. By deciding to get married, individuals signal to each other their desire for a durable relationship and their intention to behave in the appropriate fashion. Their decision to marry also signals to the outside world that they have a committed relationship. Such information is of great importance to both the individuals themselves and society in general, especially the public agencies that are concerned with family related issues. What is meant by commitment varies across and within societies. In Western countries, marriage is widely understood as a commitment to a permanent, supportive, and sexually exclusive relationship. This is what the vast majority of people wish to signal by getting married. However, modern legal and social trends have greatly reduced the credibility of this signal. It is now much easier to terminate a marriage, and the penalties for abandonment or serious misconduct, such as adultery, have been eliminated or greatly reduced, and divorce rates have mushroomed. As a result, marriage is no longer such an effective signal of commitment, either for the individuals concerned or for society at large. This represents a major loss of information that makes it more difficult to sort out the committed from the uncommitted. Even so, marriage has not entirely lost its credibility. Commitment is still much higher, on average, amongst married couples than amongst cohabiting couples, and marriage is still the best predictor of durability. It is therefore rational for individuals to get married if they wish to signal their commitment. It is also rational for public agencies concerned with the stability of families to treat married couples differently from unmarried couples. Such behavior on the part of public agencies is sometimes condemned as a form of discrimination akin to racial discrimination. This is an inappropriate analogy. Unlike race, marriage is mostly a voluntary condition, and couples who live together without getting married normally do so by choice. Same-sex couples may be an exception to this rule since legal marriage is not at present an option for them in most jurisdictions.

From a signaling point of view, there is a case for allowing same-sex couples to get legally married, as in the Netherlands, or to establish some equivalent legal institution exclusively for same-sex couples, such as civil union or registered cohabitation, as in Vermont and a number of European countries. To function as an effective signal of commitment, such an institution would have to involve significant rights and responsibilities for the homosexual partners, just as marriage does for heterosexual couples. It must be stressed that these observations on the legal recognition of same-sex unions are concerned only with certain aspects of signaling. The question of legal recognition for such unions is a complex one and involves many diverse issues that were not really explored in this chapter. The chapter should not therefore be taken as a call for the legal recognition of same-sex unions, although some of its arguments would tend to favor such a policy.

REFERENCES

Akerlof, George A. (1998), "Men without children," *Economic Journal*, 108, 287–309.
Becker, Gary S. (1976), *The Economic Approach to Human Behavior*, Chicago: University of Chicago Press.
(1991), *A Treatise on the Family*, Cambridge, MA: Harvard University Press.
Bishop, William (1984) " 'Is He Married?' Marriage as Information," *University of Toronto Law Journal*, 34, 245–63.
Black, Dan, Gary Gates, Seth Sanders, and Lowell Taylor (2000), "Demographics of the Gay and Lesbian Population in the United States: Evidence from Available Systematic Data Sources," *Demography*, 37, 139–154.
Brinig, Margaret F. (1999), "Contracting around No-Fault Divorce," in Frank H. Buckley (ed.), *The Fall and Rise of Freedom of Contract*, Durham, NC: Duke University Press.
Brinig, Margaret F. and Steven M. Crafton (1994), "Marriage and Opportunism," *Journal of Legal Studies*, 23, 869–94.
Buckley, Frank H. (1999), "Marriage and Homosexuals," in Douglas W. Allen and John Richards (eds.), *It Takes Two*, Toronto: C. D. Howe Institute.
Daly, Martin and Margo Wilson (1998), *The Truth about Cinderella: a Darwinian View of Parental Love*, London: Weidenfeld & Nicolson.
Davies, Evan and Melanie Phillips (1999), *A Fruitless Marriage? Same-Sex Couples and Partnership Rights*, London: Social Market Foundation.
Deech, Ruth (1980), "The Case against the Legal Recognition of Cohabitation," in John M. Eekelaar and Sanford N. Katz (eds.), *Marriage and Cohabitation in Contemporary Societies*, Toronto: Butterworth.
Dnes, Antony W. (1998), "The Division of Marital Assets Following Divorce," *Journal of Law and Society*, 25, 336–64.
Egerton, Brooks (2000), "Denmark Settles into Partnership Law while Gay-Union Debate Rages in U.S.," *Dallas Morning News*, 30 April.
Eissa, Nada and Hilary W. Hoynes (1999), "Good News for Low-Income Families? Tax-Transfer Schemes and Marriage," Department of Economics, University of California, Berkeley, mimeo.

Ellman, Ira M. (1989), "The Theory of Alimony," *California Law Review*, 77, 3–81.

Ellman, Ira M. and Sharon Lohr (1997), "Marriage as Contract, Opportunistic Violence, and Other Bad Arguments for Fault Divorce," *University of Illinois Law Review*, 3, 719–72.

Ermisch, John (1997), "Premarital Cohabitation, Childbearing and the Creation of One-Parent Families," in Inga Persson and Christina Jonung (eds.), *Economics of the Family and Family Policies*, London: Routledge.

Ermisch, John and Marco Francesconi (2000), "Cohabitation in Great Britain: Not for Long, but Here to Stay," *Journal of the Royal Statistical Society*, Series A, 163(2), 153–72.

Gibbons, Robert (1992), *A Primer in Game Theory*, New York: Prentice Hall.

Kiernan, Kathleen (1999), "Childbearing outside Marriage in Western Europe," *Population Trends*, London: Office of National Statistics, 11–20.

Landes, Elisabeth (1978), "The Economics of Alimony," *Journal of Legal Studies*, 7, 35–63.

Laumann, Edward O., John H. Gagnon, Robert T. Michael, and Stuart Michaels (1994), *The Social Organization of Sexuality: Sexual Practices in the United States*, Chicago: University of Chicago Press.

McRae, Susan (1993), *Cohabiting Mothers: Changing Marriage and Motherhood?* London: Policy Studies Institute.

Morgan, Patricia (2000), *Marriage-Lite: The Rise of Cohabitation and Its Consequences*, London: Institute for the Study of Civil Society.

MORI (1994), *Public Attitudes to Marriage, Divorce and Family Mediation*, London: Research Survey Conducted for the Lord Chancellor's Department.

Morse Jr., Adriaen M. (1996), "Fault: A Viable Means of Re-injecting Responsibility in Marital Relations," *University of Richmond Law Review*, 30, 515–651.

Nock, Steven L. (1998), *Marriage in Men's Lives*, New York: Oxford University Press.

Parkman, Allen M. (2000), *No-Fault Divorce: What Went Wrong?* Lanham, MD: Rowman & Littlefield.

Posner, Eric A. (1999), "Marriage as a Signal" in Frank H. Buckley (ed.), *The Fall and Rise of Freedom of Contract*, Durham, NC: Duke University Press, 245–55.

Rauch, Jonathan (1996), "For Better or Worse?," *The New Republic*, 6 May, 18–23. reprinted in Andrew Sullivan, *Same-Sex Marriage: Pro and Con*, New York: Vintage Books, 1997.

Ross, Catherine E. (1995), "Reconceptualizing Marital Status as a Continuum of Social Attachment," *Journal of Marriage and the Family*, 57, 129–40.

Rowthorn, Robert (1999), "Marriage and Trust: Some Lessons from Economics," *Cambridge Journal of Economics*, 23, 661–91.

Scott, Elizabeth S. (1990), "Rational Decision-Making about Marriage and Divorce," *Virginia Law Review*, 76, 9–94.

Scott, Elizabeth S. and Robert E. Scott (1998), "Marriage as a Relational Contract," *Virginia Law Review*, 84(7) 1225–334.

(1999), "A Contract Theory of Marriage," in Frank H. Buckley (ed.), *The Fall and Rise of Freedom of Contract*, Durham, NC: Duke University Press, 201–44.

Smart, Carol and Pippa Stevens (2000), *Cohabitation Breakdown*, London: Family Policy Studies Centre.

Spence, Michael (1974), *Competition in Salaries, Credentials, and Signaling Prerequisites for Jobs*, Stanford, CA: Stanford University Press.

Stanton, Glenn T. (1997), *Why Marriage Matters*, Colorado Springs: Pinon.

Stets, Jan E. and Murray A. Straus (1995), "The Marriage License as a Hitting License: A Comparison of Assaults in Dating, Cohabiting and Married Couples," in Murray A. Straus and Richard J. Gelles (eds.), *Physical Violence in American Families*, New Brunswick, NJ: Transaction Publishers, 227–44.

Sullivan, Andrew (1996), *Virtually Normal*, New York: Vintage Books.

(1997), *Same-Sex Marriage: Pro and Con*, New York: Vintage Books.

Trebilcock, Michael J. (1999), "Marriage as a Signal," in Frank H. Buckley (ed.), *The Fall and Rise of Freedom of Contract*, Durham, NC: Duke University Press, 245–55.

Waite, Linda (1995), "Does Marriage Matter," *Demography*, 32 (November), 483–507.

Waite, Linda and Maggie Gallagher (2000), *The Case for Marriage: Why Married People Are Happier, Healthier, and Better off Financially*, New York: Doubleday.

Wald, Michael S. (1999), *Same-Sex Couples: Marriage, Families and Children*, Seattle: Partners Task Force for Gay & Lesbian Couples.

Wellings, Kaye, et al. (1994), *Sexual Behavior in Britain*, London: Penguin Books.

Whelan, Robert (1994), *Broken Homes and Battered Children*, Oxford: Family Education Trust.

Woodhouse, Barbara Bennett (1994), "Sex, Lies and Dissipation: The Discourse of Fault in a No-Fault Era," *Georgetown Law Journal*, 82, 2524–69.

Zahavi, A. (1975), "Mate Selection – A Selection for a Handicap," *Journal of Theoretical Biology*, 55, 93–108.

9   For better or for worse? Is bargaining in marriage and divorce efficient?

Martin Zelder

Whereas the processes and mechanisms by which we get into and out of marriage have been compelling subjects for artists and philosophers for much of human history, only recently have economists turned their attention to these phenomena. Naturally, the economic approach has focused on the nature and outcomes of bargaining between potential spouses (prior to marriage) or actual spouses (during marriage or regarding divorce). This chapter endeavors to review the literature on such bargaining, concentrating on two issues: the nature of bargaining in each setting, and whether such bargaining leads to efficient outcomes. The chapter is organized in four main sections: section 1 analyzes bargaining underlying the formation of marriage; section 2 assesses bargaining within marriage; section 3 evaluates bargaining over divorce; and section 4 contains concluding thoughts.

1   Bargaining to form marriages

The analysis of bargaining in order to form a marriage has its origin as a type of assignment problem, as pioneered by Koopmans and Beckmann (1957). Becker (1973, 1974, 1991) was the first to apply this assignment model to marriages in which the division of marital output was endogenous.[1] In Becker's model, bargaining leads to the simultaneous resolution of three questions regarding marriage: whether to marry, whom to marry, and how to divide the surplus from marriage.

As originally formulated, this bargaining involves no strategic behavior: individual payoffs, either from remaining single or from a particular marriage, are public information. Consequently, marital matching is a competitive equilibrium, and individuals sort to marriages such that the aggregate social value of all marriages is maximized. In other words, the marital equilibrium in Becker's model is a Pareto optimum; any rearrangement of marital partners that improved one individual's welfare would reduce another's.

---

[1] By contrast, Becker (1991) notes that Gale and Shapley (1962) conceive of a model of marital matching in which the shares of marital output are inflexible.

Becker specifically distinguishes the *implication* of efficient marriage markets from the *assumption* of their efficiency:

I should emphasize, moreover, that the optimality of maximizing aggregate output is a theorem, not an assumption about behavior. Each man and woman is assumed to be concerned only about his or her own "selfish" welfare, not about social welfare. In pursuing their selfish interests, however, they are unknowingly led by the "invisible hand" of competition in the marriage market to maximize aggregate output. (Becker, 1991, p. 112)

Thus, there is no bargaining in the game-theoretic sense over the decision to enter marriage in this model. In particular, by emphasizing equilibrium as the outcome of individual maximization rather than being the result of social welfare maximization, Becker rejects interpretation of the marital sorting equilibrium as the outcome of a cooperative game, in which efficiency is assumed rather than deduced.

Support for Becker's efficient marriage market hypothesis is generated by Suen and Lui (1999). From 1976 Hong Kong census data, they estimate the marginal marital products of particular individual characteristics (schooling, age, wage, place of birth). From this they deduce the output-maximizing combinations among the 772 actual couples in their sample, and compare that theoretical optimum with the actual pairings. According to this comparison, the actual pairings capture 80 percent of the surplus theoretically available if the optimum were attained. They conclude, therefore, that because this 20 percent efficiency loss was found in an analysis with only four traits measured (as noted above) "the empirical model derived from the efficient marriage market hypothesis fits the data well" (Suen and Liu, 1999, p. 45).

In principle, of course, both cooperative and non-cooperative game-theoretic models of marital sorting could be constructed as alternatives to Becker's formulation. But treating the marriage market as a cooperative game is probably unrealistic, because the assumption of Pareto-optimality is difficult to defend in an environment where individual maximization is so prominent.[2] Consequently, the non-cooperative game is the logical alternative to Becker's competitive market model.

One such model, Bergstrom and Bagnoli (1993), depicts information regarding the quality of single individuals as private. Specifically, they assume that the quality of individual males (regarded heuristically as income) is not revealed until later in life, whereas the quality of females is common knowledge. They restrict individual strategies to the choice of marrying early or marrying late; remaining single in both periods is not permissible. Within this framework,

---

[2] Perhaps the cooperative-game approach might apply to arranged marriages (to be discussed below, briefly) within a small village in which there is substantial altruism.

they prove the existence of a unique equilibrium that is "stable," meaning that Pareto-improvements are impossible.

Alternative non-cooperative games, in which, for example, the strategy space is wider, might not produce unique Pareto-optimal equilibria. Indeed, one could envision a modification of Bergstrom and Bagnoli in which refusal of a particular marital match, i.e. remaining single, was an additionally available strategy. Given this elaboration, standard inefficient lemons-model equilibria – either separating or pooling – are possible in which high-quality mates are partially or entirely driven out of the market owing to adverse selection.[3]

Bergstrom (1996) addresses a second type of informational problem – moral hazard – and sketches its implications for marriage market equilibrium. The source of such moral hazard is that individuals contemplating marriage cannot credibly commit to the distribution of the marital surplus once they are married. If they could do so, the marriage market equilibrium would be Pareto-optimal. If commitments are not credible, non cooperative bargaining will not necessarily lead to a Pareto optimum. Given the state's traditional reluctance to police the incidents of an ongoing marriage or to enforce contracts regarding marital obligations, the assumption of non-credible commitments is plausible.

A specific commitment problem – the breaking of an engagement – is analyzed by Brinig (1990). She finds implicit empirical support for its importance in her ingenious investigation of a well-known engagement bonding mechanism: the diamond engagement ring. Specifically, Brinig examines the ramifications of the demise of the legal action for "breach of promise," under which an engaged woman whose fiancé reneged retained the right to sue the fiancé for damages. From 1935 onward, states gradually rescinded "breach of promise" laws, leaving jilted women in those states without tangible recourse. Hence, hypothesizes Brinig, arose the demand for diamond engagement rings to serve as bonds against male reneging. In a time-series regression for the period 1935–60, she discovers that, as the percentage of the population covered by breach of promise laws diminished, the demand for diamonds rose.[4] This implies that without any penalty for breach of promise too few marriages are formed.

An additional form of moral hazard – marital fraud – is addressed by Brinig and Alexeev (1995). Legally, marital fraud arises when deception by one spouse induces a marriage that otherwise would not have occurred. Instances of such frauds have included misrepresentation of social standing, false claims of pregnancy, concealment of a fact unknowable prior to marriage (for example, intent

---

[3] Bergstrom and Bagnoli describe their paper as "a useful first step in untangling the logic of a dynamic marital 'lemons' model" (Bergstrom and Bagnoli, 1993, p. 187). "Lemons" models depict markets in which the quality of the good being sold cannot be completely observed by buyers (as in marriage); consequently, sellers of low-quality goods ("lemons") will drive some high-quality sellers out of the market.

[4] Brinig includes per capita income and a time dummy in her simultaneous system.

not to have children), inability or unwillingness to consummate the marriage, and nondisclosure of religious preferences. Brinig and Alexeev hypothesize that fault divorce and annulment are substitutes in the termination of fraudulently obtained marriages because both allow consideration of the fraud in the determination of spousal support. In contrast, no-fault regimes often preclude consideration of fault in the awarding of support. Consequently, in jurisdictions where no-fault has replaced fault, annulments will be more common, because they are the only available mechanism to penalize fraud. Tests of this hypothesis on a pooled cross-section of the fifty US states for the period 1965–87 detected that jurisdictions that had switched to no-fault had significantly higher annulment rates. Depending on their size and the probability of their imposition, the penalties for fraud reflected in divorce settlements may elicit the efficient amount of marital fraud.

Another substantial way in which the legal system intervenes in the formation of marriage is through the tax code.[5] Specifically, many developed countries impose marriage "penalties," in that tax liability is larger for a couple if they are married than if they remain single.[6] Economists have recently considered the impact of such marriage penalties on the decision to form a marriage. Analyzing US aggregate data for 1947–88, Alm and Whittington (1995) discover that increases in the marital tax burden significantly reduce the marriage rate, although the magnitude of the effect is small. An analogous investigation (Alm and Whittington, 1999) examines whether such marriage deterrent effects are found in individual-level panel data. For the period 1968–92, they find that larger marriage tax burdens significantly decreased the probability of first marriage for women, but not for men, and that the effect for women is small in magnitude. Moreover, higher marriage penalties are found to *delay* marriage in the USA (Alm and Whittington, 1997) and in Canada, England, and Wales (Gelardi, 1996). If there are no coinciding market or government failures affecting the marriage market, of course, deadweight loss exists when there are marriages precluded or delayed by tax penalties.

Besides government intervention, suboptimal marriages may be formed when they are parentally arranged. The economics of arranged marriages, as yet formally unexplored in the economics literature (according to a search of EconLit), is an application of the principal–agent literature. In an arranged-marriage culture (where, say, children are precluded from making their own mate choices), parents are contracting agents for their children. As such, in the likely absence

---

[5] Although not reviewed in this chapter, recent research examining welfare and marital status is mixed, some papers (e.g. Moffitt, 1994, and Hoynes, 1997) finding no significant link between welfare recipiency and the likelihood of households being headed by single women, with others (e.g. Eissa and Hoynes, 1999, and Schultz, 1998) detecting such a link.

[6] While Pechman and Engelhardt (1990) detect marriage penalties in each of eleven OECD countries in 1989, Zelder and Basham (2000) discern marriage *subsidies* for some Canadian couples in 2000.

of contracts eliciting first-best spousal selections, the parents' utility maximum will differ from that of their child. In other words, in this principal–agent setting, although arranged marriages are Pareto-optimal they do not necessarily lead to a maximization of marital output.[7] Moreover, inefficiencies of this kind exist even in the presence of altruism, as Zelder (1997b) finds. Finally, arranged marriages may be Kaldor–Hicks inefficient, in that the harm to children from being mismatched may exceed the benefit to parents from controlling the match. As Becker notes of "traditional" societies, "the families of an unhappy married couple in these societies would discourage them from divorcing if these families continued to benefit from the union" (Becker, 1991, p. 346).

2   Bargaining within marriage

Once a marriage has been formed, the issue of how resources are allocated within marriage arises. Naturally, the marital resource allocation that is predicted depends on the bargaining model assumed. Four general models have been suggested: Becker's "common preference" model, the cooperative game with divorce as the threat point, the cooperative game with "separate spheres" within marriage as the threat point, and the non-cooperative game.

In a model of common preferences, it is assumed that marriage allocation decisions are made so as to maximize some joint goal, such as the husband's and wife's combined incomes. An early example of such a model is found in Landes (1978), in which the wife allocates her time between the labor market and the household so as to maximize total household income. At the marital optimum, the marginal cost of increased household time to her (and to the marriage partnership) in terms of her reduced labor market earnings and earning capacity is exactly offset by the marginal benefit from greater household production *and* the husband's enhanced labor market earnings.

Maximization of marital income is a plausible objective under either of two assumptions: divorce is impossible (or extremely rare), or no significant transactional impediments exist to writing contingent contracts over divorce output. Whereas the first criterion – highly infrequent divorce – is not met in most cultures, the possibility of the second – complete contracting – can, as Landes first pointed out, be met by an efficient divorce settlement regime. In the absence of divorce settlements (and given the unenforceability of contracts governing behavior within marriage), Landes proves that wives will invest less than is efficient both in household-specific goods and in their husbands' earning

---

[7] Exceptions to this conclusion, of course, are when parents' and children's choices coincide, and when children rationally choose to have their parents act as their agents (rather than having this contracting device imposed).

capacities. But, if the legal system provides the expectation of efficient alimony payments to the wife upon divorce, her allocation of time will be that which maximizes marital income.

This joint-maximization model was criticized as unrealistic in two game-theoretic papers from the early 1980s by Manser and Brown (1980) and McElroy and Horney (1981). The basis of this criticism was a prediction of the joint-maximization model: that additions to family income have the same impact on consumption regardless of which family member receives that income. Although evidence contrary to this prediction was not adduced until the 1990s (Lundberg and Pollak, 1996), intuition that such evidence existed undoubtedly led to the earlier theoretical models of Manser and Brown and McElroy and Horney. In their framework, bargaining over the allocation of resources within marriage is modeled as a cooperative game. This approach offers both crucial similarities and differences as compared with joint maximization. Both involve equilibria that are Pareto-optimal: joint maximization (by deduction) and the core of the cooperative game (by assumption). But the cooperative game analysis treats each spouse as possessing his or her own individual utility function, as opposed to the common preference approach of the joint-maximization model.

Any cooperative game contains a threat point; in the Manser–Brown and McElroy–Horney models, that threat point is divorce. This means that, in bargaining over the division of the marriage's output, each spouse will refuse an output share that makes him or her worse off than if divorce were to occur. How much more each spouse receives within marriage compared with the threat point depends on the bargaining rule that characterizes the division of the marital output. With a "dictatorial" bargaining rule, the non-dictator spouse receives his or her threat value plus epsilon; conversely, a symmetric bargaining rule such as the Nash solution more evenly divides the marital surplus. Regardless of the bargaining rule, however, the ultimate allocation of resources is Pareto-optimal. This property exists, of course, because it is assumed in the cooperative game framework.

The important innovation contained in these models has been interestingly modified by Lundberg and Pollak (1993). Although they retain the cooperative game setting, the substantive change they propose is in regard to the threat point. Specifically, they note that realism suggests that, for many couples, failure to agree on a division of marital output would lead not to divorce but, rather, to a non-cooperative equilibrium within marriage. This "separate spheres" threat point is characterized by voluntary contributions by each spouse to the provision of multiple household public goods. In some circumstances, this equilibrium consists of corner solutions for both spouses, where the husband ignores the wife's preferences in allocating resources to the provision of public good 1 (for example, home repair) while the wife, analogously, ignores the husband's preferences in allocating resources to the provision of public good 2 (for example, child care). Such behavior is characteristic of a Nash equilibrium and embodies underprovision of each public good. Consequently, the threat point involves inefficient allocation of resources within marriage. If, however, the threat point is avoided, the marital surplus and its division are efficient.

Alternatively, if the game characterizing the distribution of marital resources is *non-cooperative*, then non-Pareto-optimal marital allocations are possible. Lundberg and Pollak (1994) analyze a game in which spouses non-cooperatively determine their individual best response strategies for contributing to the provision of a marital public good. In this setting, they demonstrate that, even when divorce is impossible, the marital Nash equilibrium when the game is one-shot must be inefficient and, when the game is repeated, it may be inefficient. Pareto-optimal equilibria occur in the repeated game only when effective punishment is possible.

A second game structure in which inefficient marital allocations are possible is a coordination game in which the husband and wife bargain over whether or not to specialize in the provision of two household public goods, and furthermore, in the event of specialization, which good each should provide (see Lundberg and Pollak, 1994, 1996). Because there are increasing returns to specialization, there are two Nash equilibria, which differ only in the assignment of spouses to goods. If the two spouses are not interchangeable in production, however, then the equilibrium selected will be Pareto inferior if the spouses are not matched to the two public goods on the basis of comparative advantage in production.

Finally, among the numerous other potentially applicable non-cooperative games, Bergstrom (1996) discusses an adaptation of Binmore's (1985) extension of Rubinstein's (1982) sequential bargaining model. Whereas Rubinstein's model involves division of a fixed marital output only if agreement is reached, implying a threat point of (0,0), Binmore's elaboration includes a threat point with non-zero payoffs for each spouse. Binmore proves that the only subgame-perfect equilibrium of this game is Pareto-optimal. Adapting this to marriage, Bergstrom interprets Binmore's non-zero threat point as "harsh words and burnt toast" (Bergstrom, 1996, p. 1926). In such a model, Bergstrom argues, divorce is not a credible threat because of its "large irrevocable costs" (Bergstrom, 1996, p. 1926).

Other non-cooperative games, of course, might have non-Pareto-optimal equilibria. One such game is informally sketched by Brinig and Crafton (1994). They discuss a setting in which the nature of the threat posed by divorce depends on the legal regime in force. Specifically, they note that, in those no-fault states where fault is also removed as a basis for spousal support awards, divorce is a less powerful threat to the higher-income spouse. As a result, fault within marriage, such as spouse abuse, is expected to be more common in this type of no-fault jurisdiction. Brinig and Crafton test this, and discover that no-fault states exhibited a higher rate of calls to crisis centers in 1987. Thus, fault grounds appear to reduce the deadweight loss from marital opportunism such as spousal abuse.

3   Bargaining over divorce

Regardless of which mechanism is used to allocate resources within marriage, dissatisfaction of one or both partners may elicit bargaining over whether to remain married. As with the analysis in the preceding sections, the nature of equilibrium, both positively and normatively, depends on the type of bargaining, which depends not only on the degree of cooperation assumed to exist but also on the legal framework governing divorce.

The first economic analysis of divorce was found in Becker, Landes, and Michael (1977). They detect the relevance of the Coase Theorem (first articulated in Coase, 1960, and thoroughly reviewed in Zelder, 1998) for predicting equilibrium in individually maximizing non-strategic bargaining. Thus, although Becker, Landes, and Michael did not focus specifically on divorce grounds, they did deduce that "the allocation of property rights or legal liability does not influence resource allocation when the parties involved can bargain with each other at little cost" (Becker, Landes, and Michael, 1977, p. 1144). In these circumstances, the decision of whether or not to divorce depends solely on whether there are joint gains to divorce or not. In the two trivial cases where each spouse gains from remaining married, or each gains from getting divorced, they will, obviously, remain married and get divorced, respectively. When one spouse gains more from remaining married than the other does from getting divorced, marriage will (efficiently) continue under either assignment of "property rights," that is, fault (mutual consent) or no-fault (unilateral consent) divorce. In this circumstance, under fault, the divorce-seeking spouse will be unable to bribe the marriage-desiring spouse to accept divorce. Under no-fault, the marriage-desiring spouse will be able to bribe the divorce-seeker to stay put. When the tables are turned, and the divorce-seeker gains more from divorce than the other gains from remaining married, then divorce (efficiently) occurs under either legal regime.

This analysis was extended by Landes (1978), who provided the first simple mathematical proof of this proposition. Landes further recognized, however, that obstacles to Coasean bargaining could exist, particularly with regard to the payment of divorce settlements. Because of difficulties in writing contingent contracts connecting the post-divorce earnings of the "husband" and the pre-divorce investments in marriage-specific capital by the "wife," the husband, in effect, could not credibly commit to the efficient severance payment. Not only does this efficient severance payment (divorce settlement) induce the wife to make the optimal investment in the marriage (as discussed in section 2), but it also induces the efficient amount of divorce.

This Coasean model was tested against a related model involving an impediment to bargaining within marriage – marital public goods – proposed by Zelder (1989, 1993). Following a suggestion made in Landes (1978), Zelder considered whether different divorce regimes had differential divorce-rate effects when bargaining involved public goods. Specifically, Zelder designed a simple model of joint maximization within marriage in which both private and public good allocations were chosen so as to maximize one spouse's utility subject to the satisfaction of the other spouse's reservation utility. The resulting marital optimum, involving for many couples the non-zero consumption of marital public goods such as children, provides the framework for bargaining. Children were treated as a public good for the purposes of marital bargaining but as a private good for the purposes of divorce bargaining, based on the assumption that parental utility depends on co-residence with the child. Such co-residence, although complete within marriage, is apportioned by custody within divorce.

Given this complication, the standard Coasean invariance of efficiency to legal regime is altered. Efficiency now depends on divorce law because of limitations on transactions under no-fault. Because of the two spouses' joint consumption of children within marriage, gains to marriage (vis-à-vis divorce) in terms of that public good cannot be transferred from one spouse to the other within marriage. If these gains to marriage are large enough then some marriages that exhibit joint gains to marriage will be dissolved under no-fault, although not under fault. Furthermore, because these divorces occur despite the existence of joint gains to marriage, these dissolutions are Kaldor–Hicks inefficient. Empirical analysis in Zelder (1993) supports this theory, as couples with a larger fraction of marital gains in the form of child investments are more likely to divorce, but only under no fault.

As well as being affected by divorce law, the divorce decision can also, of course, be influenced by the tax code. As noted in the discussion of tax impacts on marriage in section 1, there is a growing literature evaluating connections between tax law and marital status. Because of the presence of marriage "penalties" in many countries, economists have estimated whether or not these penalties are substantial enough to encourage divorce. Examining panel data covering the period 1968–92, Whittington and Alm (1997) find that larger marriage penalties induce a small but significant increase in the propensity to divorce for women, with a smaller effect (only significant in some specifications) for men. Their findings are buttressed by the work of Dickert-Conlin

(1999), who also detects a significant but small impact of the marriage penalty on the probability of divorce in a cross-section from 1990. In the absence of coinciding market or government failures affecting the availability of divorce, of course, the additional divorces found to be induced by marriage penalties are inefficient.

Violations of the symmetry typically found in Coasean models can also occur in models of non-cooperative bargaining. In Peters (1986), private information regarding divorce opportunities creates the possibility of "costly and unproductive" bargaining (Peters, 1986, p. 442). Consequently, Peters assumes that both spouses agree, *ex ante*, to a fixed division of marital resources; that is, they agree to renounce the possibility of bargaining within marriage. Despite the fact that the state generally eschews the enforcement of bargains within marriage, Peters defends the use of a fixed-division contract rather than "[m]ore complicated game theoretic schemes," because "[t]hese schemes do not appear to be reflected in real world marriage contracts" (Peters, 1986, p. 442, n16).

Because of the fixed-division (i.e. no bargaining) rule, inefficient marriage and divorce decisions occur in this model. There are two specific implications regarding divorce decisions. In particular, the inability to bargain over marital output means that some efficient bargains to elicit divorce under mutual consent (fault) divorce are precluded, and thus too few divorces occur under fault. Conversely, under unilateral consent (no-fault) some efficient bargains to achieve continued marriage are thwarted, and thus too many divorces occur under no-fault. Within this model, therefore, there are more divorces at equilibrium under no-fault than under fault, and each divorce regime is suboptimal compared with the first-best, although which regime is second-best depends on the size of the deadweight losses under each. In any case, Peters's empirical tests find no significant difference in divorce rates under the two regimes; this result is a rarity, however, taken in the context of a number of subsequent papers that find significantly higher divorce rates under no-fault in the USA (e.g. Marvell, 1989; Allen, 1992; Zelder, 1993; Reilly, 1997; and Friedberg, 1998), Australia (Kidd, 1995), and Canada (Allen, 1998).[8]

The central feature of another non-cooperative game, found in Weiss and Willis (1993), is bargaining over transfers to children within divorce. In their model, the efficient marital status depends on the form of the bargaining game. When the parents cannot make credible *ex ante* commitments to divorce transfers, they instead bargain *ex post*. Because *ex post* bargaining would lead to lower post-divorce investments in children, they are more likely to choose to stay married in that circumstance. In contrast, when credible *ex ante* commitments

---

[8] Zelder (1997a) reviews the strengths and weaknesses of the empirical no-fault literature.

are possible, post-divorce investments in children are increased, and divorce is more likely to occur.[9]

Finally, a recent exception to Coasean invariance is presented by Clark (1999). Clark's insight is that, even when divorce is modeled as a cooperative game, Coasean invariance applies only when the marriage and divorce utility possibility frontiers do not intersect. When they do intersect, however, paradoxes analogous to the one found by Scitovsky (1941) in the context of Kaldor–Hicks efficiency occur. That is, whether marriage continues or divorce occurs *depends* on the underlying legal regime (fault or no-fault). Unlike the previous literature, however, Clark's result is not founded upon transactions costs or other impediments to transactions per se. Instead, the basis for divorce law's relevance in Clark's framework is the structure of his cooperative game and the property of intersecting utility possibility frontiers.

Clark's cooperative game contains threat points that are defined by the legal regime in force: the threat point is continued marriage under a fault regime, divorce under a no-fault regime. Because these threat points are affected by the abiding legal regime, and it is possible for the marriage and divorce utility possibility frontiers to intersect, the choice between marriage and divorce depends on the threat-point divisions of utility. Therefore, because these threat points depend on which legal regime is in place, the decision whether to remain married or to divorce depends on legal regimes; equilibrium is not invariant. Nevertheless, because of the assumed cooperative game form, equilibrium must be efficient.

4   Conclusion

This survey reveals that the economics of marriage and divorce bargaining is, relatively speaking, in its infancy. Consequently, debate naturally surrounds the selection of the appropriate model to represent marital choices. As always, sound empirical work is crucial to resolve, or at least clarify, debates of this nature. The existing literature that attempts to distinguish between cooperative game and common-preference models of marital resource allocation (for instance, Browning et al., 1994) is a good example of this. Nevertheless, econometric work on marriage and divorce is even more limited in its growth than the theoretical literature. As a result, much family policy formation has occurred in an economistic vacuum. Of course, given the multitude of equilibrium concepts found in the game theory literature, distinguishing

---

[9] Allen and Brinig (1998) also detect evidence of non-cooperative bargaining in regard to divorce in their finding that divorce propensity appears to fluctuate with intertemporal shifts in the relative sexual demands of the two spouses.

among different strategic marital choice models may be difficult. The fact that economists increasingly endeavor to test models of the family, however, and the many important family policy issues that remain contentious suggest that the flourishing of rational choice approaches to matters of the heart (and spleen) can enhance welfare in the profession, and beyond.

REFERENCES

Allen, D. (1992), "Marriage and Divorce: Comment," *American Economic Review*, 82, 679–85.
   (1998), "No-fault Divorce in Canada: Its Cause and Effect," *Journal of Economic Behavior and Organization*, 37, 129–49.
Allen, D. and M. Brinig (1998), "Sex, Property Rights, and Divorce," *European Journal of Law and Economics*, 5, 211–33.
Alm, J. and L. Whittington (1995), "Income Taxes and the Marriage Decision," *Applied Economics*, 27, 25–31.
   (1997), "Income Taxes and the Timing of Marital Decisions," *Journal of Public Economics*, 64, 219–40.
   (1999), "For Love or Money? The Impact of Income Taxes on Marriage," *Economica*, 66, 297–316.
Becker, G. (1973), "A Theory of Marriage: Part I," *Journal of Political Economy*, 81, 813–46.
   (1974), "A Theory of Marriage: Part II," *Journal of Political Economy*, 82, S11–26.
   (1991), *A Treatise on the Family*, Cambridge, MA: Harvard University Press.
Becker, G., E. Landes, and R. Michael (1977), "An Economic Analysis of Marital Instability," *Journal of Political Economy*, 85, 1141–87.
Bergstrom, T. (1996), "Economics in a Family Way," *Journal of Economic Literature*, 34, 1903–34.
Bergstrom, T. and M. Bagnoli (1993), "Courtship as a Waiting Game," *Journal of Political Economy*, 101, 185–202.
Binmore, K. (1985), "Bargaining and coalitions," in Alvin Roth (ed.), *Game-theoretic Models of Bargaining*, Cambridge: Cambridge University Press.
Brinig, M. (1990), "Rings and Promises," *Journal of Law, Economics, and Organization*, 6, 203–15.
Brinig, M. and M. Alexeev (1995), "Fraud in Courtship: Annulment and Divorce," *European Journal of Law and Economics*, 2, 45–62.
Brinig, M. and S. Crafton (1994), "Marriage and Opportunism," *Journal of Legal Studies*, 23, 869–94.
Browning, M., F. Bourguignon, P.-A. Chiappori, and V. Lechene (1994), "Income and Outcomes: A Structural Model of Intrahousehold Allocation," *Journal of Political Economy*, 102, 1067–96.
Clark, S. (1999), "Law, Property, and Marital Dissolution," *Economic Journal*, 109, C41–54.
Coase, R. (1960), "The Problem of Social Cost," *Journal of Law and Economics*, 3, 1–44.
Dickert-Conlin, S. (1999), "Taxes and Transfers: Their Effects on the Decision to End a Marriage," *Journal of Public Economics*, 73, 217–40.

Eissa, N. and H. Hoynes (1999), "Good News for Low-Income Families? Tax-Transfer Schemes and Marriage," Department of Economics, University of California at Berkeley, mimeo.

Friedberg, L. (1998), "Did Unilateral Divorce Raise Divorce Rates? Evidence from Panel Data," *American Economic Review*, 88, 608–27.

Gale, D. and L. Shapley (1962), "College Admissions and the Stability of Marriage," *American Mathematical Monthly*, 69, 9–15.

Gelardi, A. (1996), "The Influences of Tax Law Changes on the Timing of Marriages. A Two-Country Analysis," *National Tax Journal*, 49, 17–30.

Hoynes, H. (1997), "Does Welfare Play Any Role in Female Headship Decisions?" *Journal of Public Economics*, 65, 89 117.

Kidd, M. (1995), "The Impact of Legislation on Divorce: A Hazard Function Approach," *Applied Economics*, 27, 125–30.

Koopmans, T. and M. Beckmann (1957), "Assignment Problems and the Location of Economic Activity," *Econometrica*, 25, 53–76.

Landes, E. (1978), "Economics of Alimony," *Journal of Legal Studies*, 7, 35–63.

Lundberg, S. and R. Pollak (1993), "Separate Spheres Bargaining and the Marriage Market," *Journal of Political Economy*, 101, 988–1010.

    (1994), "Noncooperative Bargaining Models of Marriage," *American Economic Review*, 84, 132–7.

    (1996), "Bargaining and Distribution in Marriage," *Journal of Economic Perspectives*, 10, 139–58.

McElroy, M. and M. Horney (1981), "Nash-Bargained Decisions: Towards a Generalization of the Demand Theory," *International Economic Review*, 22, 333–49.

Manser, M. and M. Brown (1980), "Marriage and Household Decision-Making: A Bargaining Analysis," *International Economic Review*, 21, 31–44.

Marvell, T. (1989), "Divorce Rates and the Fault Requirement," *Law and Society Review*, 23, 543–67.

Moffitt, R. (1994), "Welfare Effects on Female Headship with Area Effects," *Journal of Human Resources*, 29, 621–36.

Pechman, J. and G. Engelhardt (1990), "The Income Tax Treatment of the Family: An International Perspective," *National Tax Journal*, 43, 1–22.

Peters, E. (1986), "Marriage and Divorce: Informational Constraints and Private Contracting," *American Economic Review*, 76, 437 54.

Reilly, S. (1997), "Divorce Laws and Divorce Rates: Evidence from Panel Data," Department of Economics, University of California at Berkeley, mimeo.

Rubinstein, A. (1982), "Perfect Equilibrium in a Bargaining Model," *Econometrica*, 50, 97–109.

Schulz T.P. (1998), "Eroding the Economic Foundations of Marriage and Fertility in the United States," *Structural Change and Economic Dynamics*, 9, 391–413.

Scitovsky, T. (1941), "A Note on Welfare Propositions in Economics," *Review of Economic Studies*, 9, 77–88.

Suen, W. and H.-K. Lui (1999), "A Direct Test of the Efficient Marriage Market Hypothesis," *Economic Inquiry*, 37, 29–46.

Weiss, Y. and R. Willis (1993), "Transfers among Divorced Couples: Evidence and Interpretation," *Journal of Labor Economics*, 11, 629–79.

Whittington, L. and J. Alm (1997), "Til Death or Taxes Do Us Part: The Effect of Income Taxation on Divorce," *Journal of Human Resources*, 32, 388–412.

Zelder, M. (1989), "Children as Public Goods and the Effect of No-Fault Divorce Law on the Divorce Rate," unpublished PhD dissertation, University of Chicago, Department of Economics.

(1993), "Inefficient Dissolutions as a Consequence of Public Goods: The Case of No-Fault Divorce," *Journal of Legal Studies*, 22, 503–20.

(1997a), "Did No-Fault Divorce Law Increase the Divorce Rate? A Critical Review of the Evidence," Michigan State University, Department of Economics, mimeo.

(1997b), "Rotten Altruists, Saccharine Altruists, and Saints: Altruism and Social Optimality," *Papers in Political Economy*, 87, University of Western Ontario, Political Economy Research Group.

(1998), "The Cost of Accosting Coase: A Reconciliatory Survey of Proofs and Disproofs of the Coase Theorem," in Steven G. Medema (ed.), *Coasean Economics*, Boston: Kluwer Academic Press.

Zelder, M. and P. Basham (2000), "Does Revenue Canada Play Matchmaker?" *Fraser Forum*, March, 8–10.

10   Weak men and disorderly women: divorce and the division of labor

Steven L. Nock and Margaret F. Brinig

> There are people in Europe who, confounding together the different charac-
> teristics of the sexes, would make of man and woman beings not only equal
> but alike. They would give to both the same functions, impose on both the
> same duties, and grant to both the same rights; they would mix them in all
> things – their occupations, their pleasures, their business. It may readily be
> conceived, that by thus attempting to make one sex equal to the other, both are
> degraded; and from so preposterous a medley of the works of nature nothing
> could ever result but weak men and disorderly women. . . . The Americans have
> applied to the sexes the great principle of political economy which governs
> the manufactures of our age, by carefully dividing the duties of man from
> those of woman, in order that the great work of society may be the better
> carried on.
>
> (De Tocqueville, 1835, ch. XII)

De Tocqueville's observations about the political economy of gender relations
at the beginning of the nineteenth century reflected the prevailing patterns of
employment; husbands were gainfully employed for pay, and wives cared for
home and family (see also Brinig and Carbone, 1988). In the new millennium,
this pattern no longer describes most American couples.[1] Some writers have
surmised that the divorce rate has increased because the modern marriage deal
is unfair to women (Parkman, 1998), who must do "two shifts" – their labor
force hours plus the hours of housework that remain (Hochschild and Machung,
1989). Certainly, spouses who feel their marriages are unfair may feel that divorce is a better option. The traditional marriage, which exploited each spouse's
comparative advantage, is arguably more efficient than the two-earner couple
where housework is shared (Becker, 1991). But no research considers whether
specialization can be equated not just with efficiency but with marital stability.
That is the project of this chapter.

According to economist Gary Becker, even though a man and a woman
have functioned quite similarly prior to marriage, they will begin to specialize

---

[1] The most recent statistics from the US Department of Labor suggest that 61.0 percent of women
aged 15–44 are employed, compared with 73.6 percent of men of the same ages (Bureau of Labor
Statistics News, April 2001, Table A-1; http://www.bls.gov/news.release/pdf/empsit.pdf).

once the marriage begins (Becker, 1991, ch. 2; Grossbard-Schechtman, 1993; Allen, 1992). Specialization will occur as the couple realize gains from each partner's "comparative advantage" in one or more functions. Husband and wife will engage in two kinds of labor, which Becker calls market production and household production. The spouse involved in market production divides time between labor (earning money to purchase goods) and leisure activities (spending money, or at any rate not earning more). The spouse engaged in household production divides time between the production of household (or "Z" goods) and leisure (Becker, 1991: 32–41). In "Z" good production, the spouse transforms purchased goods into ultimate consumption goods (Gronau, 1980).

It is because one spouse may have even a tiny comparative advantage at household production that Becker predicts efficient spouses will specialize (Becker, 1985). He argues that, because only women can bear children, they have the comparative advantage when it comes to household production. This advantage will increase because growing girls will invest in human capital that enhances their efficiency at producing household goods (Becker, 1973), which creates a likelihood that they will follow a traditional path (Becker, 1974). Their husbands, on the other hand, will specialize in market production. They will choose human capital investments before marriage to maximize production in the labor force. Pre-marriage specialization will also make each a more attractive mate (Becker, 1991; Duncan and Duncan, 1978). This investment in human capital can produce gendered differences in comparative advantage even without biological differences (Hadfield, 1999).

Becker and others (Parkman, 1992) assume that there is specialization between husband and wife, but not among women. They apparently believe it is less "efficient" to hire someone else to do the wash or clean the house. This view has been criticized in the literature (Brinig, 1994; Brinig and Carbone, 1988) on the ground that it does not make sense to tout specialization in the labor force generally while making an exception for tasks that are commonly performed for the household.

In related work, many critics of the specialization model advocate a more modern notion of marriage as a partnership (Smith, 1990). This alternative assumes individualism within the marriage, equality among spouses, roughly equivalent earning capacity between the spouses, and a need for flexibility over the life cycle. Those who advocate a more egalitarian marriage presume that, as married women enter the labor force, their husbands will pick up a fair share of household tasks.

Since World War II, women have markedly altered their labor force participation profiles. Men, however, have not. Prior to 1970, women typically left the labor force shortly after marriage and/or childbirth, and they maintained lower

Table 10.1 *Hours spent on housework*

	1960s	1970s	1978	1988
Women			26.7	21.3
Nonmarried			17.2	13 4
Married			29.1	23.6
Not employed	38.0–43.0	23.0–34.0	37.1	33.0
Employed	20.0–26.5	11.5–20.0	24.3	20.8
Men			6.1	7.4
Nonmarried			8.2	7.0
Married			5.8	7.5
Not employed	5.0–8.0	3.0–9.0	5.0	6.4
Employed	5.5–8.0	3.0–9.5	6.4	7.8

Sources: table derived from Blau (1998); data are drawn from the Panel Study of Income Dynamics, Institute for Social Research, University of Michigan, Ann Arbor.

rates of employment thereafter throughout the life course. But in recent decades, there has been growing convergence of life-course patterns of employment, and there is no longer a typical drop in married women's labor force participation rates when children are born (Spain and Bianchi, 1996).

Though married women have steadily increased their labor force activity, they continue to do the bulk of the housework. In table 10.1 we present summaries of time spent on housework by women and men since the 1960s. As these figures indicate, there has been little change in the relative commitment to household labor by men and women. Minor reductions in women's and minor increases in men's household labor are evident, though the magnitude of change is remarkably small.

Sociologists Goldscheider and Waite conclude their *New Families, No Families* by suggesting that Becker style "old" families will not be possible for much longer.

Why can we not return to the old balance of men's and women's work and family roles, which were "fair" to each in terms of hours, and which provided children with mothers who cared for them intensively and fathers who supported them adequately? ... The major problem for women posed by "old families" is demographic. With the increase in life expectancy and the decline in fertility, homemaking is no longer a lifetime career for women as a group. Either there has to be a division within their adult lives, with about half their time devoted to raising two or so children to adulthood and half spent in other occupations, or women have to be divided into mothers and workers, or "real" workers and "mommy track" workers. (Goldscheider and Waite, 1991, 202–3)

And what of "new" more egalitarian and sharing families? Although Goldscheider and Waite believe that this must be our future, they are less confident about the implications.

We have suggested that such families have the potential to solve critical problems facing families today. But what do we really know about them? What effects does this pioneer family form have on marriages and families and on the men, women, and children who live in them? Are more egalitarian and sharing families possible? This is largely uncharted territory. (Goldscheider and Waite, 1991, pp. 204–5)

The current research attempts to navigate some of that unknown terrain. We show how husbands' involvement in *women's* tasks and wives' involvement in *men's* tasks affect the chances of marital disruption. We also explore the extent to which attitudes, as opposed to the fair division of labor, matter for marital stability.

1   Data and methods

Data

The National Survey of Families and Households (NSFH) was first administered in the United States in 1987–8 and included personal interviews with 13,007 respondents from a national sample. The sample includes a main cross-section of 9,637 households plus an oversampling of blacks, Puerto Ricans, Mexican Americans, single-parent families, families with stepchildren, cohabiting couples, and recently married persons. One adult per household was randomly selected as the primary respondent. Several portions of the main interview were self-administered to facilitate the collection of sensitive information and to ease the flow of the interview. The average interview lasted one hour and forty minutes. In addition, a shorter self-administered questionnaire was given to the spouse or cohabiting partner of the primary respondent. We use identical questions asked of the primary respondent and his or her spouse.

The second wave of the NSFH was conducted in 1992–4, five years after the original interview. The second wave included an interview of all surviving members of the original sample via face-to-face personal interview ($N = 10,007$) and a personal interview with the current spouse or cohabiting partner almost identical to the interview with the main respondent ($N = 5,624$). The second wave included a detailed marital history sequence that we used to determine changes in marital status since the first wave.

Our sample is restricted to *couples* who were in their first marriages at wave 1. Neither partner had been previously married. This restriction was imposed to avoid problems associated with remarriages, stepfamilies, and ex-spouses.

Marital disruption

Our primary concern is marital disruption in the course of five years. We determined whether the couple divorced or separated after the initial interview. If they did, we recorded the month when the divorce or separation occurred. Of the 4,273 couples who met our criteria for inclusion in the first wave, unambiguous information about the subsequent status of their marriage was available for 3,592. Of these, 275 (6.3 percent) divorced and another 105 (2.9 percent) separated (where one spouse permanently moved out of the dwelling) in the course of the study. We treat divorce or separation as marital disruptions, and our equations combine the two. We have investigated divorces separately, and the results are essentially the same as those including separations.

Before considering the role of household labor, we control for the well-known determinants of divorce and separation (Bumpass and Sweet, 1995). Specifically, we include the following factors as controls in our equation:

1. age at first marriage for husband,
2. age at first marriage for wife,
3. the couple cohabited (with each other) before marriage,
4. number of children born to the couple,
5. husband's wage/salary income last year,
6. wife's wage/salary income last year,
7. race (of husbands, and whether the wife is the same race),
8. husband's years of schooling,
9. wife's years of schooling,
10. husband's parents are divorced, and
11. wife's parents are divorced.

To this basic set of predictors, we then add two measures of paid labor (husband's hours at paid work last week, and wife's hours at paid work last week) and four measures of household labor. In a third step, we add four related measures of perceived fairness. In a final equation, we investigate the possible interactions of perceived fairness and measures of household and paid labor.

Household labor

Our measures of household labor are intended to distinguish between those tasks traditionally performed by men and those traditionally performed by women. We relied on earlier studies (for example, Berk, 1995) to make this determination, though there was little question about the gendered nature of household labor. To verify our allocation scheme, we contrasted male and female commitments to each task with paired *t*-tests. All were statistically significant, and most showed large differences.

Table 10.2 *Average hours spent on household tasks by husbands and wives*

Household task	Husbands	Wives	N	Sig. *t*
1. Preparing meals	2.05	9.75	4,377	.001*
2. Washing dishes	1.76	6.07	4,377	.001*
3. Cleaning house	1.59	8.13	4,379	.001*
4. Outdoor tasks	4.96	1.81	4,380	.001*
5. Shopping	1.39	2.81	4,380	.001*
6. Washing, ironing	0.57	4.29	4,379	.001*
7. Paying bills	1.36	1.60	4,378	.001*
8. Auto maintenance	1.84	0.18	4,379	.001*
9. Driving others	1.15	1.39	4,372	.001*
Male tasks (4 + 8)	6.80	1.99	4,375	.001*
Female tasks (1 + 2 + 3 + 5 + 6 + 7 + 9)	9.87	33.98	4,381	.001*

Note: *paired samples *t*-test (2-tailed) is significant at $p < .001$.

Each spouse was asked to complete a page with the following questions:

The questions on this page concern household tasks and who in your household normally spends time doing those tasks. Write in the approximate number of hours per week that you, your spouse/partner or others in the household normally spend doing the following things:

1) Preparing meals
2) Washing dishes and cleaning up after meals
3) Cleaning house
4) Outdoor and other household maintenance tasks
5) Shopping for groceries and other household goods
6) Washing, ironing, mending
7) Paying bills and keeping financial records
8) Automobile maintenance and repair
9) Driving other household members to work, school, or other activities

For most household tasks, there is little question about which partner typically does most of the work. There are, however, two tasks for which there are only minor differences: Driving (#9) and Paying bills (#7). Husbands do slightly less of each than wives do (see table 10.2) and we treat both as female tasks. Given that husbands and wives commit roughly equal numbers of hours to these two responsibilities, considering them one way or the other has virtually no consequence for the analysis.

We created two summary measures of household labor. The first, *male tasks*, is the simple sum of hours spent on Outdoor and other Household Maintenance Tasks (#4) and Automobile Maintenance and Repair (#8). The second, *female tasks*, is the simple sum of hours spent on all other activities. Men and women spent significantly different amounts of time in each activity (even when the magnitude of such differences was minimal, as with Driving and Paying Bills), although none was the exclusive domain of only one gender. We calculated the number of hours husbands spent in "male" and "female" tasks, as well as the corresponding figures for wives. These four variables are our primary concern in the following equations.

The average hours spent in each of the activities is shown in table 10.2. There are clear differences between husbands and wives in their allocation of time to household tasks. Yet such efforts must be balanced against other commitments of time, especially paid labor. As others have shown (Shelton, 1992; Berk, 1995; Hochschild and Machung 1989), the aggregate (total) amount of both paid and unpaid labor by married spouses is roughly comparable because differences in unpaid labor are compensated for by differences in paid labor. Husbands in this study report spending an average 34.3 hours in paid labor weekly compared with wives, who report an average of 18.5 hours. When both paid and unpaid labor are considered together, therefore, husbands report spending a total of 51.2 hours per week compared with 54.8 hours by wives.

Fairness

The division of tasks and responsibilities is known to be a source of tension for many married couples. It is also quite likely that any consequence of time spent in tasks is conditioned by how fair the allocation is seen to be. We include four measures (two each for husbands and wives) to capture the individual spouse's assessment of the fairness of things. Each spouse was asked:

How do you feel about the fairness in your relationship in each of the following areas?

1) Household chores
2) Working for pay

Answers were: 1 = Very unfair to me, 2 = Somewhat unfair to me, 3 = Fair to both, 4 = Somewhat unfair to him/her, and 5 = Very unfair to him/her. We use the original 5-point scoring of these variables. We explored many alternative specifications, including dummy variables for each value. Despite changes in the magnitude of some coefficients, the pattern of results was invariant over different specifications. This was so even for the middle category (3 = fair to both) and indicates that respondents interpreted the questions and answers as tapping increasing levels of unfairness to their partners.

Others (Smith, Gager, and Morgan, 1998) have suggested that this question actually taps two dimensions: a relative fairness dimension, and the quality of the marriage. Their research found that couples in happy marriages are less likely than those in unhappy marriages to answer this question. However, like most researchers who have considered issues of fairness in the household (for example, Lennon and Rosenfield, 1994; Thomson, 1991), Smith et al. did not consider fairness evaluations in other domains (for example, paid labor). As we show, considering both types of fairness is essential, and failure to do so produces different results than are found when both types of evaluations are considered. Moreover, to our knowledge, we are the first to include both spouses and both types of fairness evaluations in our models.

2   Method of analysis

Cox Proportional Hazards regression is used to determine the risk of divorce associated with each variable in the equation. In the hazards model, there is a risk of marital disruption at each month of duration until the disruption occurs. The risk may be affected by other variables included in the model. The Cox procedure first determines a baseline risk that is associated with months married (every marriage has a calculable risk of dissolution that changes monthly). Then each variable is assessed for how it alters this baseline risk. Our primary question is how allocations of household labor affect the risk of marital disruption.

Specifically, the Cox regression estimates the influence of the independent variables (X) on the hazard (h) of marital disruption as:

$$h(t) = [h_0(t)]e^{(BX)},$$

where $h_0(t)$ is the baseline hazard function when the independent variables, X, are set to zero (similar to the intercept in an OLS equation, or the expected risk of marital disruption when X is zero). B is the regression coefficient – the predicted change in the log hazard for a unit increase in the independent variable.

We present the Cox regression coefficient and its exponentiated (e^B) value in our results. The latter coefficient is labeled *RISK* in the tables, and is helpful for interpreting the magnitude of the effect of a variable. For dichotomous variables such as whether a couple cohabited before marriage, *RISK* indicates the increase (or decrease) in the risk of marital dissolution associated with cohabiting. If this coefficient were 2.0, for example, it would indicate that cohabiting doubles the (baseline monthly) risk of marital disruption. If it were 0.5, it would indicate that the risk is only half as great for those who cohabit as for those who do not. For continuous variables such as the hours spent at paid labor, *RISK* indicates the percentage change in risk with each additional hour worked. Were it to be 1.02 for example, it would mean that each additional hour worked increases the (baseline) risk of marital disruption by two percentage points. Were it 0.97, it would mean that each additional hour of work is associated with a 3 percent lower risk of disruption.

Summary statistics for all variables in the Cox regression equation are reported in table 10.3. We report the results of the Cox regressions in table 10.4. The equation is developed in four steps. In the first, we enter the known

Table 10.3 *Summary statistics for all variables*

Sample characteristic	Average/percentage	Standard deviation
Years in current marriage	18.99	15.74
Percent who separated/divorced	10.58%	
Husband age at marriage	24.47	5.41
Wife age at marriage	22.26	4.87
Percent of couples who cohabited before marrying	18.34%	
No. of children born to couple	2.12	1.79
Husband wage/salary Wave I ('000)	20.76	26.81
Wife wage/salary Wave I ('000)	8.59	27.69
Husband White	78.97%	
Husband Black	10.45%	
Husband Hispanic	7.24%	
Husband Asian	1.13%	
Husband American Indian	0.36%	
Spouses different races?	13.61%	
Husband years of schooling	12.84	3.43
Wife years of schooling	12.74	2.91
Husband's parents divorced	9.26%	
Wife's parents divorced	9.15%	
Husband hours at paid work last week	34.30	21.82
Wife hours at paid work last week	18.52	19.80
Husband's hours on "men's" tasks last week	6.80	8.75
Husband's hours on "women's" tasks last week	9.87	13.71
Wife's hours on "men's" tasks last week	1.99	4.17
Wife's hours on "women's" tasks last week	33.98	23.73
Husband's fairness: household	3.21	0.56
Wife's fairness: household	2.71	0.64
Husband's fairness: paid work	3.01	0.48
Wife's fairness: paid work	2.99	0.50

Note: $N = 2,892$.

predictors of marital disruption. In the second, we add the summary measures of hours spent on men's and women's tasks by husbands and wives as well as hours spent at paid employment. In the third model, we enter the assessments of the fairness of the division of household and paid labor to determine whether they operate independently of the allocation of time committed to these tasks. In the final model, we add interactions between the measures of fairness and involvement in paid and household work. Our objective in entering these terms is to investigate whether perceptions about fairness condition the consequences of household or paid labor commitments.

The interaction terms added in the fourth model are created by multiplying each of the four fairness questions (husband's and wife's evaluation of household and paid labor) by hours in each of the three types of labor (paid, male, and female tasks), resulting in twelve terms. This strategy produces both similar and dissimilar types of task-and-fairness evaluation interactions. That is, men's evaluations of the fairness of *paid labor* are multiplied by men's involvement in *paid labor*. But men's evaluations of the fairness of paid labor are also multiplied by men's involvement in *household labor*. By investigating both types of possible interactions, we are able to determine whether one type of task spills over into another type. It is possible, for instance, that both types of interactions just described might be associated with higher or lower divorce rates. Were this so, it would suggest that the effect of hours in paid labor is conditioned by men's sense of fairness in *both* paid and unpaid tasks. On the other hand, were we to find that only the second interaction affected divorce rates, this would suggest that men's involvement in paid labor spills over into the household labor project, where men's hours at paid work matter more when household tasks are viewed as unfairly divided.

3   Findings

The first model confirms well-known results. Those who cohabit before marrying, for example, have dissolution rates that are much higher than those who do not cohabit. As table 10.4 shows, the relative RISK of dissolution is 5.88 times higher for those who cohabited prior to marriage. This value is obtained by exponentiating the value of the regression coefficient, $B = 1.7717$. In this case, $e^{1.7717} = 5.88$. Other factors found to influence marital disruption include the presence of children (reduces RISK), being Black (increases RISK), young age at first marriage (significant only for wives, owing to the high correlation between spouses' ages at first marriage), and experiencing one's parents' divorce.

In Model 2, the six measures of time allocation are added. Husband's time at paid labor increases the risk of disruption by about 1.5 percent for each additional hour worked per week. There is no corresponding effect for wife's paid employment.

Our primary interest is in the effects of household tasks performed by husbands and wives. The first such variable shows the effects of hours that men spend on traditionally male tasks. Each hour in such pursuits is associated with about 2.4 percent *reduction* in risk of dissolution. On the other hand, when men do traditionally female tasks, dissolution risks are *increased* by about 1.3 percent for each additional hour spent in such efforts. In short, for husbands who do those tasks normally done by men, the chances that their marriages will end through divorce or separation are reduced. When men venture into less traditional, more female tasks, however, the chances their marriages will dissolve are increased.

Table 10.4 Cox regressions predicting marital disruption

	Model 1		Model 2		Model 3		Model 4	
Variable	B	RISK	B	RISK	B	RISK	B	RISK
Control variables								
Cohabited	1.7717	5.8808**	1.6776	5.3528**	1.6677	5.2998**	1.6651	5.2863**
Number of children	−0.6075	0.5447**	−0.6187	0.5387**	−0.6291	0.5331**	−0.6475	0.5234**
Husband's wages	−0.0019	0.9981	−0.0047	0.9953	−0.0046	0.9954	−0.0050	0.9951
Wife's wages	−0.0101	0.9899	−0.0130	0.9870	−0.0108	0.9893	−0.0103	0.9898
Husband Black	0.4167	1.5169*	0.3728	1.4519*	0.3759	1.4562*	0.4213	1.5239*
Husband Hispanic	0.3080	1.3607	0.2441	1.2765	0.2716	1.3120	0.3054	1.3572
Husband Asian	0.3517	1.4215	0.2471	1.2804	0.2455	1.2783	0.2506	1.2848
Husband American Indian	0.5910	1.8058	0.4515	1.5707	0.3698	1.4475	0.3338	1.3962
Different races	0.0184	1.0186	0.0492	1.0505	0.0402	1.0410	0.0396	1.0404
Husband's education	0.2017	1.0017	−0.0141	0.9860	−0.0164	0.9837	−0.0219	0.9783
Wife's education	0.2017	1.0017	−0.0083	0.9918	−0.0152	0.9847	−0.0142	0.9859
Husband age marriage	0.0002	1.0002	0.0041	1.0041	0.0039	1.0039	0.0055	1.0055
Wife age marriage	−0.0757	0.9271**	−0.0689	0.9334**	−0.0700	0.9324**	−0.0745	0.9282**
Husband parents divorced	0.6762	1.9665**	0.6231	1.8648**	0.5941	1.8115**	0.5326	1.7033**
Wife parents divorced	0.6771	1.9681**	0.6203	1.8594**	0.6096	1.8396**	0.6080	1.8368**
Division of labor								
Husband hours paid work			0.0154	1.0155**	0.0154	1.0155**	0.0090	1.0091
Wife hours paid work			0.0019	1.0020	0.0015	1.0015	0.0360	1.0367
Husband hours male tasks			−0.0244	0.9759**	−0.0253	0.9750**	−0.0926	0.9115
Husband hours female tasks			0.0133	1.0134**	0.0150	1.0151**	0.1142	1.1210
Wife hours male tasks			−0.0417	0.9592	−0.0386	0.9621*	−0.2882	0.7496
Wife hours female tasks			0.0055	1.0065*	0.0066	1.0066*	0.0497	1.0510

Table 10.4 (*cont.*)

	Model 1		Model 2		Model 3		Model 4	
Variable	B	RISK	B	RISK	B	RISK	B	RISK
Sense of fairness								
Husband household					−0.1558	0.8557	0.1775	1.1942
Wife household					−0.2478	0.7805**	−0.4391	0.6446*
Husband paid work					−0.3753	0.6871**	−0.6066	0.5452*
Wife paid work					−0.0176	0.9825	0.7369	2.0895**
Fairness–hours interaction								
Husband fairness paid × hours male tasks							0.0201	1.0203
Husband fairness paid × hours female tasks							−0.0218	0.9784
Husband fairness household × hours paid							−0.0054	0.9946
Wife fairness paid × hours male tasks							0.0884	1.0925*
Wife fairness paid × hours female tasks							−0.0141	0.9860**
Wife fairness household × hours paid							0.0092	1.0093*
Husband fair household × hours male tasks							0.0029	1.0029
Husband fair household × hours female tasks							−0.0017	0.9883*
Wife fair household × hours male tasks							−0.0079	0.9922
Wife fair household × hours female tasks							−0.0002	0.9997
Husband fair paid × hours paid work							0.0083	1.0084
Wife fair paid × hours paid work							−0.0199	0.9803**
N	2,858							
−2LL	778.310							
Change (−2LL)		443.766**		44.070**		20.076**		24.066**

Note: *p < .05, **p < .01 for coefficient or for −2LL change over prior model.

Doing female tasks appears to increase the likelihood of disruption regardless of who does them. Wives' investment in traditionally female tasks leads to marginally higher risks of breakup. Though very small in magnitude (about 0.7 percent per hour), this effect was also found among husbands. Each additional hour that *wives* spend on *male tasks* is associated with a reduction of about 4 percent in the risk of dissolution. In sum, when wives do tasks typically done by husbands, their marriages appear to have lower chances of disruption. When wives increase their involvement in tasks typically done by women, however, their marriages may have higher chances of disruption.

Before interpreting the results already presented, it is necessary to consider the perceived fairness of the division of tasks. In Model 3, the coefficients for two of the four measures of fairness are statistically significant: the wife's sense of fairness in household tasks, and the husband's sense of fairness in paid labor. Both are negative, meaning that, when wives believe the division of household labor or when husbands believe the division of paid labor is *unfair to the other partner*, disruption rates are lower (alternatively, when things are seen as unfair to oneself, disruption rates are higher). These results suggest that perceptions of fairness play a role in how time spent in household and paid labor matters for marital stability. In the final model, we address this issue directly.

The final equation (Model 4) adds twelve interaction terms to investigate how perceptions of fairness moderate the various effects of household labor just described. Five interaction terms are statistically significant, indicating that household and paid labor have differing implications depending on how spouses view the fairness of their arrangements. Four of the five significant interaction effects involve wives' evaluations of fairness. Since there are so many interaction terms, and several pertain to the same variables, the results are difficult to summarize without an illustration.

The interaction effects indicate that similar investments in paid and household labor have different consequences for marital stability depending on how they are perceived (that is, on the evaluation of fairness). To summarize these results, we present the combined effects of the relevant variables in table 10.5. The entries in this table are the changes to the baseline risk of marital disruption associated with each combination of the four questions about fairness. To compute the *RISK* values reported in the table, we evaluated couples at the average (mean) level of involvement in all types of paid and unpaid labor (and at the mean of every other variable except those pertaining to fairness and interactions). Then we added the relevant fairness variables and the interaction terms to produce the change in the baseline risk of dissolution that would result. For example, the first entry in table 10.5 is 4.43. This value indicates that, when time in paid and household labor (and all other variables in Model 2 of table 4) are at the averages, the baseline risk of dissolution is 4.43 times greater when both spouses see each type of labor as "very unfair" to themselves. The

Table 10.5 *Combined effects of interactions of fairness and hours of work on risk of marital disruption*

| | Husband's sense of fairness about paid work | | | | | | | | |
| | Very unfair to me Husband fairness household work | | | Fair to both Husband fairness household work | | | Very unfair to her Husband fairness household work | | |
Wife's sense of fairness about paid work	Very unfair to me	Fair to both	Very unfair to her	Very unfair to me	Fair to both	Very unfair to her	Very unfair to me	Fair to both	Very unfair to her
Very unfair to me Wife fairness household work									
Very unfair to me	4.43	3.10	2.17	2.06	1.44	1.01	0.96	0.67	0.47
Fair to both	2.55	1.79	1.25	1.19	0.83	0.58	0.55	0.22	0.16
Very unfair to him	1.47	1.03	0.72	0.68	0.48	0.34	0.32	0.22	0.16
Fair to both Wife fairness household work									
Very unfair to me	8.48	5.93	4.15	3.94	2.76	1.93	1.83	1.28	0.90
Fair to both	8.48	3.42	2.39	2.27	1.59	1.11	1.06	0.74	0.52
Very unfair to him	2.82	1.97	1.38	1.31	0.92	0.64	0.61	0.82	0.30
Very unfair to him Wife fairness household work									
Very unfair to me	16.22	11.35	7.95	7.54	5.28	3.69	3.51	2.45	1.72
Fair to both	9.35	6.55	4.58	4.35	3.04	2.13	2.02	1.42	0.99
Very unfair to him	5.39	3.77	2.64	2.51	1.75	1.23	1.17	0.82	0.59

value 4.43 was obtained by calculating the baseline risk of marital disruption from Model 2, with all variables at their averages. Then values for the four fairness and the twelve interaction terms were varied and their effects were added to the baseline risk. The value for all questions about fairness in this example was 1.0 (very unfair to me). Other cells were computed by changing the values for all fairness questions and the associated interaction terms.

Table 10.5 highlights a central, yet simple, finding of our work: the investment of time in male or female household tasks, or in paid labor, must be understood in connection with perceived fairness when evaluating the consequences for couples. The results in table 10.5 may be summarized by comparing "best" and "worst" cases. The "worst" outcome (that is, the highest *RISK* of 16.22) is found among couples who disagree in an interesting way. Both partners think that paid work is unfair to the husband. They disagree over housework. He sees paid and household work as unfair to him. She also sees paid work as unfair to him. But she sees household work as unfair to herself. The best outcome (that is, the lowest *RISK* of 0.16) is found when the husband sees both paid work and household tasks as very unfair to his wife. She agrees about paid work (very unfair to her), but thinks housework is fair to both, or very unfair to her husband.

Perhaps the most surprising result is found in the case of agreement that paid and household tasks are fair to both partners. The middle cell of the table has a value of 1.59, indicating that this combination is associated with higher risks of divorce. Complete agreement that both spouses are treated fairly, in other words, may not be the best situation.

To gain a sense of the relative importance of the various types of fairness perceptions, we can compare the values of risk in the table. To do so, focus on blocks of nine cells defined by paid-work evaluations. The first such block consists of the nine cells defined by the husband's report that paid work is very unfair to himself, and the wife's report that paid work is very unfair to herself. Generally, the values in table 10.5 decline as one moves from left to right (that is, as husbands report that paid work is increasingly unfair to wives). Further, values increase as one moves from the top to the bottom of the table (that is, as a wife reports that paid work is increasingly unfair to herself). Thus, marriages in which husbands believe their wives bear an unfair burden for paid work and in which wives share that view are at lower risk of dissolution than other combinations. When it comes to perceptions about the fairness of household tasks, another pattern appears. At any combination of values for paid work (for example, the first block of nine cells) agreement by both partners that the arrangement is unfair to the *other person* produces the best outcomes (that is, the lowest risk of disruption). For example, when both partners feel that paid work is unfair to themselves (the first nine-cell block in the table), the risks of disruption range from 4.43 to 0.72. The highest risk obtains when partners each feel household tasks are unfair to themselves. The lowest value obtains when both feel such tasks are unfair to their partner.

Focusing first on how perceptions of fairness about *paid work* influence disruption risks, we compare comparable cells from any two blocks. Men's evaluations of the fairness of paid work alter the risks of disruption by a factor of 2.15 (e.g. 4.43 versus 2.06). Women's evaluations of the fairness of paid work, similarly, alter disruption risks by a factor of 1.91 (e.g. 8.48 versus 4.43). Men's sense of fairness about paid work, in short, is minimally more consequential than is women's.

By focusing on the cells within any block, it is possible to assess the relative importance of perceptions of fairness about *household tasks*. Doing so shows that husbands' sense of fairness about household work changes the risk by a factor of about 2.04 (moving left to right in any block of cells, such as 4.43 versus 2.17) and wives' by a factor of about 3.01 (moving from top to bottom in any block of cells, such as 4.43 versus 1.47). Women's sense of fairness about household work is considerably more consequential than is men's, and more consequential than either partner's concerns about the fairness of paid work.

4   Discussion

We sought to provide a rudimentary answer to the question asked by Goldscheider and Waite (1991): What effect does an egalitarian division of household labor have on marriages? The simplest answer is that marriages are strained when either partner does more traditionally female housework. At the same time, marriages are strengthened by time spent in traditionally male tasks. But this simple conclusion ignores the complexity of the social psychology of the household. At a minimum, "efficiency" (specialization) does not mean "stability." Doing more traditionally male tasks, such as home and auto maintenance, increases marital stability *no matter who does them* and no matter whether the worker is employed or not. This is not consistent with Becker's analysis.

What might explain the difference in the impact of "men's" and "women's" work? Traditionally male jobs, when done outside the household, are better paying than are traditionally female jobs, and tend to be (psychologically) valued more highly. Particularly for the middle-class couples at the mean of our sample, who together were earning roughly $40,000 a year in 1987–8, doing such work for the household may not seem degrading (and may actually seem rewarding). For example, the Bureau of Labor Statistics (United States Department of Labor, 1988) reports weekly earnings of $444 for carpentry and floor work, $385 for plumbing and heating, and $332 for auto repair. In contrast, for either spouse (and particularly men), doing the lower-paying, lower-status "female" work apparently lowers the value of the marriage. The same Bureau of Labor Statistics data show weekly earnings of $210 for residential care, $146 for miscellaneous personal services, $206 for laundry-dry cleaning and garment services, and $159 for retail bakeries. In 1985, men employed as repairers and mechanics earned an average of $400 weekly, compared with the $130 women earned in private household service (United States Department of the Census, 1998, table 698).

There are other, and related, explanations for the difference between the effects of "men's" and "women's" work on marital stability. "Men's work" tends to contribute directly to the value of the couple's tangible assets. For example, building an addition on a house or installing thermally efficient windows will increase the home's resale value. (It will also increase the share of the property allocated to whoever did or financed the improvement, should the couple divorce). Doing work on an automobile may save costly repairs and may increase the car's resale or trade-in value. On the other hand, ironing shirts or keeping a spotless home enhances assets in a much less direct and tangible way.

With higher possible wages, better household technology (Cohen, 1995), and fewer children, late-twentieth-century American women no longer typically dropped out of the paid labor force (Bianchi and Spain, 1996). But the answer to Hochschild's "second shift" problem is not (at least not yet) more sharing of typical homemaking tasks. Our research shows that such a solution would probably increase marital instability. It will not be possible for most couples to eliminate such tasks by, for example, hiring domestic servants. Nor is it likely that American society will suddenly begin to value "women's work" by increasing the wages of those who are engaged in such pursuits. So long as housework is devalued (Silbaugh, 1996; Hadfield, 1993), we can predict that greater sharing of such work will probably contribute to marital instability. But this gloomy assessment must be tempered by the significant role played by assessments of fairness. As our findings showed, such perceptions are critically important, and may trump any particular combination of hours committed by either partner to any particular task.

When married partners share the belief that paid work is unfair to wives and that housework is unfair to the other person, the risks of dissolution are lowered significantly. Whether such marital dynamics are sufficient to overcome any particular division of tasks, of course, cannot be answered with our results. But our results suggest that we may err by paying too much attention to the actual division of tasks and too little attention to how people understand such arrangements.

Though we cannot explain why particular combinations of fairness evaluations are associated with different risks of marital disruption, we are prepared to offer some thoughts about why perceived (mutual) fairness may be incompatible with marital stability. Why would perceived fairness in all matters by both spouses not be the best arrangement? The question is both provocative and central to our thinking about marriage and the household division of labor. As spouses, we worry about fairness or rights at times when our affections for each other or our commitment to the marriage ebb to a low point (Waldron, 1988, p. 628). When we contribute to marriage with an expectation of direct return or reward, we get less from it. Law deals with the tendency to contractualize marriage by making it unattractive. Thus cases, even relatively recent ones, consistently deny enforcement of wives' contracts to receive wages in exchange for their housework (Silbaugh, 1996). As a California case reports,

The dissent maintains that mores have changed to the point that spouses can be treated just like any other parties haggling at arm's length. Whether or not the modern marriage has become like a business, and regardless of whatever else it may have become, it continues to be defined by statute as a personal relationship of mutual support. Thus, even if few things are left that cannot command a price, marital support remains one of them.[2]

[2] *Borelli v. Brusseau,* 16 Cal.Rptr.2d 16, 20 (Cal. Ct. App. 1993).

The psychological literature reveals that spouses who see marriage in exchange terms have lower levels of satisfaction with marriage than other spouses do (Hansen, 1991). Sociological research also shows that marriages are more stable when the spouses depend upon one another (Nock, 1995). When husbands and wives are able to look beyond immediate fairness and to act for the benefit of the other, the children, or the marriage, they take what Milton Regan calls an internal stance (Regan, 1999, p. 24) which "is central to a meaningful interpersonal relationship and the growth of love" (Rempel, Holmes, and Zanna, 1985, p. 110). And this is what the very low values in the upper right-hand block of table 10.5 show. But why marriages benefit when husbands and wives agree that wives are treated unfairly, but suffer when they agree that husbands are treated unfairly (the block at the lower left of table 10.5), is still unclear. Perhaps wives are, in some fundamental sense, more unfairly treated in marriages. Possibly, the contemporary arrangement of American marriages casts women and men in asymmetrical relationships that are inherently unfair in some way. If so, then our results are easily understood. An appreciation for such unfairness, that is, apparently contributes to marital stability. Men and women, it seems, derive some benefit (in marital stability) for acknowledging this issue. Lack of appreciation for the unfair burden may cause women to file for divorce, and it is primarily they who do so (Brinig and Allen, 2000).

Can we have egalitarian marriages? Is it possible to envision a pattern of housework and paid labor that is fair to both partners and that does not undermine the stability of the union? Our results suggest that mutual perceived fairness or an exchange-type relationship may not be the most desirable situation if stable marriages are the desired outcome. *Stable marriages, that is, may not be experienced as fair marriages.* And, although stable marriages are possible with greater sharing of housework, such sharing may not produce desirable outcomes unless both partners understand that wives bear an unfair burden.

REFERENCES

Allen, Douglas (1992), "What Does She See in Him? The Effect of Sharing on the Choice of Spouse," *Economic Inquiry*, 3(1), 57–67.
Becker, Gary S. (1973), "A Theory of Marriage, Part I," *Journal of Political Economy*, 81(4), 813–46.
——— (1974), "A Theory of Marriage: Part II," *Journal of Political Economy*, 82(2), S11–26.
——— (1975), *Human Capital: A Theoretical and Empirical Analysis, with Specific Reference to Education*, 2nd edn., New York: National Bureau of Economic Research, Columbia University Press.
——— (1985), "Human Capital, Effort, and the Sexual Division of Labor," *Journal of Labor Economics*, 3, S33–58.
——— (1991), *A Treatise on the Family*, Cambridge, MA: Harvard University Press.

Becker, Gary, Elisabeth M. Landes, and Robert T. Michael (1977), "An Economic Analysis of Marital Instability," *Journal of Political Economy*, 85(6), 1141–87.

Berk, Sarah Fenstermaker (1995), *The Gender Factory: The Apportionment of Work in American Households*, New York: Plenum Press.

Bianchi, Suzanne M. and Daphne Spain (1996), "Women, Work, and Family in America," *Population Bulletin*, 51(3), 2–48.

Blau, Francine W. (1998), "Trends in the Well-Being of American Women, 1970–95," *Journal of Economic Literature*, 36, 112–65.

Brinig, Margaret F. (1994), "Comment on Jana Singer's Alimony and Efficiency," *Georgetown Law Journal*, 82, 2461–79.

Brinig, Margaret F. and Douglas W. Allen (2000), "These Boots Are Made for Walking: Why Most Divorce Filers are Women," *American Law and Economics Review*, 2, 126–69.

Brinig, Margaret F. and June Carbone (1988), "The Reliance Interest in Marriage and Divorce," *Tulane Law Review*, 62, 853–905.

Bumpass, Larry L. and James A. Sweet (1995), "Cohabitation, Marriage and Union Stability: Preliminary Findings from NSFH2," NSFH Working Paper No. 65, Madison, Center for Demography and Ecology.

Bumpass, Larry, Teresa Castro, and James A. Sweet (1990), "Recent Trends in Marital Disruption," *Demography*, 26(1), 37–52.

Cohen, Lloyd (1995), "Rhetoric, the Unnatural Family, and Women's Work," *Virginia Law Review*, 81, 2275–305.

Duncan, Beverly and Otis D. Duncan (1978), *Sex Typing and Social Roles: A Research Report*, New York: Academic Press.

Goldscheider, Frances K. and Linda J. Waite (1991), *New Families, No Families? The Transformation of the American Home*, Berkeley: University of California Press.

Gronau, Reuben (1980), "Home Production – A Forgotten Industry," *Review of Economics and Statistics*, 62(3), 408–16.

Grossbard-Schechtman, Shoshana (1993), *On the Economics of Marriage: A Theory of Marriage, Labor, and Divorce*, Boulder, CO: Westview Press.

Hadfield, Gillian K. (1993), "Households at Work: beyond Labor Market Policies to Remedy the Gender Gap," *Georgetown Law Journal*, 82, 89–107.

(1999), "A Coordination Model of Sexual Division of Labor," *Journal of Economic Behavior and Organization*, 40, 125–53.

Hansen, Gary L. (1991), "Moral Reasoning and the Marital Exchange Relationship," *Journal of Social Psychology*, 131, 71–81.

Hochschild, Arlie and Anne Machung (1989), *The Second Shift*, New York: Viking Penguin.

Lennon, Mary Clare and Sarah Rosenfield (1994), "Relative Fairness and the Division of Housework: The Importance of Options," *American Journal of Sociology*, 100, 506–31.

Nock, Steven L. (1995), "Commitment and Dependency in Marriage," *Journal of Marriage and the Family*, 57, 503–14.

Parkman, Allen W. (1992), *No-Fault Divorce: What Went Wrong?* Boulder, CO: Westview Press.

(1998), "Why Are Married Women Working So Hard?" *International Review of Law and Economics*, 18, 41–9.

Regan, Milton C. (1999), *Alone Together: Love and the Meaning of Marriage*, Oxford: Oxford University Press.

Rempel, John K., John G. Holmes, and Mark P. Zanna (1995), "Trust in Close Relationships," *Journal of Personality and Social Psychology*, 49, 95–120.

Shelton, Beth Ann (1992), *Men, Women, and Time: Gender Differences in Paid Work, Housework and Leisure*, New York: Greenwood Press.

Silbaugh, Katharine (1996), "Turning Labor into Love: Housework and the Law," *Northwestern University Law Review*, 91, 1–86.

Smith, Bea (1990), "The Partnership Theory of Marriage: A Borrowed Solution Fails," *Texas Law Review* 68, 689–743.

Smith, Herbert L., Constance T. Gager, and S. Philip Morgan (1998), "Identifying Underlying Dimensions in Spouses' Evaluations of Fairness in the Division of Household Labor," *Social Science Research*, 27, 305–27.

Spain, Daphne G. and Suzanne M. Bianchi (1996), *Balancing Act: Motherhood, Marriage, and Employment Among American Women*, New York: Russell Sage Foundation.

Thomson, Linda (1991), "Family Work: Women's Sense of Fairness," *Journal of Family Issues*, 12, 181–96.

Tocqueville, Alexis de (1835), *Democracy in America*. New York: Vintage Books, ed. 1954.

United States Department of Labor (1988), Bureau of Labor Statistics, *National Employment, Hours and Earnings*, Series ID: EEU80729004, etc.

United States Department of the Census (1998), *Statistical Abstract of the United States*, Rockville, MD.

Waldron, Jeremy (1988), "When Justice Replaces Affection: The Need for Rights," *Harvard Journal of Law and Public Policy*, 11, 625–47.

11 The impact of legal reforms on marriage and divorce

Douglas W. Allen

1 Introduction

With several countries currently reconsidering the status of their existing marriage and divorce legislation, there has begun an increased interest in the "facts" regarding the actual impact of laws on marriage and divorce behavior. For those interested in a simple answer, a simple perusal of the economic literature will not be very satisfactory. There, some argue that the law merely reflects the social norms of the time, and is impotent in changing any behavior. Others argue that the law is critical in establishing the constraints and threat points that couples bargain under, and therefore the laws do influence behavior. Presumably an empirical analysis of these issues could settle this dispute, but unfortunately, though the questions are relatively straightforward, the answers seem very difficult to pin down. Furthermore, although the effect of marriage laws must filter into all types of household decisions – from the choice of living together or becoming married, to the choice over what career path to take – almost all of the academic attention has been devoted to the effect of no-fault divorce laws on the divorce rate, with relatively minor attention paid to female labor force participation.

When it comes to marriage law, as detailed as that subject is, most people simply mean the no-fault divorce laws that swept the Western world in the early 1970s. Although another significant aspect of the law relates to how marital property is divided at divorce, over time community and common law distinctions have converged to the point where there is little difference. Hence, in addition to the grounds under which a divorce might occur, some attention has been given to the rules under which property is divided at the time of divorce. With this in mind, in this chapter I intend to provide a broad discussion of the economic effects of no-fault divorce laws on three economic decisions: the divorce rate, labor force participation, and the age at which individuals marry. For the most part I will provide a survey of the literature; however, for the question regarding the age at marriage I do provide some new evidence.

The bottom line regarding the effects of divorce laws is that the effects are quite straightforward but not that large in absolute size. No-fault divorce does

Thanks to Bob Rowthorn for comments.

raise the divorce rate, but accounts for only about 17 percent of the increased stock of divorces over the past thirty years by the best estimate. No-fault divorce does raise the age of first time marriage, but by only about six to nine months. Likewise, no-fault divorce contributes about a 2 percent increase in the labor force participation of married women. In the conclusion of the chapter I discuss the possibility that the divorce law in part shapes our culture as well as our culture shaping it, and how the simple econometric models used thus far have ignored this.

2   The simple economics of fault and no-fault divorce

The essence of a fault-based divorce law is that one party must breach the marriage contract by committing a specific act in order for a divorce to occur. At the turn of the twentieth century these faults mostly consisted of adultery, desertion, and cruelty in common law localities. Some jurisdictions had more faults, others less, and the tendency throughout the twentieth century in all jurisdictions was to add to the list.[1] In Canada, the 1968 Divorce Act, for example, added fifteen faults for divorce. Prior to this, faults for divorce in Canada were a provincial responsibility. Eight provinces essentially legislated adultery as the only ground, whereas Quebec and Newfoundland required private acts of parliament's Senate to dissolve a marriage.[2] The addition of "insanity" was a turning point in US faults because it was the first instance where legislatures recognized that a marriage could be over without the culpability of one partner.

Essentially a fault-based law assigns the property right, or power to divorce, to the spouse *least wanting to divorce*.[3] Divorces that result from violence and abuse, in cases where this is reported, actually account for a very small number of divorces. Foster and Freed (1973/4, p. 446) state: "It is not an oversimplification to say that such statutes convert the system from one where divorce most often is a matter of mutual consent into one where it is available upon unilateral demand." In addition to determining whether a divorce would take place, fault could often play a role in determining the property settlement. For example, spouses who committed a fault might be punished in terms of child custody or loss of marital property.[4] However, one of the major consequences of fault-based divorce was the incentive it provided for privately negotiated

---

[1] The list of faults can become quite colorful. In Lebanon if one belongs to the Greek Orthodox community, fault includes, among other things, "willful destruction by the wife of the husband's seed; if wife . . . attends banquets or bathes with men in mixed baths, all against the husband's order; if she goes to the races, theaters, or gambling halls surreptitiously or against the husband's orders" (*Martingale-Hubbell Law Digest*, 1991, p. LEB-5).

[2] See Allen (1998) for more details.

[3] Economists have generally assumed that the wife has been most committed to the marriage. Recent research by Allen and Brinig (1998), however, has shown that, of those who divorce, women are more likely to behave opportunistically.

[4] In fact, even in many "no-fault" states, fault still plays a role in custody and property settlement. This is part of the reason for the debate over state legal classification. Brinig and Buckley (1998),

divorce settlements. Since many marriages "died" for reasons other than those listed by legislation, and since even when a legal fault was committed it was difficult to prove, in actual practice the husband and wife often negotiated a private divorce settlement and simply agreed to a fault. Throughout the twentieth century, prior to the introduction of no-fault divorce, the preferred fault to agree on was cruelty. When the couple proceeded with an uncontested divorce and with an agreed property settlement, the agreement would supersede the state or provincial laws on marital property. This practice described the vast majority of divorce cases.[5] No-fault divorce laws essentially eliminated the grounds for divorce by introducing a unilateral ground such as separation or irreconcilable differences. The critical feature of these grounds is that one party can instigate a divorce without the consent of the other spouse. As was mentioned, the ability unilaterally to divorce might be tempered by penalties in terms of child custody or property settlement if an actual fault has been committed. Barring these restraints, however, a no-fault law transfers the right to divorce to the individual *most wanting a divorce*.

In order to analyze the impact of divorce laws on the decision to divorce, suppose the dollar values in table 11.1 can be placed on a marriage. This number simply reflects the utility that the husband and wife obtain from their marriage.[6] Likewise suppose there is a dollar value for both the husband and the wife for being single. If the joint value of being single (that is, the sum of the husband's and wife's single values) is greater than the joint value married, then a divorce is efficient. When the opposite is true (that is, when the joint value of staying together is greater than being apart), and yet the couple still divorces, then this is called an inefficient divorce. Presumably the law should allow efficient divorces because this raises social values. On the other hand, the law should discourage inefficient divorces for the opposite reason – they lower social value. In viewing marriages as simply good or bad, and in thinking that only bad marriages end in divorce, the proponents for divorce reform made the simple conclusion that no-fault divorce was efficient.

In 1977 an influential article was published by Gary Becker et al. that gave a theoretical justification for why the only divorces that occur are efficient ones. It is an argument based on the work of Ronald Coase (1960). Consider the dollar values in table 11.1 as representing the values of a couple in and out of

---

for example, argue that states with tough property penalties for fault should be counted as fault states, regardless if divorce is unilateral or not.

[5] According to Fain (1977, p. 34): "Well over 90 percent of American divorces were uncontested. Marital fault usually was significant only as it affected the negotiation process and provided leverage for financial or property terms eventually agreed upon." Freed and Foster (1979, p. 107) state the same, saying: "Under the traditional nineteenth and early twentieth century grounds for divorce, over 90 percent of divorces were uncontested and hence there was divorce by mutual agreement and *de facto* created a mutual consent divorce law."

[6] I want to stress that this dollar value is *not* a mere reflection of the financial value of the marriage; it is just a convenient measure of the *total* utility the husband and wife obtain from marriage.

194   *Douglas W. Allen*

Table 11.1. *Sample payoffs in an efficient marriage ($)*

	Husband	Wife	Total
Married	50	50	100
Divorced	60	30	90

Source: This example is taken from Allen (1995).

marriage. Since the total value of the marriage is greater than the total value of the couple when they are single, this is an efficient marriage and the couple should not divorce. Suppose the law is a fault law. The husband must come to his wife and purchase the right to divorce. The husband is better off by $10 due to the divorce, but the wife is worse off by $20. In other words, the husband is willing to pay the wife $10 for the right to divorce, but the wife will not accept anything below $20. As a result a divorce will not happen and the socially efficient result occurs. On the other hand, suppose the law is no-fault. Now the husband need not purchase the right and can just leave. However, the wife prefers the husband to stay, and is willing to pay for him to do so. Clearly there is room for bargaining since the $20 the wife is willing to pay exceeds the $10 that the husband requires. Once again the marriage remains together. In other words, it did not matter what the law said, the same efficient outcome occurred. If we had started with a marriage that was inefficient (that is, where the numbers were reversed), then the marriage would have ended in divorce under both laws. For example, if we switch the row labels such that the value of marriage is $60 for the husband and $30 for the wife, and the value of a divorce is $50 each, then the wife will seek and obtain a divorce under both laws. With fault law she is better off by $20 from divorce compared with her husband's loss of $10. If she pays her husband $11 they are both better off with a divorce. If the law is no-fault, she leaves and the husband is unwilling to compensate her to stay. Hence, once again the law has no effect on the divorce outcome. This bears reiterating: regardless of the law, when parties are free to bargain, only efficient divorces occur. The empirical implication of this is that the change in divorce law should have had no effect on the divorce rate.

This is a powerful result, and one that gave theoretical justification to the preliminary assessments of the new laws. Yet something about it rings untrue. The critical assumption in the above analysis is that property rights or ownership are complete. Economists say that the *transactions costs* are zero in order for the result to hold.[7] The problem is that marriage is one exchange where the

---

[7] Transactions costs are the costs of establishing and maintaining property rights (ownership). See Allen (1991) for an elaboration.

transactions costs are quite high. As a result it is often possible that divorces happen in no-fault situations that are *inefficient*.

The number and types of transactions costs that may result in inefficient divorces under no-fault divorce laws would seem to be quite large. First, quirks in property laws at the time of divorce can easily create situations whereby efficient marriages dissolve. For example, if a wife contributes to the education of her husband, but the courts do not consider a degree as property, then that contribution is not considered in the marital property settlement. Likewise pension funds, insurance policies, and lost workforce opportunities may or may not be considered property in a given jurisdiction. In some US states there is an automatic split of marital property 50:50, despite contribution. In other states the courts make an effort to establish each spouse's contribution to the marriage. In every case imperfect rules are made that allow one spouse to take advantage of the other. The history of divorce legislation since the enactment of no-fault divorce has been the adoption of one band-aid remedy after another. No sooner is one type of asset ruled on as marital property than another example emerges. As long as it is costly to write laws and as long as transactions costs are positive, no law will ever define property accurately enough, and the possibility of inefficient divorces arises.

Second, government failures to enforce support payments for children and spouse allow instigating parties to avoid some of the costs of their actions. Hence the private values of the party leaving the marriage can be out of line with the joint value of the marriage. This phenomenon of the "deadbeat dad" imposes costs not only on the mother and children but also on the state, which is often required to assist the family through welfare.[8] To the extent welfare creates its own set of disincentives, the wife and children are further made worse off.

Third, many family assets may be indivisible or may be public goods, making them difficult and costly to bargain over at the time of divorce. Zelder (1993) makes the case that children are always quasi-public goods, and as a result their presence almost always makes the divorce inefficient. "Public good" is an economic term that essentially means one's consumption of a good does not hinder the consumption by another. With children, the fact that a father gets utility from a child does not mean the mother cannot also gain utility from a child. This affects divorce because a father can leave a marriage and still get utility from being a father. The mother, in using the child as an enticement to stay, is limited by the fact that the child is partly a public good. To the extent that utility from children is tied to access, this reduces the public good nature of children. Unfortunately, for many fathers this does not appear to be the case.

---

[8] Moir (1999) makes the case that failure to make payments may reflect the fact that one man cannot support the original household at the same standard of living when he establishes a second household, rather than a lack of responsibility on the part of the husband.

Fourth, violent reactions by a spouse may make renegotiating the terms of the marriage too costly, and an inefficient divorce or marriage may occur. Inefficient bargains are always the result of a failure to respect the property rights of others. Given the physical difference between husbands and wives, and given the privacy in which they interact, violence is often a possibility. Either party is capable of threats of violence in order forcibly to dissolve a marriage and enforce a property settlement that does not reflect the true contributions of the parties. Likewise, both parties can force a divorce by destroying the marital capital if they stay together by being abusive or irresponsible and dissipating financial assets. Similarly, one party may be able to maintain a marriage through threats of force. When violence or threats of violence are involved, inefficient divorces and marriages are likely.

Finally, contracts based on a promise not to leave are essentially unenforceable in court, so this restricts the ability to bargain for the person least wanting to leave and can result in an inefficient divorce (Brinig and Buckley, 1998).

Allen and Brinig (1998) provide another reason for bargaining failures based on biological differences between the life-cycle demands for sex for men and women. Marriage is such a complicated contract that the list of transactions costs that could lead to breach is probably very long. This is particularly a problem for women. Though wives make many contributions to a marriage, a major one is pregnancy and the rearing of children. Though a mother may also work, the presence of more than one child causes major disruptions in workforce participation, and hence a reduction in her financial contribution to the household. Because this contribution takes place early in a marriage, the wife makes a sunk investment in the marriage and places herself in considerable jeopardy. The husband, on the other hand, makes no such investment. In fact, typical male incomes increase throughout his working life. Middle-aged husbands, then, can realistically expect a new spouse after divorce, whereas the same is not true for middle-aged wives.[9] Under these conditions it is easy to see why the inability to enter a binding contract with the husband is detrimental to wives. Thus the question of what happens to the divorce rate when the law changes from fault to no-fault is ultimately an empirical one that hinges on the level of transactions costs. If transactions costs are high, for example because marital property is difficult to define or child payments are hard to enforce, then the divorce rate should increase with the introduction of no-fault.

Given that there are a number of factors at work that increase the chance that bargaining to prevent a divorce will break down, it seems unlikely that the divorce rate should remain constant. In addition, there is a reciprocal reason

---

[9] After 40 the male/female sex ratio also begins to turn against women, and the increased competition hurts the bargaining position of wives.

for increased divorce rates, namely, the old fault law allowed for inefficient *marriages*. The reason is that similar transactions cost problems hold true for inefficient marriages under fault divorce. For example, suppose a couple marries, neither of their expectations are met, and, although one partner wishes to remain married, total wealth is higher if they separate. If the husband wants the divorce, the wife may not agree if she believes the husband will default on alimony and the state will not enforce the divorce agreement. In other words, the potential transactions costs of privately enforcing a separation agreement may prevent the agreement in the first place. Transactions costs may also arise over non-transferable wealth, from indivisibilities in marital property or children, or from violence or threats of violence, that again may prevent a bargain from taking place. Hence the presence of transactions costs implies some inefficient marriages when there is fault divorce and some inefficient divorces under no-fault divorce. Both of these factors imply that the divorce rate should increase when no-fault laws are introduced.

If no-fault divorce allows for the creation of inefficient divorces, and if this problem is greater than the inefficient marriages that might result from fault law, then no-fault laws essentially raise the costs of getting and remaining married. This has a number of relatively straightforward implications for other marriage decisions. Given that there are still gains from marriage, when the protection offered by fault laws is absent individuals will substitute other forms of private protection of the rents generated throughout the marriage. For example, with no-fault divorce women should be more likely to increase the number of hours in the workforce, they should be more likely to participate in the workforce, and they should be more likely to choose careers that can support them if they do become divorced. Cohabitation might become more likely, especially for individuals with physical wealth heading into the marriage or individuals who expect to earn large quasi-rents during the marriage. Finally, individuals will marry later in order to evaluate their potential spouse better.

Perhaps because it has taken so long to converge to an answer on whether or not no fault divorce influenced the divorce rate, most of these latter issues have not been studied. In the next section I survey the research that has been done on the divorce rate and labor force participation. I also provide some new results on the effect of no-fault divorce on the age at marriage.

3   The evidence

The divorce rate

In order to understand the empirical evidence on the effect of no-fault laws on the divorce rate, it is important to divide the literature into those studies published before and after 1986, when Elizabeth Peters' work was published in the *American Economic Review* (Peters, 1986). Her work was the capstone of a series of articles that concluded no-fault laws made no difference to divorce rates. Because it was the first to use a large data set and sophisticated econometric techniques, it appeared to provide the ultimate empirical verification of the work done by Becker a decade before.

Yet this triumph was short lived, and the demise was foreshadowed a year earlier with the publication of Weitzman's book, *The Divorce Revolution* (Weitzman, 1985). Although Weitzman's book contained no random samples or complicated regressions, its commonsense reporting rang true. In contrast to Peters, Weitzman's interviews and numbers suggested that divorce rates were higher with no-fault, and that divorce was a financial disaster for women. Jacob (1988, p. 162) was one of the last major social scientists to assert that no-fault laws had no impact on the divorce rate by quite tersely stating: "no-fault itself did not add to the rising wave of divorce."[10] Parkman (1992a), in a book highly critical of no-fault divorce, also tersely reviewed the literature on the divorce rate. In citing only Becker (1981) and Peters (1986), he concluded: "No-fault divorce did have a feedback effect that led to an increase in the divorce rate for a period shortly after its introduction, but the divorce rate then returned to its earlier trend" (p. 79). Parkman was unaware of the studies that were about to refute this conclusion. Since the publication of Peters' work, not a single study on divorce rates has agreed with her finding. In fact, her results have been shown to depend on a misclassification of data.

There were at least seven studies on divorce rates and no-fault laws prior to 1986.[11] In retrospect, many of the early ones are reminiscent of blind people feeling the different parts of the elephant. Not only were there no computers or software to work with, there were practically no data! Goddard (1972) was first, and concluded that no-fault laws in California increased the divorce rate because the number of divorces in 1970–1 was higher than "expected." Schoen, Greenblatt, and Mielke (1975) visually compared the California trend in divorce with the US trend and concluded that there was no lasting effect.[12] Gallagher (1973) provided another example of simplistic methods. He concluded that divorce rates in Delaware soared as the result of no-fault laws based on a table of divorce decrees for seven years across three counties.[13] Gallagher was incorrect in stating that "[n]o-fault divorce is a concept that has been recognized

---

[10] Jacob argues elsewhere (Jacob, 1989) that there was no effect on the welfare of women either; which makes one wonder why he chose *The Silent Revolution* as the title of his book.

[11] See Zelder (1992) for a critical assessment of these early studies.

[12] This type of experiment was repeated by Becker (1981) using econometric methods, and he basically arrived at the same conclusion.

[13] Gallagher, for a lawyer, doesn't even get the classification quite right. In analyzing no-fault divorce laws, the most important feature is that the law allow for *unilateral* divorce.

in Delaware since 1957 when voluntary separation for three years became a
ground for divorce" (1973, p. 873). Since the separation was to be voluntary,
the Delaware divorce law amounted to a mutual divorce law – which is the
opposite of a unilateral law. This is seen when he states: "lawyers found that a
contested voluntary separation action was usually difficult for a plaintiff to win.
The controversy often evolved into a claim by the plaintiff that the separation
was voluntary against a disclaimer of voluntariness by the defendant. In most
contested cases, the plaintiff lost" (1973, p. 873). The studies by Wright and
Stetson (1973), Frank, Burman, and Mazur-Hart (1978), and Sepler (1981),
although better, still amounted to simple correlations and visual inspection of
graphed divorce rates.

Five years passed between the publication of Becker's work on California
and Peters' 1986 work. Unlike the earlier studies, Peters began with the 1979
Current Population Survey (CPS) published by the US Bureau of Labor, which
had a special supplement related to divorce. From these data she drew a sample
of approximately 20,000 women from all fifty US states – some of whom had
been divorced, all of whom had been married just once. She then ran logit
regressions with these data, controlling for age, number of children, education,
region of residence, etc., along with a variable indicating whether the state was
no-fault or not.[14] What she found was that the no fault variable was essentially
zero – the probability of divorce did not depend on the law. Allen (1992)
showed that the Peters cross-section regression is very sensitive. What made
the CPS data so valuable was that they were collected between 1975 and 1978,
a time when some states were no-fault and others were not. This is crucial for
a cross-section regression. A problem arises, however, over how to classify the
states that changed *during* the 1975–8 period. It turned out that three states
(Massachusetts, Rhode Island, and Wyoming), amounting to only 38 divorces
in the whole sample of 20,000 women, were misclassified. Simply correcting
this problem changed Peters' result from the law having no statistical effect
to the law having a positive and significant one. Suddenly, all of the evidence
to suggest the law did not matter was reduced to the earlier crude graphs of
divorce rates.[15]

Since 1986 there has been a flood of research on the effect of no-fault laws
on divorce rates, reflecting higher-quality data, better econometric programs,
and better legal definitions. Marvell (1989) conducted the first systematic and
complete time-series analysis of divorce rates across the USA. He used the aggregate state-wide divorce data by year, along with other variables that measured

---

[14] Given the primitive state of computers and software in the early 1980s, this regression was quite
an accomplishment.
[15] Like the case of Gallagher (1973), many of these early studies are plagued with data problems
and incorrect classification of states. See Marvell (1989) for a discussion.

average state incomes, etc.[16] He concluded that "[n]o-fault laws, ... had a significant impact on divorce rates, with the major thrust delayed for a year" (p. 563). Anderson and Shughart (1991) were the first to consider the effect of property laws and the distinction between no-fault laws that allow unilateral divorce and those that do not. They also used aggregate time-series data from the USA, and conclude that "states that do not provide a no-fault divorce option, have lengthy residency requirement, and impose mandatory separation periods tend to have lower divorce rates" (p. 143).

Other significant studies in recent years have continued to look at more subtle issues. Nakonezny, Shull, and Rodgers (1995) looked at no-fault divorce and how it interacts with income, education, and religiosity, and concluded that "the enactment of no-fault divorce law had a clear positive influence on divorce rates" (p. 487). Weiss and Willis (1989) were the first to use a panel data set that follows a cohort through time, and consistently found that no-fault laws increased the rate of divorce. Finally, Brinig and Buckley (1998) used aggregate longitudinal data with the most careful legal classification of states thus far. They concluded that the "principal finding is that divorce levels are positively and significantly correlated with state laws which do not penalize marital misbehavior at the time of divorce. ... Our study of 1980–91 divorce rates provides the strongest evidence to date that no-fault divorce laws are associated with higher divorce levels" (1998, p. 16).

It is beyond the purpose of this chapter to analyze each one of these papers in any detail. However, three recent papers are of particular importance for the argument made here. The first is a study by Leora Friedberg (1998) in the *American Economic Review*. Friedberg took up the Peters–Allen debate in an effort to provide a definitive answer to the question of divorce laws affecting divorce rates. To do so she amassed a data set that included "virtually every divorce in the U.S. over the entire period of the law changes." Her data were a panel of state-level divorce rates, which means not only that she compared differences in divorce rates across states, as did Peters and Allen, but that she could also control for changes in divorce behavior across time. Friedberg used a series of state and time dummy variables that control for fixed differences across time and states. She concluded that "[t]he estimation reveals a strong influence of unilateral divorce: divorce rates would have been about 6 percent lower if states had not adopted unilateral divorce, accounting for 17 percent of the overall increase between 1968 and 1988" (1998, p. 17). In addition,

---

[16] Data on divorce usually take one of two forms. Either large individual random samples are used, or state-wide data are used. The advantage of the former is that individual characteristics can be used, but the data are only cross-sectional and therefore fixed effects are ignored. The advantage of the latter is that cross-sectional time-series regressions can be used that control for exogenous changes in the divorce rate over time and across space, but only crude averages can be used to control for demographic variables.

Friedberg used the legal definitions produced by Brinig and Buckley (1998) in order to test the different impacts of the different state laws. Some states have no-fault laws that require mutual agreement, whereas others are true unilateral no-fault laws. Friedberg found that:

> the type of unilateral divorce a state adopted mattered. The strictest unilateral divorce, without separation requirements or fault considerations in property division, raised the divorce rate by 0.549 per thousand people – 11.9 percent of the average of 4.6 during the sample period.... Overall, the results strengthen conclusions about the impact of switching to any type of unilateral regime. (1998, p. 12)

The Friedberg study is likely to go down as the definitive answer in the no-fault divorce debate. Some might consider changes in divorce rates, brought about exclusively by the change in law, of around 5–10 percent to be too small to worry about. However, as Friedberg noted, this accumulates to 17 percent of the divorces over the no-fault era.[17]

Changing the law is one of the few instruments available to reduce divorce rates, no matter how small. But ultimately, the issue is not how large the effect is, but whether or not these divorces should be allowed. In other words, is the rise in divorce a result of inefficient or efficient divorces? If the law contributes to a 10 percent rise in the number of inefficient divorces, then presumably this should be prevented.

Two studies have attempted to identify the presence of inefficient divorces caused by the change in the law. Zelder (1993) argued that children are a public good in marriages and that, as a result, their presence can lead to inefficient bargains over divorce. With the presence of public goods the marriage can be efficient but, if one party unilaterally decides to leave, the *private* transferable wealth of the other spouse may be inadequate to prevent the divorce. The presence of public goods allows the divorce instigator to gain all of the benefits of being single, while still consuming the public goods of the marriage. These divorces are inefficient and should not be allowed. To test this, Zelder constructed a variable that measures the total expenditure on children divided by the non-child assets in the household, which presumably proxies the importance of children in the marriage. This variable was then multiplied by a no-fault dummy to capture the inefficient divorces. Zelder tested this using the data set from the Panel Study of Income Dynamics and found that this variable is positive and significant, even when a dummy variable for no-fault divorce is included. He concluded that the presence of children and the bargaining problems they cause at divorce are a significant source of inefficient divorces.

---

[17] Keep in mind that in the USA there was and is a spectrum of laws in the fault and no-fault eras. Forty years ago many states had laws that were quite liberal, and today many no-fault states are quite conservative. Hence, unlike Canada where the change in law was very discrete and profound, the change in US law was less dramatic. This may explain why the number appears low.

Zelder's finding is of particular importance to the no-fault debate because children are found in virtually all marriages. If it is true that children create public goods problems that generate inefficient divorces, then the divorce law should not allow divorce at the will of one party except in cases of childless couples.

Allen (1998) took a different approach in finding evidence for inefficient divorces by modeling costly information about future contributions of potential spouses which results in mistakes in the choice of spouse. This article used variables that measure pregnancy before marriage, workforce participation, and the variance in workforce participation, all multiplied by a no-fault dummy to estimate the probability of an inefficient divorce.[18] In terms of the no-fault divorce debate, the critical finding here is that other factors besides the presence of children can proxy inefficient divorces. Since marriage involves commitments of specific human capital over long periods of time to one single person and relationship, the opportunities for inefficient dissolutions are many. Furthermore, Allen and Zelder pointed out that measuring these factors involves measuring the *interaction* of the no-fault dummy variable with specific demographic variables. This helps put the 17 percent Friedberg number into perspective.

When Friedberg ran her regressions she used straight dummy variables to control for differences across states and time. The 17 percent rise in divorce represents the increase in the divorce rate that was attributed to the no-fault dummy variable alone. Friedberg and others also included demographic variables in their regressions. For example, it is common to include some measure of economic performance since it is well known that the number of divorces increases in economic downturns. However, it is important to note that many of these divorces would not have occurred had the no-fault law not been present. This holds, in fact, for all other demographic and dummy variables in these regressions. The no-fault law interacts with everything, and thus the 17 percent number that Friedberg arrived at should be considered a lower bound. In both the Zelder and Allen studies no-fault divorce laws were found to produce inefficient divorces. These divorces result because transactions costs are too high and prevent family members from convincing the exiting spouse to stay. These two results are important because they deflect the concession that, although no-fault divorce leads to more divorces, these are marriages that should end anyway. Allen's (1998) was also the only paper to analyze the Canadian experience with no-fault divorce. The fact that divorce is a federal responsibility in Canada allowed for a unique opportunity to test the standard question. There is no doubt that Canada's no-fault law raised the divorce rate

---

[18] The actual econometric technique, though not complicated, is space consuming to explain, and irrelevant for the point being made here. Interested readers can refer to the articles.

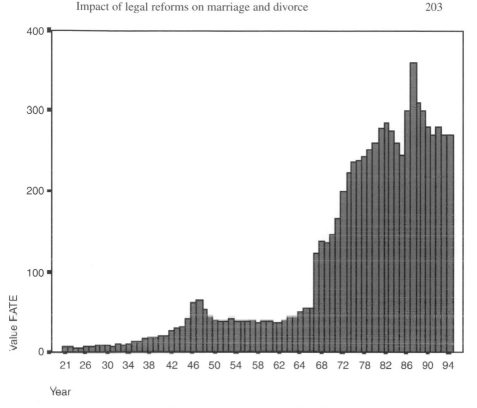

Figure 11.1   Canadian divorce rate per 100,000: 1921–94.

(see figure 11.1). Even looking at the crude divorce rate in figure 11.1, it is obvious that something significant happened in 1968. In the conclusion of the chapter I discuss some reasons for the econometric evidence in favor of legal variables and the divorce rate being so small. One reason is that many of the legal changes have not truly been exogenous. The Canadian experience, however, may be a better test. Canada not only changed its law for all provinces at once, but also was the first country to move to a no-fault law. The Canadian law no doubt caught many people by surprise and could be considered exogenous.

Labor force participation of women

Though there has been a relatively surprising amount of disagreement over the effect of no-fault divorce on the divorce rate, there is remarkable agreement in the work done on the effect of divorce laws on the labor force participation of women (LFPR). Women have been increasingly joining the workforce for over a century, with the bulk of the increase coming after World War II. Until 1970, most of this increase in participation could be attributed to the growth in female real wages. However, a puzzle arose after 1970. Although female participation in the workforce continued to increase, real wage growth was flat. Robert Michael (1985) was the first to suggest that the rise in the participation rate was caused by increases in divorce. Because divorced women are more likely to work, and because the divorce rate was increasing after 1970, he suggested this could explain the anomaly. To test this he observed a lagged relationship between increases in the divorce rate and the increases in the female participation rate of married women with young children.

Peters (1986), in the same article on divorce rates, was the first person to link the no-fault divorce law to the LFPR of women. Peters argued that married women make specific family investments when they stay home and look after the children. If these marriage-specific investments are not accounted for in the divorce property settlement, then the wife is made worse off at divorce, and as a result she tries to protect herself by working during marriage. Using the same CPS data that she used for the divorce rate, Peters ran the LFPR against a series of demographic variables and a dummy variable for whether or not the individual lived in a no-fault state. She found that labor force participation increased by 2 percent in no-fault states.

Allen Parkman (1992b) also investigated the effect of no-fault divorce on the LFPR using the same CPS data as Peters. His main concern was not with the fact that women would increase their LFPR to insure against a divorce, but with how this mechanism worked. Parkman argued that it was not the marriage-specific investments that married women worried about, but that, by being married and staying home with the children, married women decreased their human capital, and this would not be compensated for at the time of divorce. Parkman showed that the increase in LFPR was mostly among married women "who could experience larger reductions in their human capital if they reduced their participation in the labor force." These were young white women. Although Parkman disagreed about the mechanism described by Peters, he found a similar effect for the law.

Parkman (1998) expanded on his earlier work and looked at the total amount of time that women are working. He considered not only the increased workforce participation of women, but also increases in the household work over all. Parkman used a times-series data set that spanned 1975–81 and contained data on household work. He found that women living in a no-fault state worked on average four hours more per week than their counterparts in fault-based states. In contrast, the husbands in these states actually reduced the amount of hours per week by almost two hours. Parkman argued that this refutes the notion that women work simply to increase the family budget, and that women's increased workload is a mechanism for women to use the labor force as a means of obtaining insurance against the threat of divorce.

One final important study is by Johnson and Skinner (1986).[19] As mentioned earlier though, thirteen US states have classifications in conflict with what are normally thought of as no-fault states, and so it is difficult to know what to make of their findings. They used a panel study from Michigan to analyze the effect of divorce on the LFPR. They found that women increase their participation in the workforce before a divorce occurs, which begs the question: did the increase occur because the women were trying to insure against divorce, or was the labor force participation destabilizing to the marriage? They tested these two hypotheses using a simultaneous model of future divorce probability and current labor supply on married women, and concluded that working has no real impact on divorce probabilities, but that an anticipated divorce has a relatively large impact on working. Their results accounted for 2.6 percent of the 15 percent growth in labor force participation that is not explained by real wages and other factors.

The age at marriage

Virtually all of the attention paid to the effect of no-fault divorce law has been directed at either the divorce rate or, to a lesser extent, the labor force participation rate of women. The one exception to this rule is Allen Parkman's book (Parkman, 1992a). In chapter 5 of that book, Parkman explored several other implications of making divorce easy, under the assumption that women generally favor marriage over divorce. For example, Parkman argued that the financial status of women is hurt by no-fault divorce. Since the publication of his book, this has been well documented. Finnie (1995) did an extensive study of post-divorce wealth levels and found that poverty rates are 2.5 times greater for women than for men in the first year of divorce. Brinig and Allen (2000) have found that, when men file for divorce, they do so when they can take many of the financial assets of the marriage with them. Women file for divorce when they can gain full custody of the children. Both of these factors imply a reduced financial status at the time of divorce for women.

Parkman argued that women seek more education and job skills to insure against divorce, that the quality of married life decreases for women, and that the quality of family life also diminishes. He also claimed that individuals will marry later to ensure they have chosen the right spouse, given that divorce is

---

[19] There is also a study by Gray (1998), who added property settlements to the definition of the law and found similar results on the LFPR.

Table 11.2. *Variable definitions*

Variable	Definition
NOFAULT	= 1 if state is no-fault, based on Friedberg (1998)
AGEDIFF	= husband's age minus wife's age
MIXED RACE	= 1 if husband or wife were of different race
B-NUM-MAR	= number of previous marriages of bride
G-NUM-MAR	= number of previous marriages of groom
B-PREVIOUS	= 1 if bride was previously married
G-PREVIOUS	= 1 if groom was previously married
TIME	= 1 if marriage in 1989
	= 2 if marriage in 1990
	...
	= 7 if marriage in 1995

costly, but easy, under no-fault. In each of these cases, Parkman either was making an analytical argument or using some very crude numbers to back himself up. In this section I report numbers on the age at marriage that support this last claim by Parkman.

I use the marriage records collected by the US National Center for Health Statistics for 1989–95. These records contain information on every marriage in the USA during this period. The sample size was 1,250,460 observations, but I took a 10 percent random sample to reduce the run times.[20] Although there are many observations, the number of variables per record is quite small. Essentially one knows the ages at marriage, race, and the locations of the marriages. I use the state classifications for no-fault found in Friedberg (1998). Definitions of the variables used are in table 11.2.

Table 11.3 reports several OLS regressions of age at marriage on a number of variables for a number of different samples for women, while table 11.4 does the same for various samples of men. The results from the female sample are virtually identical to the male sample results. The only difference is that men marry slightly younger women on average. The regressions show that couples who are mixed in race marry later. This may be due to higher search costs across races, or may reflect the higher probability of future divorce for these marriages. The *TIME* trend variable shows that individuals continue to marry later over time. The other control variables merely show the arithmetic result that individuals marrying a second or third time are older on average. The result of interest, however, is the coefficient for no-fault. Clearly no-fault has a modest impact on the age of marriage. Depending on which regression we consider, the age at marriage increases by six to nine months if one lives in a no-fault state.

---

[20] The data come on a CD and are downloaded using a very slow DOS program.

Table 11.3. *OLS regression. dependent variable = bride's age at marriage*

Variable	All marriages	First time marriage	More than one marriage
NOFAULT	0.47	0.36	0.36
	(10.23)	(8.32)	(4.64)
AGEDIFF	−0.32	−0.37	−0.28
	(−77.39)	(−66.24)	(−28.13)
MIXED RACE	1.78	1.63	1.72
	(35.69)	(36.55)	(9.34)
B-NUM-MAR	2.17		1.97
	(36.47)		(18.83)
G-NUM-MAR	1.84		1.56
	(29.81)		(14.71)
B-PREVIOUS	5.23		
	(56.04)		
G-PREVIOUS	4.96		
	(52.00)		
TIME	0.16	0.119	0.198
	(13.98)	(11.31)	(5.57)

Table 11.4. *OLS regression: dependent variable = groom's age at marriage*

Variable	All marriages	First time marriage	More than one marriage
NOFAULT	0.47	0.35	0.68
	(10.33)	(8.31)	(4.74)
AGEDIFF	0.66	0.62	0.71
	(158.88)	(113.16)	(71.46)
MIXED RACE	1.77	1.62	1.72
	(35.69)	(36.65)	(9.35)
B-NUM-MAR	2.15		1.97
	(36.25)		(18.79)
G-NUM-MAR	1.86		1.58
	(30.18)		(14.84)
B-PREVIOUS	5.22		
	(55.99)		
G-PREVIOUS	4.97		
	(52.18)		
TIME	0.16	0.119	0.195
	(13.93)	(11.36)	(5.50)

These numbers are similar to numbers relating to the divorce rate and to labor force participation. No-fault laws have statistically significant impacts, but the magnitude of the effect is relatively quite small.

4   Conclusion

The evidence on the impact of no-fault divorce on marriage and divorce leaves something of a paradox. If we assume that the world has positive transactions costs and that marriage is subject to these costs, then it is not very surprising to suggest that divorce should become more common when it is made easier, and that individuals will take private precautions to avoid a bad marriage and, consequently, a bad divorce. Added to this we have the common perception that divorce is rampant and individuals are taking great efforts to mitigate its effects. For example, in British Columbia, there was a 20 percent increase in the number of common law relationships between 1984 and 1994, and, in 1997, 46 percent of women between the ages of 18 and 30 who left singlehood entered a common law union. Yet, when empirical work is done on the effect of no-fault divorce, though the signs are correct, the magnitudes are quite small. What is going on?

Part of the answer may be that virtually all of the testing is done using data from the United States. Several problems arise from this. First, there is the problem of state classification. Some states are clearly no-fault or fault states, but many lie in the middle. If a state requires three years of separation for a divorce, is this fault or no-fault? What about five years of separation, or if fault is used as a consideration in relation to property?[21] A similar problem stems from not measuring the "degree of change" from fault to no-fault. Just as some no-fault states are quite rigorous and limiting, some old fault laws were quite liberal. If a liberal fault state becomes no-fault and a strict fault state becomes a strict no-fault one, there may be only a marginal change in the law. Without controlling for this effect, the estimated coefficients for the no-fault dummy variable will be biased downwards.

Finally, there is likely a problem with endogeneity. The US transition to no-fault took fifteen years. The cultural environment in 1970 regarding divorce, women in the workforce, single parenthood, and common law marriages was much different than in 1985 when South Dakota finally changed. In 1984, the divorce rate in South Dakota must have been influenced by what Barbara Whitehead (1997) calls "the Divorce Culture." The question is, how much of this divorce culture was caused by the earlier changes in divorce laws elsewhere?[22]

---

[21] Friedberg is the only one to my knowledge who attempts to control for this problem by using two classifications of the law.

[22] Rowthorn (1999) makes the same point.

The current generation of young men and women entering the stage of their life where marriages are begun is the first cohort who have grown up with no-fault laws always existing and who are completely familiar with all of the effects. The propensity for this cohort to divorce must be different than that of an earlier generation, and this is indirectly an effect of the original no-fault law. Hence, it would appear that using the same dummy variable for South Dakota as for California is an inadequate test of the effect of no-fault.

With these considerations, Canada might appear a better environment in which to conduct such test. As figure 11.1 showed, there was a clear and large impact from the legal change. Given that Canada was the first modern jurisdiction to introduce no-fault divorce, and given that it was a federal law, the assumption of an exogenous change seems more reasonable. Hence, although the empirical estimates arrived at so far are small, it is likely that they are a lower bound of the true impact of easy divorce. No doubt, though the direction of impact is clear, debates over these magnitudes will continue.

REFERENCES

Allen, Douglas (1991), "What Are Transaction Costs?" *Research in Law and Economics*, 14, 1–18.
    (1992), "Marriage and Divorce: Comment," *American Economic Review*, 82, 679–85.
    (1995), "Some Comments Regarding Divorce, Lone Mothers, and Children," in John Richards and William Watson (eds.), *Family Matters: New Policies for Divorce, Lone Mothers, and Child Poverty*, Toronto: C.D. Howe Institute.
    (1998), "No-Fault Divorce in Canada: Its Cause and Effect," *Journal of Economic Behavior and Organization*, 37, 129–49.
Allen, Douglas and Margaret F. Brinig (1998), "Sex, Property Rights and Divorce," *European Journal of Law and Economics*, 5, 211–33.
Anderson, Gary and William Shughart II (1991), "Is Breaking up Hard to Do? Legal Institutions and the Rate of Divorce," *Journal of Public Finance and Public Choice*, 2, 133–45.
Becker, G. (1981), *A Treatise on the Family*, Cambridge, MA: Harvard University Press.
Becker, G., E. Landes, and R. Michael (1977), "An Economic Analysis of Marital Instability," *Journal of Political Economy*, 85, 1141–87.
Brinig, M. and Douglas Allen (2000), "These Boots Are Made for Walking: Why Most Divorce Filers Are Women," *American Law and Economics* Review, 2, 126–69.
Brinig, M. and F. Buckley (1998), "No-Fault Laws and At-Fault People," *International Review of Law and Economics*, 18, 325–40.
Coase, R. (1960), "The Problem of Social Cost," *Journal of Law and Economics*, 3, 1–49.
Fain, Harvey (1977), "Family Law – Whither Now?" *Journal of Divorce*, 1, 31–42.
Finnie, Ross (1995), "The Economics of Divorce," in John Richards and William Watson (eds.), *Family Matters: New Policies for Divorce, Lone Mothers, and Child Poverty*, Toronto: C.D. Howe Institute.
Foster Jr., H. and D. Freed (1973/4), "Divorce Reform: Brakes on Breakdown?" *Journal of Family Law*, 13, 443–93.

Frank, A., J. Berman and S. Mazur-Hart (1978), "No Fault Divorce and the Divorce Rate: The Nebraska Experience – An Interrupted Time Series Analysis and Commentary," *Nebraska Law Review*, 58, 1–99.

Freed, D. and H. Foster Jr. (1979), "Divorce in the Fifty States: An Overview as of 1978," *Family Law Quarterly*, 13, 105–28.

Friedberg, L. (1998), "Did Unilateral Divorce Raise Divorce Rates? Evidence from Panel Data," *American Economic Review*, 88, 608–27.

Gallagher, H. (1973), "No-Fault Divorce in Delaware," *American Bar Association Journal*, 59, 873–5.

Goddard, W. (1972), "A Report on California's New Divorce Law: Progress and Problems," *Family Law Quarterly*, 6, 405–8.

Gray, J.S. (1998), "Divorce Law Changes, Household Bargaining, and Married Women's Labor Supply," *American Economic Review*, 88, 628–42.

Jacob, H. (1988), *The Silent Revolution: The Transformation of Divorce Law in the United States*, Chicago: University of Chicago Press.

(1989), "Another Look at No-Fault Divorce and the Post-Divorce Finances of Women," *Law and Society Review*, 23, 95–115.

Johnson, W. and J. Skinner (1986), "Labor Supply and Marital Separation," *American Economic Review*, 76, 455–69.

Martingale-Hubbel Law Digest (1991), New Providence, NJ.

Marvell, T. (1989), "Divorce Rates and the Fault Requirement," *Law and Society Review*, 23, 543–67.

Michael, R. (1985), "Consequences of the Rise in Female Labor Force Participation Rates: Questions and Probes," *Journal of Labor Economics,* 3, S117–46.

Moir, D. (1999), "A New Class of Disadvantaged Children: Reflections on 'Easy' Divorce," in Douglas Allen and John Richards (eds.), *It Takes Two: The Family in Law and Finance*, Toronto: C.D. Howe Institute.

Nakonezny, P., R. Shull, and J. Rodgers (1995), "The Effect of No-Fault Divorce Law on the Divorce Rate Across the 50 States and Its Relation to Income, Education, and Religiosity," *Journal of Marriage and the Family*, 57, 477–88.

Parkman, A.M. (1992a), *No-Fault Divorce: What Went Wrong?* Boulder, CO: Westview Press.

(1992b), "Unilateral Divorce and the Labor-Force Participation Rate of Married Women, Revisited," *American Economic Review*, 82, 671–8.

(1998), "Why Are Married Women Working So Hard?" *International Review of Law and Economics*, 18, 41–9.

Peters, H.E. (1986), "Marriage and Divorce: Informational Constraints and Private Contracting," *American Economic Review*, 76, 437–54.

Rowthorn, R. (1999), "Marriage and Trust: Some Lessons from Economics," *Cambridge Journal of Economics*, 23, 661–91.

Schoen, R., H. Greenblatt, and R. Mielke (1975), "California's Experience with Non-Adversary Divorce," *Demography*, 12, 223–43.

Sepler, H. (1981), "Measuring the Effects of No-Fault Divorce Laws across Fifty States: Quantifying a Zeitgeist," *Family Law Quarterly*, 15, 65–102.

Weiss, Y. and R. Willis (1989), "An Economic Analysis of Divorce Settlements," unpublished manuscript, Population Research Center, University of Chicago.

Weitzman, L. (1985), *The Divorce Revolution: The Unexpected Social and Economic Consequences for Women and Children in America*, New York: Free Press.

Whitehead, B. (1997), *The Divorce Culture*, New York: Knopf.

Wright, G. and D. Stetson (1973), "The Impact of No-Fault Divorce Law Reform on Divorce in American States," *Journal of Marriage and the Family*, 40, 575–81.

Zelder, M. (1992), "Did No-Fault Divorce Law Increase the Divorce Rate? A Critical Review of the Evidence," unpublished manuscript, Northwestern Law School.

(1993), "Inefficient Dissolutions as a Consequence of Public Goods: The Case of No-Fault Divorce," *Journal of Legal Studies*, 22, 503–20.

12   European divorce laws, divorce rates, and their consequences

Ian Smith

1   Introduction

Most investigations of the links between the liberalization of divorce laws and the dramatic rise in divorce rates have tended to focus on North America. With the exceptions of Goode (1993), Glendon (1989), and Phillips (1988), there is relatively little recent comparative literature on legal change and divorce rates in Europe and even less formal empirical analysis. Following some early descriptive studies of the divorce data (Chester, 1977; Commaille et al., 1983), the only notable recent statistical contribution is that of Castles and Flood (1991). In the light of this relative neglect, the primary aim of the chapter is to re-evaluate the association between divorce statutes and divorce rates in the European context.

In addition to the appropriate legal grounds for marital dissolution, rules governing the division of marital property and child support payments continue to receive legislative attention in many jurisdictions. Policy innovations in settlement rules have significant implications not only for incentives to divorce but also for the living standards of broken families. In particular, the financial impact of divorce on lone parents and their children has generated considerable concern. Since the economic burden of marital disruption varies substantially within Europe, the chapter will also comment on these cross-country differences in the financial consequences of divorce.

Data

Total divorce rates for a selection of European countries with readily available data are presented in table 12.1. The total divorce rate estimates the proportion of current marriages that will end in divorce.[1] One caveat with respect

I would like to thank Tony Dnes and Bob Rowthorn for helpful comments and suggestions.
[1] It is obtained by adding together the divorce rates at each length of marriage in any given year. In other words, it represents a projection of the proportion of couples whose marriages would eventually end in divorce if they were to experience the entire set of these marital duration-specific divorce rates. Since this estimate controls for the composition of the married population in terms of marriage duration, it is more satisfactory than a crude divorce rate that simply divides the number of divorces by the number of married couples or, more commonly, deflates by total population.

Table 12.1 *Total divorce rates in selected European countries*

Country	1960	1970	1975	1980	1985	1990	1995
Austria	0.14	0.18	0.20	0.26	0.31	0.33	0.38
Belgium	0.07	0.10	0.16	0.20	0.27	0.31	n/a
Denmark	0.19	0.25	0.37	0.40	0.46	0.44	0.41
England and Wales	0.07	0.16	0.30	0.38	0.42	0.42	0.43
Federal Republic of Germany	0.10	0.15	0.22	0.22	0.30	0.29	0.34
Finland	0.11	0.17	0.26	0.28	0.28	0.41	0.49
France	0.09	0.12	0.16	0.22	0.31	0.32	0.38
Greece	n/a	0.05	0.05	0.06	0.11	0.12	0.15
Italy	0.00	0.05	0.03	0.03	0.04	0.08	0.08
Netherlands	0.07	0.10	0.20	0.26	0.34	0.28	0.32
Norway	0.09	0.13	0.21	0.25	0.33	0.43	0.46
Sweden	0.16	0.23	0.50	0.42	0.45	0.43	0.50
Switzerland	0.13	0.15	0.21	0.27	0.30	0.33	0.38
Total number of divorces (thousands)	152	248	410	470	565	565	638

Sources: Commaille, et al. (1983), Council of Europe (1990).
Notes: n/a = not available.
Total divorce rates are estimates of the probability of divorce based on a weighted average of duration-specific divorce rates.

to the use of divorce rates is that they capture only the legal termination of marriages rather than rates of actual marital breakdown. In countries where obtaining a divorce is more difficult or costly, irretrievable marital failure is less likely to be translated into a legal divorce. Given international differences in the accessibility of divorce, the variation between countries in actual levels of marriage breakdown is smaller than that indicated by the divorce statistics in table 12.1. Moreover, the figures do not include judicial separations available in some countries as a less costly alternative to divorce but without the benefits of the option to remarry. Indeed, a direct association would be expected between the strictness of divorce law and rates of judicial and *de facto* separation. For the same reasons, the growth in failed marriages over time is likely to be exaggerated by these data, especially when comparing divorce rates before and after major legal reforms.

2   The law and divorce

Table 12.1 indicates that the 1970s display the most rapid sustained growth in the aggregate level of European divorce, particularly prior to 1975, though not all individual countries conform to the same pattern. It is natural to associate this remarkable rise with parallel legislative changes that significantly lowered the barriers to divorce. Before examining this time-series relationship, it is important to appreciate that even in 1960 or 1970, prior to the wave of liberal divorce reforms, there was already substantial variation in divorce rates across this sample of countries. The Scandinavian nations of Sweden and Denmark had the highest rates, followed by the German-speaking countries of Switzerland, Austria, and the Federal Republic of Germany. Divorce was not permitted in Italy until 1970, while Belgium, the Netherlands, and England and Wales displayed the lowest divorce rates.

The variance in divorce rates in the 1960s was paralleled by considerable variation in the legal provision for divorce. To investigate the links between divorce law and rates, it is fruitful to ask first whether any association can be established across Europe before the major legal reforms were enacted. This also provides a framework within which to discuss subsequent developments. Three types of divorce grounds can be distinguished and attributed to particular groups of European countries. Although the divorce rules within each group are not uniform, the variation between groups is much greater.

Separation grounds

Separation grounds provide for divorce after a waiting period during which the couple live apart. It was notably the Scandinavian countries that used separation as the main legal basis for divorce in the 1960s. In Sweden, for example, the longstanding marriage code of 1920 permitted divorce on the basis of three years' *de facto* separation. Alternatively, a legal separation could be obtained and after one year either spouse could apply for a divorce (Trost, 1977). This was the most popular option, accounting for 81 percent of divorces in 1960. The attraction of the judicial separation option was its shorter waiting period and its earlier formalization of legal consequences in terms of financial transfers and child custody. Divorce was also available using one of eight fault grounds, but these were infrequently selected. A similar pattern of primarily (judicial) separation-based divorce was evident elsewhere in Scandinavia.

Strong fault grounds

Under a strong fault regime, the right to file for divorce is available unilaterally to an innocent party if his/her spouse is guilty of a serious marital offense such as adultery. It is necessary to present proof of fault in court before a judge, and the determination of guilt by the court is of decisive importance for the right to spousal maintenance. The guilty party cannot apply for divorce directly but may be able to use bargaining devices such as income transfers to induce the innocent spouse to consent to petitioning. Indeed, even without the commission of a fault, divorce could be secured if the parties agreed that one partner would plead guilty to a fabricated offense, a strategy designated the "big lie practice" in the Netherlands (Kooy, 1977). The key point of fault divorce is that, without this consent and cooperation, legally innocent marriage partners cannot be divorced against their will. However, a guilty spouse might be able to induce "constructive" consent simply through behaving intolerably (Weiss and Willis, 1993).

In the 1960s, the strong fault regime was central to the divorce procedures available in France, England and Wales, Scotland, the Netherlands, and Belgium among others (Chester, 1977). Very few jurisdictions permitted divorce explicitly on mutual consent grounds since this would dispense with matrimonial offense and its legal consequences. An exception was found in the Civil Code of Belgium. Even in this case, however, the procedure was long and costly, requiring several court appearances, and limited by restricted eligibility.

Weak fault grounds

Weak fault is characterized by the specification of a rather open-ended, non-specific fault ground that can flexibly accommodate a wide range of provable matrimonial offenses, possibly even of a relatively minor character. The implication is that a spouse could be divorced against his/her will even without committing a serious fault, depending on both the standards of proof required and the strictness of judicial interpretation and practice.

In the 1960s, the German-speaking countries included a portmanteau fault ground alongside the traditional offenses. In Austria, for example, divorce was available on the basis of "other serious matrimonial offences," which accommodated an assortment of possible faults (Haller, 1977). Likewise in the former West Germany, divorce could be secured on the broad ground of serious marital offense (Künzel, 1977). In Switzerland, divorce was obtainable for non-specific irretrievable marital breakdown due to a complex variety of causes (Kellerhals, Perrin, and Voneche, 1977). In all three countries, this weak fault ground was the most frequently used, constituting 90 percent of divorces in Austria in 1960, 70 percent in Switzerland, and 87 percent in West Germany. In each case, divorce on the basis of a three-year separation was also available, but it was unpopular owing to the greater time costs and, unlike Scandinavia, a divorce petition citing separation could be denied if an innocent spouse objected.

3   Divorce regime and rate correspondence

There was clearly a rough correspondence in the 1960s between the type of legal regime and the divorce rate. On average, rates tended to be highest in the Scandinavian countries where separation grounds without consent were available, followed by the German-speaking jurisdictions where weak fault prevailed, while divorce rates were lowest in strong fault countries. This ranking is consistent with the key distinction between the regimes, namely, the ease with which a spouse can unilaterally dissolve a marriage. It might be expected that, the more readily an unhappy partner can legally terminate a marital relationship in a given jurisdiction, the greater the divorce rate, all else equal. Presumably divorce is most readily obtainable under a no-fault separation rule. If fault must be proved in court, a dissatisfied innocent spouse is most able to file unilaterally for divorce when the scope of permissible faults that can be cited is wide and judicial demands for proof are loose.

Note, however, that the correspondence between divorce regime and rate is rather stylized and certainly not as clean as might be suggested by the categorization. In the Scandinavian case, for example, the total divorce rates in 1960 varied from the high of 0.19 in Denmark through to 0.09 in Norway. Indeed, the rate for Norway is the same as that in (strong fault) France, despite the fact that most Norwegian divorces were granted after a prior one-year (with mutual consent) or two-year (without consent) period of legal separation, waiting periods that were six months shorter than those in Denmark.

Note also that it can be argued that, under certain strict conditions, the divorce rate is theoretically unrelated to the grounds for divorce. This result derives from applying the Coase Theorem (Coase, 1960) to show that, with perfect information and costless bargaining, it should not matter which spouse has the legal entitlement to dissolve the marriage (Peters, 1986). Divorce will occur only when it is efficient, that is, when the joint value of the marriage is less than the sum of the values of the post-divorce opportunities of each spouse. If divorce is inefficient then spouses can induce each other through private bargaining over marital gains to remain married, even if a pure unilateral divorce regime is in operation. This application of Coase's theorem, however, is a special case (Clark, 1999; Allen, 1998). In general, the result breaks down once the conditions of the theorem are relaxed. To the extent that the legal regime affects how far couples invest themselves in their marriages, for example, this will influence the average quality of marriage and the incidence of divorce (Rowthorn, 1999).

For those who doubt that the correlation between the legal regime and the cross-section pattern of divorce rates establishes causality, an alternative non-legal account of the association is required. One approach is to argue that both the grounds for divorce and divorce rates across countries are jointly determined by common factors. Two possibilities present themselves: the influence of religion, and women's economic status.

Cross-country variation in religious influence

The religious history of a country naturally shapes the evolution of its divorce legislation. A recent example is the case of the Republic of Ireland, a strong

Catholic monopoly, which introduced divorce only in the Family Law (Divorce) Act of 1996. This followed a referendum in which the vote to relax the prohibition on divorce passed by the narrowest of margins.[2] Indeed, Catholicism, far more so than Protestantism, has held a strictly negative view of divorce, a factor that increases its psychological costs for Catholic spouses. Catholicism has also proved significantly more successful than European Protestant denominations in retaining high levels of religious participation, especially compared with the state Lutheran churches in Scandinavia, where regular church attendance is extremely low (Smith, Sawkins, and Seaman, 1998). Hence, it is particularly in Catholic countries that religious influence would be expected to lead to both strict divorce laws and low divorce rates. So, according to this theory, the association between divorce statutes and outcomes is not primarily causal but reflects the common influence of religious belief.[3] Castles and Flood (1991) performed some statistical tests on the determinants of the liberality of the divorce law. Their results support the view that, for the 1960s, the most powerful predictor is the percentage of the population affiliated to the Catholic Church. However, they did not test whether both the variance in divorce incidence and legal strictness are jointly determined by religious belief.

Cross-country variation in women's economic status

Variations in the strictness of divorce law may also be explained by its economic impact on women. Becker and Murphy (1988) argue that, historically, divorce legislation can be characterized as state intervention in marriage to protect domestically specialized wives from being divorced against their will. Because mothers usually have child custody, protecting mothers also protects the welfare of dependent children. On this view, the strictness of divorce legislation is correlated with the economic burdens of divorce. Stricter grounds would be expected in those jurisdictions where family size is large, where the state social safety-net is limited, where mechanisms for enforcing maintenance payments from former husbands are weak, and labour market opportunities for women are few. In such circumstances, married women and their children are economically severely vulnerable in the event of divorce, especially older women whose value in the remarriage market diminishes rapidly with age.

Variations in the divorce rate may also be considered to reflect differences in the financial costs of divorce for women. If the percentage of married women

---

[2] The Irish ground for divorce is a separation period of four out of the previous five years (Walls, 1997).

[3] More generally, the apparent link between divorce incidence and laws may reflect the degree of moral and social stigma attached to marital breakdown. As moral censure eased so the divorce rate climbed and the law liberalized. However, shifts in moral norms are themselves partly determined by trends in religious adherence, though other factors are also important, as the highly religious yet divorce-prone United States illustrates.

in paid employment is high in a particular country, the accompanying low gains from a typical marriage and the relative financial independence of women are mirrored in a high rate of marital breakdown (Ermisch, 1993). Indeed, the correlation between female economic independence and divorce is visible in many traditional cultures. Some illustrative examples of high divorce rates in societies where wives have considerable economic autonomy are provided by Fisher (1992). When divorce is financially feasible for women, they make use of the legal provisions for marital dissolution.

Thus both the pattern of divorce rates and the strictness of legislation can be jointly explained in terms of the economic costs of divorce for women and their children. So this hypothesis would predict relatively high (low) married women's labor market participation rates associated with low (high) barriers to divorce and high (low) levels of marriage failure, as in Sweden (Italy). Note, however, that the direction of causation may not be only from the labor market to law. Positive feedback from the ease of marital exit to paid employment rates is also likely as married women insure themselves against higher risks of divorce (Johnson and Skinner, 1986). Moreover, as Castles (1994) observes, married women's employment may itself be partly determined by the strength of traditional religious attitudes towards the sexual division of labor within the family, so that religion remains the fundamental explanatory variable.

In sum, without formal testing, it is difficult to determine the extent to which divorce law had an independent effect on divorce levels across Europe even prior to the divorce revolution. Alternatively, both these variables may be jointly explained by religious or labor market factors.

4   The divorce revolution

The wave of widespread and permissive divorce law reform, initiated since the end of the 1960s, transformed marriage in many European countries by considerably easing access to divorce. In brief:

Scandinavia.   Most radical of all the reforms was the 1973 legislation in Sweden, which replaced the mixed fault and separation system with a simple unilateral divorce law without fault, ground, consent, legal separation, or a long *de facto* waiting period. The only exception arises if the divorce petition is opposed, or if there are dependent children under 16, in which case a six-month period of (re)consideration must be observed unless the spouses have already been separated for at least two years. A similar reform in Finland was implemented in 1987 (Bradley, 1998).[4]

---

[4] In Denmark, divorce is still obtainable on fault grounds but most couples choose to divorce after a six-month legal separation with mutual agreement or unilaterally after a one-year legal separation. In Norway, a new marriage law implemented at the beginning of 1993 shortened to one year the required legal separation period after which divorce is available on demand.

German-speaking countries. In German-speaking countries, there was a shift away from (weak) fault towards the separation system. The 1976 West German reform replaced fault with separation grounds of either one year (by mutual consent) or three years (without consent).[5] Likewise in Austria divorce by mutual agreement was established in 1978, after at least a six-month separation, and unilateral divorce was made available after six years apart. Although the previous fault grounds were left in place, by 1992 approximately 90 percent of Austrian divorces used the six-month separation provision (Simotta, 1995).

Other western European jurisdictions. Among the jurisdictions that adhered to strong fault in the 1960s, the most radical liberalization occurred in the Netherlands. Under the new law of 1971, divorce grounds were reduced to the assertion of the permanent disruption of the marriage and a waiting period of six months (Vlaardingerbroek, 1995).

In France, the Divorce Reform Law of 1975 introduced divorce by mutual consent, while fault divorce was retained in the weak form of behavior that made the maintenance of marital life intolerable. Unilateral divorce was also permitted after a six year separation, though such a long delay inevitably renders the provision unattractive, and it accounts for less than 1 percent of divorces. In Belgium, reform was much less permissive. An additional divorce ground came into effect in early 1975 permitting divorce on the basis of a ten-year (!) separation and guilt still had an effect on alimony; this period was reduced to five years in 1982.

In the case of England and Wales, the Divorce Reform Act implemented in 1971, although still permitting divorce using the traditional facts of adultery and desertion, introduced separation grounds and the weak fault fact of unreasonable behavior. The subsequent innovation of a special procedure for processing petitions removed the court from investigating the grounds for divorce, replacing it with an administrative paper transaction in which a quick divorce was available on (weak) fault grounds.

The southern European countries. For three southern European Catholic countries, divorce statutes were introduced for the first time in Italy (1970), Portugal (for Catholic marriages, 1975), and Spain (1981) on the basis of long-term separation. In the Italian case, legal separation has long been available but divorce became legally possible only at the end of 1970, chiefly on the basis of a five-year legal separation established on fault grounds (six years without consent or seven years if the petitioner is the guilty partner). The fault prerequisite was abolished in 1975, and the minimum separation period was

---

[5] Recently, the German Civil Code (Bürgerliches Gesetzbuch, paragraph 1579) was amended to reintroduce fault as a consideration in the determination of alimony at the discretion of the judge (Krause, 1998).

reduced to three years in 1987 (Ceschini, 1995). Note that legal separation and later divorce petitions remain relatively costly in both time and money because two separate court appearances are required. Many petitioners choose to stick at legal separation because this maintains a number of spousal rights including inheritance.

5   Liberalization and the divorce explosion

Divorce rates rose following liberalization in all countries and Haskey (1992) and other commentators suggest a direct causal relationship. Visual inspection of table 12.1 provides some support for this view. Total divorce rates doubled during the five-year period between 1970 and 1975 in Sweden and the Netherlands, the same two countries that had introduced the most radical reforms. England and Wales also witnessed substantial growth in divorce following liberalization. However, the picture is uneven. The German total divorce rate, for example, remained stable, comparing 1975 with 1980, despite the substitution of fault by separation in the 1976 reform.

By the 1990s, the regional patterns evident in the 1960s persisted largely unchanged. Scandinavian countries, in which access to divorce is available after very short waiting periods, if any, all display total divorce rates between 40 percent and 50 percent. England and Wales is ranked alongside Scandinavia, possibly reflecting the comparable availability of the "quickie" administrative divorce, but on weak fault grounds. For the remaining western European countries, divorce rates lay between 32 percent and 38 percent in 1995. Interestingly, although proof of fault in court is still a significant path to divorce in France and Belgium, the divorce rates in these countries were no lower in the 1990s than those in the Netherlands or the former West Germany, which abandoned fault. It is in southern Europe that divorce remains comparatively infrequent.

Some writers, such as Goode (1993), are rather skeptical regarding the role of changes in the legal environment. Switzerland provides perhaps the best example of a jurisdiction where the (weak) fault grounds for divorce did not change during the period of liberalization elsewhere, yet the divorce rate rose in tandem with that in countries experiencing considerable reform (Graham-Siegenthaler, 1995).

No one denies, however, that the legal environment will have effects on the timing of divorce. There is often a temporary boost to divorce rates as a backlog of long dead marriages are given an opportunity for legal burial under new legislation. In Belgium, for example, the annual number of divorces climbed spectacularly from 22,026 in 1994 to 34,995 in 1995, though declining somewhat to 26,800 by 1997. The large jump in the divorce figures primarily reflected the introduction of legislation simplifying the conditions on the use of the mutual consent ground to two years' separation.

The key issue is whether there are any permanent effects of legislative innovations on the volume of divorces or, more fundamentally, on the incidence of actual marital breakdown. Econometric studies using time-series data for European countries are rare. Those conducted by van Poppel and de Beer (1993) for the Netherlands or by Smith (1997) for Britain, struggle to detect evidence of permanent legal effects. However, as Rowthorn (1999) emphasizes, it is inherently difficult for statistical studies to capture the very long-run and diffuse impact of divorce reform on marriage failure.

The American evidence has been investigated far more extensively than the European data and most studies identify some role for legal reform. Gray (1998) is a recent exception who finds no effect of the shift from fault or mutual consent to unilateral divorce in US states on divorce probabilities. In contrast, Friedberg (1998) reports a statistically significant legal impact on divorce rates, though it is not large. She estimates that the move towards unilateral divorce explained 17 percent of the increase in divorce rates between 1968 and 1988. Although this proportion is not trivial, it would appear that non-legal factors explain the majority of the divorce rate increase.

Moreover, causation may not be unidirectional. Trends in divorce rates themselves can provide a powerful stimulus to legal change. Most conspicuous is the case of England and Wales, where the implementation of the Divorce Reform Act in 1971 followed a doubling in the total divorce rate during the previous decade. In the American case, both Peters (1992) and Friedberg (1998) find that prior state divorce rates are a reasonable predictor of whether or not a state adopted unilateral divorce and the strictness with which this was formulated. There are several possible channels by which changes in divorce behavior can precipitate legal reform.

First, rapidly increasing divorce levels place a heavy burden on any legal system that seriously attempts to investigate in court the reasons for marital breakdown and to impose fault-based sanctions. If the judicial process faces capacity constraints, a backlog of cases soon accumulates and naturally generates demand for legal and procedural revisions from an overextended legal profession.

Second, to the extent that the state subsidizes divorce through legal aid schemes providing financial assistance for those on lower incomes, escalating divorce petitions place a significant financial strain on the public purse. There is a powerful incentive for governments to transform divorce into an administrative process that demands less judicial time and less legal aid. In France, for example, proposals to reduce the role of the judiciary in divorce by substituting an administrative procedure are currently under consideration.

Third, in so far as growth in demand for divorce reflects the increasing financial independence of women and the waning influence of religion, liberalizing divorce law becomes socially more efficient and politically more feasible. Allen (1998) argues that, in the case of Canada, unanticipated increases in female labor force participation during the 1950s and 1960s reduced the gains from marriage, causing a significant number to become inefficient. Since these could not be legally dissolved without proof of serious marital misconduct under (strong) fault law, many couples who had not committed matrimonial offenses found themselves unable to escape their marital bonds except by fabricating evidence. Such factors naturally motivated the demand for legal reform. If the social costs from inefficient marriages under fault law outweigh those expected from inefficient divorces under a more liberal regime, then revising the legal provisions would minimize social losses.

Whether it was the limited capacity of the legal system, constraints on public money, or the cumulative number of inefficient marriages that precipitated statutory reform, these were all problems generated by a rapid growth in marital breakdown. In other words, legislative change functioned primarily to codify and regulate economic and social developments rather than initiating them. The ubiquity and timing of this trend towards simpler divorce procedures across countries indicate that common and powerful forces were operating, resulting in the failure of stricter divorce laws to survive. Even if they had been maintained, it is dubious whether this would have had a major impact on marriage preservation. As Agell (1992) argues, the conditions for divorce are not efficient tools for preventing marital failure. In so far as the secular trend in divorce chiefly reflects socio-economic factors, the strictness of divorce law has only a marginal effect on actual marriage breakdown.

6   The economic consequences of divorce

Whatever the causes of increasing divorce, its consequences for the living standards of broken families, especially lone mothers, have attracted considerable attention from social policy makers (OECD, 1990). European differences in the resources available to mothers who have not re-partnered and their children depend primarily on settlement rules, child support payments, labor market opportunities, and state welfare provision. Although there are insufficient data with which to make systematic cross-country comparisons, some qualitative distinctions can be briefly highlighted.

Settlement rules

Divorce settlements differ across European jurisdictions according to the role of alimony, the range of assets included in the legal definition of property to be divided, and the basis upon which this division is conducted. There is also variation in terms of the use of fixed rules and judicial discretion and the relative weights given to equity and equality.

In most common law legal systems, such as England and Wales, the equitable division of marital resources is determined by the discretion of judges when couples have failed privately to agree financial arrangements. In practice, the principle of need is the decisive criterion.[6] This contrasts with the civil codes of most European countries where marital property is divided according to a fixed rule of equal division, recognizing that, although spousal financial contributions may be very unequal, marriage is an equal economic partnership. There are differences between the systems according to the scope of the property available for division. The Nordic countries operate a system of deferred community of property, which provides for separate administration and control of assets during marriage combined with universal community of any and all property on marital dissolution. The German system, on the other hand, provides for a community of marital property increase (Rheinstein and Glendon, 1980). This entails that the spouse with the smaller increase in the monetary value of his/her property acquired during marriage is entitled to half of the difference in the value of the respective property increments. Germany is also notable for including pensions in the definition of marital property as long ago as 1977 (Voegeli and Willenbacher, 1992).

Such fixed division rules are open to criticism regarding the fairness of the outcomes that they generate. Since an equal division approach, for example, does not take future needs into account, it may generate less favorable outcomes for a custodial parent or an older homemaker than a discretionary property allocation system. Another potential inequity is that of "divorce into money" where, after a relatively short marriage, one spouse secures a divorce and obtains substantial property gains from his/her share of the partner's wealth.[7]

France operates a mixed system of rules and discretion. Marital assets acquired during marriage (a community of acquests) are divided equally but if there is great disparity in the post-divorce needs and resources of the former

---

[6] The landmark House of Lords judgment in the case of *White v. White* in October 2000 has revolutionized the yardstick used to divide matrimonial assets, especially in the case of wealthy couples whose contributions to family assets are very unequal in economic value. Previously, if the husband had been chiefly responsible for the accumulation of family wealth, he retained the majority of the couple's joint assets and his former wife received an allocation sufficient to provide for her reasonable requirements. The new ruling establishes a yardstick of equal division as the baseline, from which departures are permitted on the grounds of fairness. The court of appeal in the case of *Cowan v. Cowan*, for example, allocated 62 percent of the £12 million family fortune to the husband, justifying this uneven split on the basis of his exceptional entrepreneurial flair, inventiveness, and hard work.

[7] The Swedish Marriage Code of 1987 attempts to resolve this by introducing an element of discretion, permitting a spouse to retain more than half of the marital property if equal division would prove unreasonable or inequitable (Bradley, 1990).

partners, in particular if the wife and children experience economic deprivation, the judge may require the husband to make a compensatory payment, in the form of either a capital sum or a regular income transfer (Boigeol, Commaille, and Roussel, 1977). For most jurisdictions, however, alimony payments to economically weaker wives play only a very limited role since increasingly the emphasis has shifted to establishing a clean break and self-sufficiency. Even in the French case, compensatory payments tend to be unenforced, infrequent, and usually quite small, especially if the husband's income is low.[8] This is particularly problematic for the domestically specialized older woman with weak links to the labor market and little property available for division on divorce.

As with property settlement, systems of child support differ according to the roles played by private ordering, judicial discretion, and fixed payment rules. Experience suggests that the discretionary approach is vulnerable to underpayment to the extent that the true costs of raising children are underestimated or the payments are irregular and weakly enforced. The burden subsequently carried by state benefits has led several European countries, including Belgium, Denmark, France, Germany, and Britain, to establish child support agencies to secure payments from absent fathers. The best systems operate an efficient collection system with automatic wage withholding in case of default. For example, in Sweden, if payment default occurs, then the state advances maintenance contributions to compensate and attempts to collect from the non-custodial parent (Glendon, 1987).

Labor market attachment and opportunities

The labor market typically provides the main source of income for the employed. For mothers, especially divorced mothers, cross-country differences in earning capacity will reflect, among other things, opportunities to combine work and family. Within Europe, there is considerable variation in the percentage of mothers employed. The statistics for women whose youngest child was aged between 7 and 15 in 1988 stood at 44 percent in Italy, 41 percent in the Netherlands, 53 percent in Belgium, 50 percent in the Federal Republic of Germany, 67 percent in France, 70 percent in Great Britain, 85 percent in Denmark, and 88 percent in Sweden (Joshi and Davies, 1992).

Provisions for paid maternity leave and public day-care facilities are among the principal factors explaining differences in the labor supply of mothers.[9] In

---

[8] See Bastard and Cardia Voneche (1992) for illustrative case studies of French divorces.

[9] Of course, other factors also affect the availability of jobs and the earning capacity of mothers. Even among women without children there is still considerable variation in labor market participation across Europe. In countries such as Sweden and Italy, the relatively large public sector has provided employment opportunities for women. In Britain and the Netherlands, the availability of low-paid part-time service sector jobs has assisted in balancing the demands of motherhood and employment.

the exceptionally flexible case of Sweden, for example, a parent is entitled to up to 450 cash benefit days at home per child, with income replaced at 90 percent of salary for 360 days and thereafter at a reduced rate (Meisaari-Polsa, 1997). For mothers who prefer to avoid an extended break from work, there are more than 7,300 publicly funded, all-day child-care centers available.

Likewise, with respect to school-age child care, Sweden is noted for its heavily subsidized provision in the form of day-care centers, child minders, and after-school centers. In addition, cash benefits are available for a parent to stay at home to care for each child under 12 years old for sixty days annually, as well as leave to care for sick children. The result for Sweden is that the presence of dependent children has relatively little effect on the aggregate labor market participation rate of mothers. Although this may contribute to relatively high rates of marital dissolution, the economic consequences are less problematic than would otherwise be the case. Indeed, divorce is no longer viewed as a serious social concern in Sweden (Bradley, 1998), notwithstanding the possible negative psychological effects of marital failure.

In contrast, when labor market opportunities for mothers are relatively few and publicly funded child care is very limited, one would anticipate low rates of marital dissolution but potentially serious economic consequences. In Italy, for example, divorce and separation are still comparatively rare by European standards, but the economic impact may be severe for lone parents given the greater difficulties in finding employment supported by access to child care (Chesnais, 1996).

In the British case, a recent longitudinal study by Jarvis and Jenkins (1999) confirms previous findings that a marital split is accompanied by substantial falls in the average real income of women and children, whereas that for husbands changes much less.[10] Divorced or separated mothers, in particular, are likely to be relatively dependent on social welfare payments, to receive little maintenance, and to have relatively low labor market participation rates. Indeed, many would not gain significantly from paid work owing to the loss of benefits and the costs of private child care that it entails.

In the Federal Republic of Germany, where divorce rates are comparatively low by western European standards, women's financial losses from divorce are as great as, if not greater than, in the divorce-prone United States (Burkhauser et al., 1990). This is perhaps not surprising given the continued predominance of the traditional breadwinner/homemaker family arrangement in Germany. Moreover, kindergarten, the main form of public child care, is available only in the mornings for pre-school children aged over 3 years (Federkeil, 1997). And,

[10] Since their study focuses on changes in income following divorce, capital transfers between spouses are included only in so far as they generate current income. This ignores the effect of such transfers on post-divorce wealth. Indeed, the reported unfavorable financial impact of marital splits on women relative to men may be smaller when total assets are factored into the accounting.

since the school day in Germany is only four or five hours in length, this restricts even part-time employment for mothers of older children, especially given the closure of schools at lunchtime and the lack of after-school care centers.

France, on the other hand, has an extensive network of child care for young children, offering day nurseries and subsidized child minders. Nearly all children aged 3 to 6 attend nursery school, with provision made for care both before and after school hours. For older children, the school day is eight hours in duration, facilitating the relatively high labor force participation rate of French mothers (Muller-Escoda and Vogt, 1997).

Evaluation

A high divorce rate is of greatest concern when it is accompanied by large average economic losses for lone parents and their children, as in Britain. This contrasts with countries where high levels of marital dissolution occur precisely because potential negative economic consequences are cushioned by labor market opportunities and state policies. Poverty in lone parent families, for example, is rare in Sweden, where only 5 percent of children live in one-parent households with less than half median household income, whereas the comparable figures for Britain and Germany lie between 20 percent and 30 percent (Chesnais, 1996).

Despite the long-term financial costs of divorce incurred by lone parents in most countries, an important but neglected point is that the increase in divorce is primarily driven by the initiative of married women wishing to escape unsatisfactory marriages. Admittedly, the rise of explicitly consensual or separation-based divorce makes this observation difficult to document, especially following the reforms of the 1970s. Indicative, however, is the fact that in the Federal Republic of Germany the proportion of divorce petitions filed by women rose from 52 percent in 1950 to 71 percent in 1972 (Künzel, 1977). Likewise in England and Wales, the share of divorce actions initiated by wives rose from 55 percent in 1959 to 69 percent by 1976. Goode (1993) doubts whether such sex differences in divorce petitions are a good index of which marital partner is less satisfied. However, these trends suggest that the increasing gains from divorce particularly favor women. Indeed, such women may still perceive themselves better off in terms of well-being and satisfaction from escaping a bad marriage, despite the negative financial consequences. It is less clear whether the same argument can be applied to dependent children.

7   Conclusions

There is significant variation in the evolution of divorce rates and laws across European countries. Although legal innovations certainly reflect and regulate changing behavioral patterns, it is difficult to establish that the considerable liberalization of divorce legislation in most European jurisdictions is primarily responsible for rising divorce rates since the late 1960s. Indeed, both the strictness of divorce laws and divorce rate levels may be jointly determined by religious influences and women's and children's economic losses from marital dissolution. A rigorous empirical study using a panel of data from European countries is required to facilitate discrimination between these hypotheses.

The historical trajectory of legislation on the grounds for divorce is towards no-fault, separation-based marital dissolution. In an age of mass divorce, this is unlikely to be reversed given constraints on both the legal system in processing fault petitions and public money in subsidizing them. There are certainly no European initiatives comparable to the introduction of covenant marriage in some American states. Rather than using the law to discourage divorce, the trend in the European context is to focus on measures that minimize its social and economic costs. Family policy initiatives in many countries are concerned, for example, with the enforcement of child support transfers from fathers, the splitting of assets on divorce, and the provision of child-care subsidies. Paradoxically, insulating women and children from the adverse consequences of divorce reinforces incentives for marital dissolution in so far as the effective reduction in its costs increases its likelihood. There appears to be something of a trade-off between protecting the institution of marriage and protecting the casualties of marital breakdown.

REFERENCES

Agell, A. (1992), "Grounds and Procedures Reviewed," in L.J. Weitzman, and M., Maclean, (eds.), *Economic Consequences of Divorce: The International Perspective*, Oxford: Clarendon Press.

Allen, D.W. (1998), "No-fault Divorce in Canada: Its Cause and Effect," *Journal of Economic Behavior and Organization*, 37, 129–49.

Bastard, B. and Cardia Voneche, L. (1992), "Attitudes to Finance after Divorce in France," in L.J. Weitzman, and M. Maclean (eds.), *Economic Consequences of Divorce: The International Perspective*, Oxford: Clarendon Press.

Becker, G.S. and K.M. Murphy (1988), "The Family and the State," *Journal of Law and Economics*, 31, 1–18.

Boigeol, A., J. Commaille, and L. Roussel (1977), "France," in R. Chester (ed.), *Divorce in Europe*, Leiden: Netherlands Interuniversity Demographic Institute, Martinus Nijhoff Social Sciences Division.

Bradley, D. (1990), "Marriage, Family Property and Inheritance in Swedish Law," *International and Comparative Law Quarterly*, 39, 370–95.

  (1998), "Politics, Culture and Family Law in Finland: Comparative Approaches to the Institution of Marriage," *International Journal of Law, Policy and the Family*, 12, 288–306.

Burkhauser, R.V., G.J. Duncan, R. Hauser, and R. Berntsen (1990), "Economic Burdens of Marital Disruptions: a Comparison of the United States and the Federal Republic of Germany," *Review of Income and Wealth*, 36, 319–33.

Castles, F.G. (1994), "On Religion and Public Policy: Does Catholicism Make a Difference?" *European Journal of Political Research*, 25, 19–40.

Castles, F.G. and M. Flood (1991), "Divorce, the Law and Social Context: Families of Nations and the Legal Dissolution of Marriage," *Acta Sociologica*, 34, 279–97.

Ceschini, R. (1995), "International Marriage and Divorce Regulations and Recognition in Italy," *Family Law Quarterly*, 29, 567–75.

Chesnais, J.-C. (1996), "Fertility, Family, and Social Policy in Contemporary Western Europe," *Population and Development Review*, 22, 729–39.

Chester, R. (ed.) (1977), *Divorce in Europe*, Leiden: Netherlands Interuniversity Demographic Institute, Martinus Nijhoff Social Sciences Division.

Clark, S. (1999), "Law, Property and Marital Dissolution," *Economic Journal*, 109, C41–54.

Coase, R. (1960), "The Problem of Social Cost," *Journal of Law and Economics*, 3, 1–44.

Commaille, J., et al. (1983), "Le Divorce en Europe Occidentale: La Loi et le nombre," GIRD (International), CETEL (Geneve), INED (Paris).

Council of Europe (1998), *Recent Demographic Developments in Europe 1998*, Strasbourg: Council of Europe.

Ermisch, J. (1993), "Familia Oeconomica: A Survey of the Economics of the Family," *Scottish Journal of Political Economy*, 40, 353–74.

Federkeil, G. (1997), "The Federal Republic of Germany: Polarization of the Family Structure," in F.-X. Kaufmann, A. Kuijsten, H.-J. Schulze, and K.P. Strohmeier, (eds.), *Family Life and Family Policies in Europe: Volume 1*, Oxford: Clarendon Press.

Fisher, H.E. (1992), *Anatomy of Love*, New York: W.W. Norton.

Friedberg, L. (1998), "Did Unilateral Divorce Raise Divorce Rates? Evidence from Panel Data," *American Economic Review*, 88, 608–27.

Glendon, M.A. (1987), *Abortion and Divorce in Western Law*, Cambridge, MA: Harvard University Press.

(1989), *The Transformation of Family Law*, Chicago: University of Chicago Press.

Goode, W.J. (1993), *World Changes in Divorce Patterns*, New Haven, CT: Yale University Press.

Graham-Siegenthaler, B. (1995), "International Marriage and Divorce Regulation and Recognition in Switzerland," *Family Law Quarterly*, 29, 685–700.

Gray, J.S. (1998), "Divorce-Law Changes, Household Bargaining, and Married Women's Labor Supply," *American Economic Review*, 88, 628–42.

Haller, M. (1977), "Austria," in R. Chester (ed.), *Divorce in Europe*, Leiden: Netherlands Interuniversity Demographic Institute, Martinus Nijhoff Social Sciences Division.

Haskey, J. (1992), "Patterns of Marriage, Divorce, and Cohabitation in the Different Countries of Europe," *Population Trends*, 69, 27–36.

Jarvis, S. and S.P. Jenkins (1999), "Marital Splits and Income Changes: Evidence from the British Household Panel Survey, *Population Studies*, 53, 237–54.

Johnson, W.R. and J. Skinner (1986), "Labor Supply and Marital Separation," *American Economic Review*, 76, 455–69.

Joshi, H. and H. Davies (1992), "Day Care in Europe and Mothers' Forgone Earnings," *International Labor Review*, 132, 561–79.

Kaufmann, F.-X., A. Kuijsten, H.-J. Schulze, and K.P. Strohmeier (eds.) (1997), *Family Life and Family Policies in Europe, Volume 1*, Oxford: Clarendon Press.

Kellerhals, J., J.F. Perrin, and L. Voneche (1977), "Switzerland," in R. Chester (ed.), *Divorce in Europe*, Leiden: Netherlands Interuniversity Demographic Institute, Martinus Nijhoff Social Sciences Division.

Kooy, G. (1977), "The Netherlands," in R. Chester (ed.), *Divorce in Europe*, Leiden: Netherlands Interuniversity Demographic Institute, Martinus Nijhoff Social Sciences Division.

Krause, H.D. (1998), "On the Danger of Allowing Marital Fault to Re-emerge in the Guise of Torts," *Notre Dame Law Review*, 73, 1355–68.

Künzel, R. (1977), "The Federal Republic of Germany," in R. Chester (ed.), *Divorce in Europe*, Leiden: Netherlands Interuniversity Demographic Institute, Martinus Nijhoff Social Sciences Division.

Meisaari-Polsa, T. (1997), "Sweden: a Case of Solidarity and Equality," in F.-X. Kaufmann, A. Kuijsten, H.-J. Schulze, and K.P. Strohmeier (eds.), *Family Life and Family Policies in Europe, Volume 1*, Oxford: Clarendon Press.

Muller-Escoda, B. and U. Vogt (1997), "France: the Institutionalization of Plurality," in F.-X. Kaufmann, A. Kuijsten, H.-J. Schulze, and K.P. Strohmeier (eds.), *Family Life and Family Policies in Europe, Volume 1*, Oxford: Clarendon Press.

OECD (1990), *Lone Parent Families: the Economic Challenge*, Paris: Organisation for Economic Co-operation and Development.

Peters, H.E. (1986), "Marriage and Divorce: Informational Constraints and Private Contracting," *American Economic Review*, 76, 437–54.

(1992), "Marriage and Divorce: Reply," *American Economic Review*, 82, 686–93.

Phillips, R. (1988), *Putting Asunder: A History of Divorce in Western Society*, Cambridge: Cambridge University Press.

Poppel, F. van and J. de Beer (1993), "Measuring the Effect of Changing Legislation on the Frequency of Divorce: The Netherlands, 1830–1990," *Demography*, 30, 425–41.

Rheinstein, M. and M.A. Glendon (1980), "Interspousal Relations," *International Encyclopedia of Comparative Law, IV: Persons and Family*, Tübingen: J.C.B. Mohr.

Rowthorn, R.E. (1999), "Marriage and Trust: Some Lessons from Economics, *Cambridge Journal of Economics*, 23, 661–91.

Simotta, D.-A. (1995), "Marriage and Divorce Regulation and Recognition in Austria," *Family Law Quarterly*, 29, 525–40.

Smith, I. (1997), "Explaining the Growth of Divorce in Great Britain," *Scottish Journal of Political Economy*, 44, 519–44.

Smith, I., J.W. Sawkins, and P.T. Seaman (1998), "The Economics of Religious Participation: A Cross-country Study," *Kyklos*, 51, 25–43.

Trost, J. (1977), "Sweden," in R. Chester (ed.), *Divorce in Europe*, Leiden: Netherlands Interuniversity Demographic Institute, Martinus Nijhoff Social Sciences Division.

Vlaardingerbroek, P. (1995), "Marriage, Divorce, and Living Arrangements in the Netherlands," *Family Law Quarterly*, 29, 635–44.

Voegeli, W. and B. Willenbacher (1992), "Property Division and Pension-Splitting in the FRG," in L.J. Weitzman, and M. Maclean, (eds.), *Economic Consequences of Divorce: The International Perspective*, Oxford: Clarendon Press.

Walls, M. (1997), "Ireland Gets Divorce," *Family Law*, April, 271–73.

Weiss, Y. and R.J. Willis (1993), "Transfers among Divorced Couples: Evidence and Interpretation," *Journal of Labor Economics*, 11, 629–79.

Weitzman, L.J. and M. Maclean (eds.) (1992), *Economic Consequences of Divorce: The International Perspective*, Oxford: Clarendon Press.

Index